Berlin
in Early Berlin-Wall Era
CIA, State Department, and Army Booklets

Compiled by

T.H.E. Hill

The author of

*The Day Before the Berlin Wall: Could We Have Stopped
It? — An Alternate History of Cold War Espionage*

T.H.E.Hill

T.H.E. Hill, compiler

Berlin in Early Berlin-Wall Era CIA, State Department, and Army Booklets

Subject headings:

Cold War

Intelligence service

Berlin Wall, Berlin, Germany, 1961

Includes index, B&W illustrations, maps.

ISBN-10: 1496158334

ISBN-13: 978-1496158338

First published in the United States of America for the twenty-fifth anniversary of the Fall of the Berlin Wall, 9 November 2014.

Cover design by the compiler.

www.VoicesUnderBerlin.com/1961.html

1 2 3 4 5 6 7 8 9 0

Contents

Chronology of the Wall

- 15 June 1961: "No one has the intention of constructing a wall."
  — Walter Ulbricht

- 30 July 1961: "The East Germans have the right to close their borders"
  — J.W. Fulbright

- 1 August 1961: "If the border were to be closed, the Americans and West Germans would be pleased." — Nikita Khrushchev

- Early August: Khrushchev "will have to do something to stop the flow of refugees—perhaps a wall. And we won't be able to prevent it. I can hold the Alliance together to defend West Berlin but I cannot act to keep East Berlin open." — John F. Kennedy

- 13 August 1961: The Berlin Wall goes up.

- 26 June 1963: "Ich bin ein Berliner." — John F. Kennedy

- 12 June 1987: "Mr. Gorbachev, tear down this wall!" — Ronald Reagan

- 19 January 1989: "The Wall will be standing in 50, and even in 100 years, if the reasons for it still have not been removed." — Erich Honecker

- 18 October 1989: Honecker resigns

- 9 November 1989: The Berlin Wall falls

- 3 October 1990: Formal reunification of Germany and Berlin

Annamarie Doherr (*Frankfurter Rundschau*): *„Bedeutet die Bildung einer Freien Stadt Ihrer Meinung nach, daß die Staatsgrenze am Brandenburger Tor errichtet wird?"*

"In your opinion, does the creation of a free city mean that the State frontier will be set up at the Brandenburg Gate?"

„Ich verstehe Ihre Frage so, dass es in Westdeutschland Menschen gibt, die wünschen, dass wir die Bauarbeiter der Hauptstadt der DDR dazu mobilisieren, um eine Mauer aufzurichten. Mir ist nicht bekannt, dass eine solche Absicht besteht. Die Bauarbeiter unserer Hauptstadt beschäftigen sich hauptsächlich mit Wohnungsbau, und ihre Arbeitskraft wird dafür voll eingesetzt. Niemand hat die Absicht, eine Mauer zu errichten!"

"As I understand your question, there are people in West Germany who wish that we would mobilize the construction workers of the capital of the GDR for the purpose of erecting a wall. I am not aware of the existence of any such intention. The construction workers of our capital are primarily engaged in the building of housing, and all their efforts are directed toward this goal. No one has the intention of building a wall."
— Walter Ulbricht, Press Conference on 15 June 1961

Walter Ulbricht (1893-1973)
General Secretary of the Socialist Unity Party of Germany
(*Sozialistische Einheitspartei Deutschlands* or *SED*)

"I think that that might certainly be a negotiable point. The truth of the matter is, I think, the Russians have the power to close it [the Berlin Escape Hatch] in any case. I mean you are not giving up very much because I believe that next week if they chose to close their borders they could, without violating any treaty. I don't understand why the East Germans don't close their border because I think they have a right to close it. So why is this a great concession? You don't have that right now."

— J. William Fulbright, during the television news program *Issues and Answers*, 30 July 1961, quoted in *The New York Times*, 3 August 1961, page 2.

James William Fulbright (1905-1995)
The longest serving chairman in the history
of the Senate Foreign Relations Committee

„Ich denke, das könnte ein bemerkenswerter Punkt (eines Kompromisses) sein. Ich meine, man gibt nicht viel auf, weil sie (die DDR und die Sowjetunion) ohnehin die Macht haben (die Zugänge) auf jeden Fall zu schließen. Sie könnten das ohne Verletzung irgendeines vertraglich festgelegten Rechts tun ... Ich verstehe nicht warum die Ostdeutschen nicht ihre Grenzen schließen, weil ich denke, daß sie ein Recht dazu haben, sie zu schließen."

— *Neues Deutschland*, 3 August 1961, front page, with the headline:

Fulbright: „Die Ostdeutschen haben das Recht, ihre Grenzen zu schließen" / Wutgeschrei in Bonn

Fulbright: "The East Germans have the right to close their borders" / Cries of Rage in Bonn

Early in August, Kennedy privately told his Deputy Special Assistant for National Security Affairs (Walt Rostow):

> "Khrushchev is losing East Germany. He cannot let that happen.... He will have to do something to stop the flow of refugees—perhaps a wall. And we won't be able to prevent it. I can hold the Alliance together to defend West Berlin but I cannot act to keep East Berlin open."

— W.W. Rostow, *The Diffusion of Power: An Essay in Recent History* (New York, 1972), p. 231.

John Fitzgerald Kennedy (1917-1963) [right]
the 35th President of the United States
Served from January 1961 until he was assassinated in November 1963

Nikita Sergeyevich Khrushchev (1894-1971) [left]

"If the border were to be closed, the Americans and West Germans would be pleased. Ambassador Thompson told me that the refugee flow is inconveniencing the West Germans. Were you to establish this control, everyone would be pleased."

— Khrushchev, in a phone conversation with Ulbricht on 1 August 1961.

Nikita Sergeyevich Khrushchev (1894-1971) [left]
First Secretary of the Communist Party of the Soviet Union
Served from 1953 to 1964

Walter Ulbricht (1893-1973) [right]

The Army of Occupation Medal

Awarded for thirty or more consecutive days of duty as a member of the occupation forces after World War II. While in Austria and most of Germany the period of qualifying service for award of the medal ended in 1955, Berlin was legally an occupied territory until the Reunification of Germany in October 1990. This is one of the things that made Berlin a unique place to be stationed.

Dedicated to the countless men and women of Berlin Command and Berlin Brigade who stood resolutely shoulder-to-shoulder with the West Berliners during the Cold War, ensuring that the Island of Freedom known as "West Berlin" remained free. In June 1963, from a platform erected on the steps of Rathaus Schöneberg in Berlin, John F. Kennedy made his world-famous statement that is often shortened in quotation to: "Ich bin ein Berliner" (*I am a Berliner*). What Kennedy actually said was: "Today, in the world of freedom, the proudest boast is 'Ich bin ein Berliner'." The men and women of Berlin Command and Berlin Brigade felt this same sense of pride in being Berliners, perhaps, even more strongly than Kennedy, because they actually lived in Berlin, sharing the fate of those whom it was their impossible duty to defend. They knew the dangers of brinksmanship better than most, because they would have been the first casualties if the post-war peace in Europe failed. Yet for almost fifty years (1945-1994) they never flinched. They can proudly say that they held their *Outpost of Freedom* until relieved.

To learn more about the Cinderella Commemorative Stamps for

The 50th Anniversary of the Berlin Wall,

please visit: http://voicesunderberlin.com/Stamps4.html

Compiler's Foreword

This book is a by-product of the research for a novel about the crisis that became the epicenter of the Cold War. *The Day Before the Berlin Wall: Could We Have Stopped It?* is the story of one of the American soldiers who worked hard to collect intelligence about East German and Soviet intentions on the eve of the construction of the Berlin Wall in August 1961. It asks the question of why this intelligence was not used, and speculates about what could have happened, if it had been used. That is what makes the novel *An Alternate History of Cold War Espionage.*

The booklets reproduced in this volume define the historical context of *The Day Before the Berlin Wall.* They cover the period from 1958 to 1966, spanning the critical year in which the Wall was built: 1961.

The decision to reproduce these booklets was based on a number of considerations. The CIA *Berlin Handbook* is not available in print. The copy of the State Department booklet on Berlin at the National Archive is incomplete. The missing pages have been filled in from my own personal archive. The booklets from Berlin Brigade are not to be found on WorldCat, the on-line catalogue of a consortium of libraries, headed by the Library of Congress. Nor are they to be found at the National Archive. Reprinting will make them all available for research libraries to add to their collections.

The second consideration is that—when presented in a single volume— these booklets have a historical value that is greater than the sum of the individual booklets in isolation. The booklets all represent three different perspectives of Berlin: **practical**, **rhetorical**, and **pragmatic**.

The CIA *Berlin Handbook* is **practical**. It presents factual data on Berlin, ranging from statistics on the number of East German refugees to the military order of battle for the Group of Soviet Forces, Germany. It lists which railroad bridges on the lines to Berlin are "chambered for demolition," and presents the statistics on how many refugees have left East Germany since 1949.

The State Department *Background Berlin* is **rhetorical**. It presents the legal status of the Four-Power occupation of Berlin in a way that a lawyer would love, replete with original documents of the time, and quotes from Presidents and Secretaries of State. It considers the consequences of "closing the escape hatch" from East Germany, and ponders the effects of West Berlin as a "lighthouse of freedom in a dark totalitarian sea. ... [that] demonstrates the material superiorities of a free society which allows and encourages individual initiative."

Berlin Brigade Special Services Presents Berlin is **pragmatic**. It presents a guide of how to get on with life in Walled Berlin, ranging from the history of Berlin to where to go shopping and sightseeing. This is the point of view of the Americans who actually lived in Berlin, sharing the fate of those whom it was their impossible duty to defend, because—as the *Berlin Handbook* says—"the Soviets and East Germans could seize West Berlin at any time."

Making it easy to compare these perspectives in a single volume is one of the "values added" by this reprint of these booklets. Another is that the State Department and Berlin Brigade booklets create a sense of living history. The differences between pre-Wall and post-Wall editions are presented in-line so that the reader can see how things changed in Berlin between those two points in time.

It is things like this that make it appealing for those interested in the history of Berlin to read these early Berlin-Wall Era booklets in parallel. There is an index to make this easier. No attempt has been made to re-edit the texts. Only blatant typographical errors have been corrected.

T.H.E. Hill,
March 2014

The Day Before the Berlin Wall: Could We Have Stopped It?
— An Alternate History of Cold War Espionage

From T.H.E. Hill, the author of:

Voices Under Berlin: The Tale of a Monterey Mary

Reunification: A Monterey Mary Returns to Berlin

The plot of *The Day Before the Berlin Wall* is based on a "legend" that was still being told by members of Field Station Berlin in the mid-1970s. According to the legend, we had advance knowledge of the construction of the Wall, including the fact that the East German troops who were going to build it had been told to halt construction if the Americans were to take aggressive action to stop them.

The Day Before the Berlin Wall was written because I could not believe that we had the intelligence that would have allowed us to stop the Wall being built and did not take action on it. I wanted to explore the possibilities of keeping Berlin from becoming the epicenter of the Cold War, and liberating a whole generation of East Germans from tyranny.

In this award-winning fictional version of the tale, a young American sergeant is the one who gets this piece of intelligence, but he is in East Berlin and has to get back to his unit to report it. The Stasi (the East German secret police) are prepared to kill to keep him from reporting it. They have killed his postmistress, and framed him for her murder. Now it is not only the Stasi, and the Vopos (the East German "People's" Police), but also the West-Berlin municipal *Polizei* and the U.S. Army MPs who are after him. It's the day before construction is scheduled to start, and time is running out, so the sergeant is running as fast as he can to prevent the wall from being built, and to keep himself out of jail.

The key question of the novel is "even if he is lucky enough to make it back across the border, will anybody in the West believe what he has to say and take action on it before it is too late?" History says that he either didn't make it, they didn't believe him, or they ignored his information. This alternate history of Cold War espionage explores what might have happened.

The Legend? — Or was it fact?

> The attraction of secret histories is "the ineradicable popular belief that the real facts of history are never given."
>
> — John Sutherland
>
> *Bestsellers*, London: Routledge & Kegan Paul, 1981, p. 173.

On her "Our Whiskey Lullaby" blog, Katherine writes, "I truly believe that this wasn't a legend at all. I think the United States knew about the wall before it was built, but we kept our mouths shut. [*The Day Beofre the Berlin Wall*] is a great voice to us all and even though the story itself is fictional, the basis behind it, in my opinion, isn't."[1]

In July 2013, the Interagency Security Classification Appeals Panel (ISCAP) declassified more information in the NSA history, *American Cryptology during the Cold War*, which reveals that a 9 August 1961 intercept of East German Communist Party (SED) communications provided information on plans to begin blocking all foot traffic between East and West Berlin. The interagency intelligence Watch Committee assessment said that this intercept "might be the first step in a plan to close the border," which had long been predicted.[2]

This is the "legend" upon which this novel is really based. Before this information was declassified, it was not possible to broach this topic any other way, except to call it a "legend." The Berlin Wall was not an intelligence failure. It was a political failure.

In his "Bitter Measures: Intelligence and Action in the Berlin Crisis, 1961,"[3] Dr. Donald P. Steury observes that: "The possibility of some sort of Soviet action to restrict access to West Berlin—either as a repetition of the 1948 blockade, or as some other form of action—figured strongly in intelligence reporting throughout the last half of the 1950s. In November 1957, CIA's Office of Current Intelligence (OCI) warned that the Soviets might seal the sector borders between East and West Berlin as a means of applying pressure on the West.[4] On 28 May 1959, OCI warned that East Germany—not the Soviet Union—might restrict traffic at the border crossings, to reduce or eliminate uncontrolled access to West Berlin, force the West Berlin government to negotiate on issues of access, and reduce the labor shortage in East Germany."[5]

Stephen A. Koczak, an officer at the US Mission in Berlin had been warning that the Communists were going to close the border long before the events of 13 August proved him right.[6]

Shortly after the border closing on 13 August, the British Ambassador said: "I personally have always wondered that the East Germans waited so long to seal this boundary."[7]

In his memoirs (*The Service*), General Reinhard Gehlen, then head of West German Intelligence, rejects the criticisms of "politicians" that his organization "failed to provide warning of the Communist plans to build the Berlin Wall on 13 August 1961. The truth is that in countless individual reports before that date we indicated that" the refugee situation "was worsening, and that East Berlin would have to stem the mass flight of labor, which was costing them far too many of their skilled workers and specialists; otherwise the Ulbricht regime would face a catastrophe. ... We reported to Bonn that a *totale Absperrung*, or total shutdown, was imminent."[8]

A declassified BND (West German equivalent of the CIA) document dated 11 August 1961 contains a prediction of the closing of the border, giving the time frame for this action as 12-18 August 1961. (Appendix: Document 1)

Egon Bahr, the Press spokesman for the Berlin Senate, led at that time by Mayor Willy Brandt, recalls that, in the first week after the Wall went up, the Berlin evening newspaper *Der Abend* printed a story which suggested that the allies had known in advance about the Wall and had decided not to do anything about it. Bahr demanded that the U.S. issue a denial of the story within thirty minutes. Bahr got his denial even a bit faster than he had demanded.[9]

Bahr was clearly misinformed, because declassified information on the BND webSite from the 17 August Session of Chancellor Adenauer's Cabinet notes that the American and British Commandants of Berlin had been informed about the plans to close the border no later than mid-day on 12 August. (Appendix: Document 2)

Peter Wyden's non-fiction book *Wall: The Inside Story of Divided Berlin* (1989) shows that there were sources other than the SED intercept and the BND intelligence that predicted the closing of the sector borders in Berlin.

> On Wednesday 9 August, four days prior to the construction
> of the Wall, Colonel Ernest Von Pawel, the Chief of the U.S.
> Military Liaison Mission to the Commander Group of Soviet
> Forces, Germany predicted the construction of a wall at the

weekly meeting of the Berlin Watch Committee, but he had no hard evidence to back up his prediction.[10]

Unlike the Chief of USMLM, LTC Thomas McCord, the Chief of the 513th Military Intelligence Group (Berlin), had a HUMINT source who predicted the correct date of the start of construction. A report had come in from a new source on 6 August, a week before construction. The source was a functionary in the SED.[11]

The French also had a source who told his case officer that "They're going to erect barriers right in the middle of Berlin." This source, unfortunately, had no information about the date of the operation.[12]

In the "East German Countermeasures" section of a partially declassified CIA Memorandum of 10 August on the subject of "THE EAST GERMAN REFUGEES," paragraph 10 stated that:

10. There is some evidence that the regime is considering harsher measures to reduce the flow.

- 5 -

Approved For Release 2004/10/08 : CIA-RDP79S00427A000500040020-9

East German propaganda on 10 August suggested that a decree promulgating new and more vigorous control meas- ures would be forthcoming from the meeting of the East German Peoples Chamber on 11 August.

(Appendix: Document 3)

Why Nothing Happened

Freedom of movement for East Germans was already on the American list of bargaining chips. The ~~TOP SECRET~~ "Minutes of the Inter-Departmental Steering Group on Berlin" for 26 July 1961 summarized the negotiating proposals presented by Dean Acheson. The first item in the numbered list reported in the minutes was: "(1) there could be a discouragement of movements of population as distinct from acts of genuine political refuge."[13]This proposal was restated in the ~~SECRET~~ memorandum "Berlin: A Political Program" (31 July 1961) as "a general undertaking to discourage excessive movements of population, so long as a reasonable freedom of movement is permitted within the city, including freedom to live in one part and work in another without economic or other penalty."[14] This line of thinking was aimed squarely at the refugee flow and border crossers. (Consult the index to learn the difference between "freedom of movement" and "free access.")

The goal of any successful diplomatic negotiation is to extract the maximum counter-concession from your opponent for each bargaining chip you are prepared to give up. On 30 July 1961, Chairman of the Senate Foreign Relations Committee Senator J. William Fulbright, speaking on the television news program *Issues and Answers*, told the Soviets that they could have the number one bargaining chip in the American negotiation strategy for free:

> "I think that that might certainly be a negotiable point. The truth of the matter is, I think, the Russians have the power to close it [the Berlin escape hatch] in any case. I mean you are not giving up very much because I believe that next week if they chose to close their borders they could, without violating any treaty. I don't understand why the East Germans don't close their border because I think they have a right to close it. So why is this a great concession? You don't have that right now."
> — quoted from *The New York Times* issue of 3 August 1961, p. 2.[15]

This statement was loosely quoted in the East German Communist Party Newspaper *Neues Deutschland* in a three-column spread on the front page of the 3 August 1961 issue, with the headline:

Fulbright: "The East Germans Have the Right to Close their Borders" / Cries of Rage in Bonn

Fulbright: „Die Ostdeutschen haben das Recht, ihre Grenzen zu schließen" / Wutgeschrei in Bonn

„Ich denke, das könnte ein bemerkenswerter Punkt (eines Kompromisses) sein. Ich meine, man gibt nicht viel auf, weil sie (die DDR und die Sowjetunion) ohnehin die Macht haben (die Zugänge) auf jeden Fall zu schließen. Sie könnten das ohne Verletzung irgendeines vertraglich festgelegten Rechts tun ... Ich verstehe nicht warum die Ostdeutschen nicht ihre Grenzen schließen, weil ich denke, daß sie ein Recht dazu haben, sie zu schließen."

The border around West Berlin was closed 10 days later, on 13 August, within Fulbright's time frame of "next week," which was not included in the translation published by *Neues Deutschland*. If that had been in the German translation of Fulbright's statement, the exodus that followed would have been even greater.

Even without Fulbright's time frame of "next week" to warn them just how little time they had, the East Germans could clearly read the message hidden in the prominence given to Fulbright's statement by placing it on the front page of *Neues Deutschland*.

47,700 refugees poured into the West during August,[16] which was in essence only a half month. The average daily number of refugees after 13 August dropped to 112.[17] Fulbright's statement could have been the event that triggered the decision to leave for many East Germans. The average monthly total for the first seven months of 1961 was only 19,000. The total for the first half of August was almost two and a half times that.

August 1961 registered the highest monthly total of refugees recorded since 1949—with the exception of March 1953, when Stalin died—at which time there were 58,605 refugees.[18] If the refugee flow had continued at the same pace for the second half of August 1961, the monthly total would have surpassed that of March 1953, climbing to approximately 95,400.

A cable from US Embassy Bonn reported that "rarely has a statement by a prominent American official aroused so much consternation, chagrin and anger." (Appendix: Document 5)

Willy Brandt's Press Secretary Egon Bahr is quoted as saying: "We privately called him Fulbricht."[19]

The name "Fulbricht" is a pun based on the surname of the East German leader Walter Ulbricht, who would have seen—and perhaps personally approved the publication of Fulbright's remarks in *Neues*

Deutschland. He interpreted them as a signal that the West would not react to the closing of the sector borders in Berlin.

Fulbright was clearly not the only one in the West making such comments. At a press conference on 15 June 1961, Ulbricht had alluded to this when he said: "As I understand your question, there are people in West Germany who wish that we would mobilize the construction workers of the capital of the GDR for the purpose of erecting a wall. I am not aware of the existence of any such intention. The construction workers of our capital are primarily engaged in the building of housing, and all their efforts are directed toward this goal. No one has the intention of building a wall."

In a phone conversation with Khrushchev on 1 August, Ulbricht said:

> *„Der Gegner spürt, dass wir uns darauf vorbereiten, die Grenze zu schließen. Gestern hat mich zum Beispiel ein englischer Korrespondent gefragt: Würden Sie heute die Grenze schließen? Ich habe gesagt, dass das von den Westmächten abhängt."* [20]

> "The enemy senses that we are preparing to close the border. Yesterday, for example, and English correspondent asked: "Would you close the border today?" I said that depends on the Western Powers."

In the now declassified ~~SECRET~~ Department of State Memorandum of 28 June 1961 entitled "The Berlin Crisis" that was prepared for President Kennedy, Dean Acheson clearly presented US priorities in Berlin:

> "It is plain that, if carried to its conclusion, the Berlin offensive strikes at the power and world position of the United States. Even its more limited purposes are gravely damaging to the United States and the Western Alliance. This is the nature of the crisis which confronts us; not the fate of a city, or of its two and one-half million people, or even the integrity of our pledged word. … Nothing could be more dangerous than to embark upon a course of action of the sort described in this paper in the absence of a decision to accept nuclear war rather than accede to the demands which Khrushchev is now making, or their substantial equivalent." [21]

The fact that Kennedy was not prepared to take that risk is demonstrated by his widely quoted statement: "It's not a very nice solution, but a wall is a hell of a lot better than a war."

Early in August, Kennedy privately told his Deputy Special Assistant for National Security Affairs (Walt Rostow):

"Khrushchev is losing East Germany. He cannot let that happen.... He will have to do something to stop the flow of refugees—perhaps a wall. And we won't be able to prevent it. I can hold the Alliance together to defend West Berlin but I cannot act to keep East Berlin open."[22]

In a phone conversation between Khrushchev and Ulbricht on 1 August 1961, Khrushchev said:

„Wenn die Grenze geschlossen wird, werden Amerikaner und Westdeutsche zufrieden sein. Botschafter Thompson hat mir gesagt, dass diese Flucht den Westdeutschen Ungelegenheiten bereitet. Wenn Sie also diese Kontrolle errichten, werden alle zufrieden sein."[23]

"If the border were to be closed, the Americans and West Germans would be pleased. Ambassador Thompson told me that the refugee flow is inconveniencing the West Germans. Were you to establish this control, everyone would be pleased."

A declassified BND document from mid-August 1961 reports that:

„In seiner Unterredung mit dem Bundeskanzler ließ SMIRNOW gewisse Andeutungen über eine vorherige sowjetische/amerikanische „Verständigung" bezüglich Absperrmaßnahmen fallen."

In his discussion with the Federal Chancellor [Konrad Adenauer], [Ambassador Andrey Andreyevich] Smirnow let certain hints fall about a prior Soviet-American "Understanding" on measures to cordon things off. (Appendix: Document 6)

In an interview on Amazon,[24] Frederick Kempe—the author of *Berlin 1961*—explains why Kennedy did nothing. He says that his "book builds the best cases to date that Kennedy acquiesced to the border closure and the building of the Wall. The record shows that in many respects he wrote the script that Khrushchev followed—as long as Khrushchev restricted his actions to Soviet-controlled East Berlin and East Germany, Kennedy would accept his actions. Kennedy falsely believed that if East Germany could end its refugee stampede, Khrushchev might become a more willing negotiator on a set of other issues. It was a tragic misreading of the man and of the situation. Berlin paid for it—as did tens of millions of people."

While Kennedy projected a face of shocked depression to the press and the public, his sense of relief at the building of the Wall was evident to those who were closest to him.[25]

Rueger observes that "It is a painful and often omitted fact that ... the order to ready the sector closure in August came only after the West had communicated loudly and clearly that it would defend West Berlin, but not care about the sectoral border."[26]

Campaigning for election as Chancellor of Germany in Nuremberg, West Berlin's Mayor Willy Brandt said that the streams of refugees pouring into Berlin every day were driven by the fear that "the Iron Curtain will be cemented shut" and that they will be left "locked into a giant prison. They are agonizingly worried that they might be forgotten or sacrificed on the altar of indifference and lost opportunities."[27]

The Frenchman Georges Pâques (1914-1994), who spied for the Soviets for over 20 years, and who had access to Allied contingency plans for Berlin that were agreed upon at the Foreign Ministers' Conference in early August 1961, reportedly passed these on to the Soviets. This let the Soviets know that if they and/or the East Germans were to build a "barrier" to close off East Berlin, the Western Allies were not prepared to use force to stop them.[28]

In her talks with Gorbachev in the Kremlin, Margaret Thatcher told the Soviet leader: "The reunification of Germany is not in the interests of Britain and Western Europe." She could not say this publicly, because it was counter to NATO policy. "We don't want a united Germany ... because such development would undermine the stability of the whole international situation and could endanger our security."[29]

What Could Have Happened?

On 15 September, Ulbricht wrote to Khrushchev: "The tactic of gradually carrying out the measures made it more difficult for the enemy to orient himself with regard to the extent of our measures and made it easier for us to find the weak places in the border. I must say that the enemy undertook fewer countermeasures than was expected."[30]

General Gehlen remarked that "In the beginning, the barrier was a light and temporary structure, which could have been withdrawn at the least sign of force from the three Western powers."[31]

The East German military units installing the barbed wire barriers had rifles, but no ammunition.[32]

> Order of the East German Minister of Defense (Nr. 01/61 Strausberg, 12. August 1961):[33]
>
> *„Die Anwendung der Schußwaffe ist kategorisch verboten und erfolgt nur auf meinen Befehl."*
> "The use of firearms is categorically forbidden and will only be upon my orders."

It was only "three days later, after it had turned out that the West would protest but not actively respond, [that] GDR construction teams began replacing the barbed wire with bricks and mortar."[34]

Hagen Koch, a former member of the East German Stasi, confirms the other part of the "legend." "If the Americans had let General (Lucius D.) Clay knock down our barbed-wire barriers, we were under orders to do nothing," Koch said. "Most of DDR personnel believed the Americans would call our bluff. They didn't. It might have been different if the American president was Reagan instead of Kennedy."[35]

The West German commentator on Soviet Affairs Wolfgang Leonhard stated "We know now — we learned later from refugees — that the leadership in East Berlin would have backed down if the West had stood up to them."[36]

Lucius D. Clay, the former military governor of the U.S. Zone, Germany (1947–49) and the "father" of the Berlin Airlift (1948–1949), felt that "we might have been able to have stopped the Wall from being built that night," if the American Commandant of Berlin had taken action, "even if he had been in violation of his instructions, he would have succeeded and he would have been forgiven and he would have become a very great man."[37]

The senior statesman Dean Acheson, former U.S. Secretary of State under President Harry S. Truman (1949 to 1953), was of the same opinion. "If we had acted vigorously ... we might have been able to accomplish something."[38]

Military Police Lieutenant Vern Pike—like many of those stationed in Berlin at the time—believed that "Kennedy and Johnson could have simply pushed the wall down before it was built without the Soviets doing much more than whimper about it."[39]

Hagen Koch, a former member of the East German Stasi, confirmed Pike's belief "that the communists gambled and won in putting up the Wall in 1961."[40]

Notes:

---

[1] http://ourwhiskeylullaby.blogspot.com/2011/02/day-before-berlin-wall-review.html

[2] National Security Archive Electronic Briefing Book No. 441 (Posted – September 25, 2013): http://www2.gwu.edu/~nsarchiv/NSAEBB/NSAEBB441/ lvo 27 February 2014.

[3] www.foia.cia.gov/sites/default/files/document_conversions/16/BitterMeasures.pdf

[4] Steury's footnote: Memorandum for the DDI; Subject: "The Berlin Situation," 1 November 1957 (MORI: 44001 in Ibid., pp. 536-37.

[5] Steury's footnote: Current Weekly Intelligence Summary: "East Germany May Move against East German Sector Border Crossings," 28 May 1959; Ibid., pp. 493-94.

[6] *Congressional Record — House* (31098), volume 113, p. 208, November 3, 1967; Honoré Marc Catudal, *Kennedy and the Berlin Wall Crisis: A Case Study in U.S. Decision Making*, Berlin: Verlag Arno Spitz, 1980, p. 247; Norman Gelb, *The Berlin Wall: Kennedy, Khrushchev, and a Showdown in the Heart of Europe*, Times Books, 1986, p. 192; Current News: *Espionage*, Issue 1612, Department of Defense, Department of the Air Force, 1987, p. 8.

[7] Steel to Foreign Office, 14 August 1961, The National Archives (TNA), FO371/160509.

[8] Reinhard Gehlen, *The Service: The Memoirs of General Reinhard Gehlen*, David Irving (trans.), New York: World Publishing, 1972, p. 239.

[9] Egon Bahr, *Zu meiner Zeit*, Munich: Karl Blessing Verlag, 1996, p. 134.

[10] Peter Wyden, *Wall: The Inside Story of Divided Berlin*, New York: Simon and Schuster, 1989, p. 91.

[11] Wyden, pp. 92-93.

[12] Wyden, p. 93.

[13] ~~TOP SECRET~~: "Minutes of the Inter-Departmental Steering Group on Berlin," The White House, July 31, 1961, 5:15 p.m., p. 1. Via the National Archive. (See the appendix: Document 6.)

[14] ~~SECRET~~: "Berlin: A Political Program," July 31, 1961, pp. 8-9. Via the National Archive. (See the appendix: Document 7.)

[15] The question and answer were quoted in the *Congressional Record — Senate*, 1 August 1961, pp. 14222-14224. (See the appendix: Document 4)

[16] *Berlin Handbook*, CIA Office of Current Intelligence, 27 December 1961, p. 79 in the original, and p. 92 in this volume.

[17] Berlin Brigade *ISUM* #10, 311600 Aug 61 — 71600 Sep 61, paragraph 6.

[18] *Berlin Handbook*, p. 78 in the original, and p. 88 in this volume.

[19] Fabian Rueger, *Kennedy, Adenauer and the Making of the Berlin Wall, 1958-1961*, Stanford University, 2011, p. 210; See also Jürgen Petschull, *Die Mauer: August 1961 — 12 Tage zwischen Krieg und Frieden*, Hamburg: Stern Bücher, 1981, p. 205. The „Fulbricht" quote was expunged when the book was republished in 1990 as *Die Mauer: August 1961 — November 1989 vom Anfang und vom Ende eines Deutschen Bauwerks*, Hamburg: Ein Stern Buch, p. 259. (See the appendix: Document 8)

[20] www.chronik-der-mauer.de/index.php/57305/Media/TextPopup/id/1576253/old Action/Index/oldId/943776/oldModule/Start/page/0 lvo 27 February. Original is in German.

[21] pp. 2, 4. Available from the National Archive.

[22] W.W. Rostow, The Diffusion of Power: An Essay in Recent History (New York, 1972), p. 231.

[23] www.chronik-der-mauer.de/index.php/57305/Media/TextPopup/id/1576253/old Action/Index/oldId/943776/oldModule/Start/page/0 lvo 27 February. Original is in German.

[24] www.amazon.com/dp/product-description/0399157298/ref=dp_proddesc_0/177-5212899-2492430?ie=UTF8&n=283155&s=books LVO 27 February 2014

[25] Frederick Kempe, *Berlin 1961*, New York: Putnam Adult, 2011, p. 379.

[26] Rueger, p. 254

[27] Kempe, p. 338.

[28] Honoré M. Catudal, *Kennedy and the Berlin Wall Crisis*, Berlin: Berlin Verlag, 1980, pp. 244-245.

[29] Michael Binyon, "What Thatcher and Gorbachev really thought when the Berlin Wall came down," *The Times*, September 11, 2009.

[30] *Inside the Warsaw Pact*, Washington, D.C.: Woodrow Wilson International Center for Scholars, 1992, p. 31.

[31] *The Service*, p. 239.

[32] Rueger, p. 226. See also: Christof Münger, *Kennedy, die Berliner Mauer und die Kubakrise: die westliche Allianz in der Zerreissprobe* 1961-1963, Ferdinand Schöningh, 2003, p. 101.

[33] www.chronik-der-mauer.de/index.php/57305/Media/TextPopup/id/592873/old Action/Index/oldId/943794/oldModule/Start/page/0 lvo 27 February 2014. Original is in German.

[34] Rueger, p. 226.

[35] http://edcolumn.blogspot.com/p/ex-stasi-officer-helped-make-berlin.html

[36] *Newsweek*, volume 114 (1989), p. 38; Michael R. Beschloss, *The Crisis Years: Kennedy and Khrushchev (1960-1961)*, New York: Harper Collins, 1991, p. 282.

[37] Beschloss, p. 281.

[38] Beschloss, p. 281.

[39] Kempe, p. 388.

[40] http://edcolumn.blogspot.com/p/ex-stasi-officer-helped-make-berlin.html

27 December 1961

CENTRAL
INTELLIGENCE
AGENCY

BERLIN HANDBOOK

PREPARED BY OFFICE OF CURRENT INTELLIGENCE

Compiler's Preface to

Berlin Handbook

Berlin Handbook was originally classified S̶ ̶E̶ ̶C̶ ̶R̶ ̶E̶ ̶T̶ ̶ ̶N̶O̶F̶O̶R̶N̶, but has been declassified.

What is of particular interest is the presentation of the issues of Berlin without the rhetoric inherent in public statements on the topic.

The Soviet Union "indicated that a separate Four Power agreement on a new status of West Berlin, guarantees for that status and continuing access could be negotiated prior to the conclusion of a peace treaty if the West is willing to end formally the military occupation of West Berlin and sever the city's political ties with Bonn."

"**London** can be expected to support an initially 'tough' Western position as long as a slight *detente* in East-West tension endures. Any intensification of the crisis, however, would generate pressure for greater concessions."

"Although [**Paris**] issued a public statement regretting the West's failure to take more positive action when the Berlin wall was erected on 13 August, Paris subsequently has sought to ease around direct confrontations in Berlin, rather than provoke Soviet retaliation."

Chancellor Adenauer "has strongly and consistently opposed any withdrawal of Allied forces from Germany or disengagement of the Federal Republic from NATO. Berlin, although very important, is secondary, and Adenauer is believed to be extremely reluctant to risk nuclear war over the city."

"Generally speaking **Berlin Mayor Brandt** goes further than Adenauer in insisting that all ties between West Berlin and the Federal Republic be maintained, and has criticized the Chancellor for not being vigorous enough in maintaining them."

Ulbricht "emphasized that East Berlin belongs *de jure* to the GDR and that lines of communication between West Berlin and West Germany are to be used only on the basis of 'contractual' arrangements with the GDR."

Placing the word "contractual" in quote marks is, alas, an indication of the difficulty of bridging the language gap in cases like this. The correct translation of *"contractual" arrangements* should have been *treaty arrangements*. The German word *Vertrag* can mean either *treaty* or *contract*, depending on the context. The exact same mistake is found in the Embassy Bonn cable about Senator Fulbright's comments on East Germany's right to close the sector border. (Appendix: Document 5) What Fulbright actually said is: "If they chose to close their borders, they could, without violating any **treaty right** I know of." The cable—which was a reaction to the West German press coverage of the Senator's remarks, without the aid of his original remarks in English—said: "They (the Russians) in my opinion could close the borders whenever they wished without violating a **contractual right**." (**Emphasis** added.)

The conclusion of a German peace treaty—with either one or both Germanies—was a key issue in the Berlin crisis of 1961. (See the "Index.") Failing to recognize that point by giving the word *Vertrag* the correct translation of *treaty* is a major blunder.

Berlin Handbook has been reformatted from its original size (8.5 X 11) to fit the format of this book (6X9). No other editing has been done to the text. Only blatant typographical errors have been corrected.

The quality of the photographs and the maps are limited by the quality of the available originals.

A Handbook on the Berlin Problem

This handbook is intended as a factual study of Berlin. Its purpose is not to analyze Soviet intentions or estimate the future. While the factual data in this handbook includes the latest information available to the compilers, minor details such as pertain to the condition of access routes or border controls, are constantly changing. In its essentials, however, this study is believed to reflect accurately the current situation.

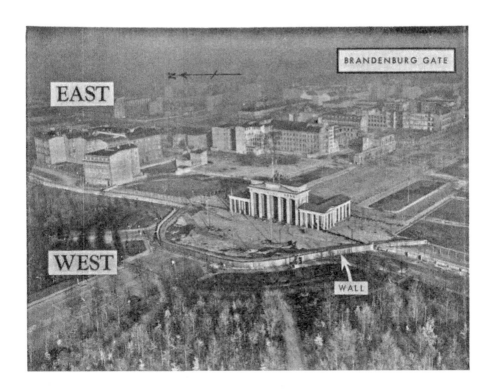

Table of Contents

S E C R E T   NOFORN

Charts

Photographs

SECTION I

The Soviet Position

The current Soviet position on Berlin and Germany is essentially the same as that put forward in November 1958, and modified at the Geneva Foreign Ministers Conference in May 1959. In their Vienna memorandum of 4 June 1961, the Soviets demanded a German peace treaty, the establishment of a free city of West Berlin and guarantees that this new status would be respected. They offered two alternatives—a single treaty with both German states, or a peace settlement based on two separate but similar treaties which would be signed at their discretion by some or all of the members of the wartime coalition.

Moscow contends that the peace treaty, or treaties, would end the occupation of West Berlin and establish it as a free, demilitarized and neutral city, guaranteed by the Four Powers who could station "symbolic contingents" in the city. The Vienna memorandum provided for the stationing of neutral troops under the auspices of the United Nations, in West Berlin. Access to the free city from the West would be permitted, but the Vienna memorandum left the manner in which it would be arranged vague, stating only that the free city of West Berlin could "freely effect its communications with the outside world," and that the US would have "every opportunity" to maintain and develop relations with the free city.

As an alternative to such a permanent solution, the Vienna memorandum proposed that "an interim solution could be adopted for a definite period—apparently for no longer than six months—on condition that meanwhile the two German states agree on the terms of a single peace treaty. In the event they failed, the wartime allies would undertake "measures" to conclude a treaty with one or both Germanies. Barring this, the Vienna memorandum repeated the threat of a separate Soviet bloc peace treaty with East Germany—which the Soviets maintain would end the occupation of West Berlin and mean that land, water and air access to Berlin would "have to be settled in no other way than through appropriate agreements with the GDR."

Khrushchev subsequently elaborated this position—or, at least, shifted his emphasis. While injecting a note of ultimatum by warning that a separate treaty would be signed in 1961, Khrushchev emphasized that any guarantees desired by the western powers probably would be acceptable. On 28 June, he said that free-city guarantees could be provided by the presence of Four-

Power neutral or United Nations troops. He repeated this on 8 July, adding that "if the Western powers have a better version of guarantees let them propose them." At the same time, be did not allude to the possibility of an interim solution and spoke of settling the "question of West Berlin itself"—which, he declared on 11 August, was "not so difficult to solve." He indicated that there could be "other variations of guarantees" for a free city. A significant modification appeared to be Khrushchev's statement that "we [presumably the USSR] are prepared to give firm guarantees not only to the population of West Berlin but also to Western powers" concerning no interference in Berlin and free access. The Soviets later indicated that they might underwrite East Germany's acceptance of such an arrangement.

Since the beginning of September, Soviet and bloc statements appear to have emphasized a separate Berlin agreement, which would be incorporated into a bloc peace treaty with East Germany. The Soviets have indicated that a separate Four Power agreement on a new status of West Berlin, guarantees for that status and continuing access could be negotiated prior to the conclusion of a peace treaty if the West is willing to end formally the military occupation of West Berlin and sever the city's political ties with Bonn. Moscow purposely has left vague the manner and form in which East Germany might be associated with such an agreement. One variation might be a Soviet-East German agreement to ensure East German recognition of the Four Power accord. In return, however, the Soviets have insisted that East German sovereignty must be "respected" which probably means at least tacit recognition of the Ulbricht regime.

British Position on Berlin

The British government supports fully the West's right to be in Berlin and enjoy restricted access to the city and its determination to defend the freedom of the West Berliners. London makes no attempt to hide its eagerness for a negotiated settlement, but is careful to conceal the issues on which they are prepared to concede.

The Foreign Office prefers a "narrow" approach to talks on an Allied-Soviet agreement on West Berlin access prior to the signing of any bilateral USSR-GDR treaty, but would not oppose broader discussions if Moscow so desired. London hopes that any limited understanding would open the way to a subsequent four-power conference on Germany and European security. It insists that any temporary arrangement contain an acceptable formula for eventual German reunification—no matter how remote.

While they refuse to consider formal recognition of the GDR, the British have not spelled out what concessions they do envisage, making only the vague suggestion that informal "modalities" might be worked out with the Soviets to permit the GDR to exercise nominal access controls. Although London has asserted its unwillingness to compromise on the question of possible limitations on West German rearmament, the strong anti-German feeling that frequently comes to the surface in the press and in statements in Parliament may indicate another area of concession. The transfer of some or all UN agencies to Berlin, as well as a UN role in any settlement, is included in the British list of useful negotiating tactics.

The British were relieved when the US took the lead in explorations with the Soviets. Late in 1961, however, due in part to parliamentary questions from Labor spokesmen, the government grew somewhat restive over delays in formulating a Western position. The Macmillan government believes that recent signs of "give" in the Soviet position provide an adequate basis for opening negotiations and would be prepared to "go it alone" with the US if De Gaulle refuses to participate.

Growing press and Labor Party demands will keep the Macmillan government pressing for negotiations. London can be expected to support an initially "tough" Western position as long as a slight *detente* in East-West tension endures. Any intensification of the crisis, however, would generate pressure for greater concessions.

French Position on Berlin

France's position on Berlin and Germany is based on the desire to maintain the *status quo* and promote its "alliance" with Bonn as the foundation of De Gaulle's increasingly Europe-oriented policies. France fears a reunited Germany, free to rearm and thereby pose a threat to France. It also rejects reunification under any East-West agreement to neutralize Germany, because this would sever France's close links with the Federal Republic and leave a reunited Germany free to seek accommodation with the USSR. Paris. therefore, seeks to keep firm ties with Bonn and opposes any change which would alter adversely its relative power status *vis-à-vis* Germany, or weaken the security of Western Europe *vis-à-vis* the Soviet bloc. De Gaulle has stated privately that he is no friend of German reunification; he maintains, however, that the West must stand firm on Berlin and avoid any appearance of publicly foreclosing an eventual reunification so as not to discourage the West Germans, who might then incline toward neutralism. The French insist the Berlin problem can be solved only within the context of the whole German problem—the solution of which they maintain is neither urgent nor immediately possible.

De Gaulle consistently has sought to divert East-West negotiations away from the Berlin and German problems to "new ground" i.e., disarmament, and other means of improving relations. It insists that meaningful negotiations cannot be conducted under threat of force, or with one side proposing all of the conditions. The importance he attributes to this point is evident in France's determination to adhere to it, rather than accept US and UK views in order to avoid disclosing publicly Western differences over negotiations. De Gaulle believes that Khrushchev does not want war, and that the West must stand firm in Berlin, maintain its rights and be willing to meet force with force, if necessary.

Although it issued a public statement regretting the West's failure to take more positive action when the Berlin wall was erected on 13 August, Paris subsequently has sought to ease around direct confrontations in Berlin, rather than provoke Soviet retaliation. Generally speaking, the French, whose identification procedures are similar to those of the US, have preferred to deny themselves entry into East Berlin rather than force the issue or submit to East German controls.

At the same time France has opposed altering the Four-Power status of Berlin. It has favored increased three-power control over West German legislation applicable to the city and opposes meetings of the Bundestag and Bundesrat in Berlin on the grounds that such ties undermine legal arguments for continued Allied presence. On the other hand, Paris opposes weakening the existing relationship between West Berlin and the Federal Republic because of the adverse effect it presumes this would have on West Berlin and, ultimately, West German morale. French leaders often have emphasized the importance they attach to maintaining unrestricted Allied access to West Berlin.

Because France has found itself in the position of being the most outspoken opponent of East-West negotiations on Berlin, the points in which it might be willing to bargain are obscure. Paris feels that any bargaining points should be reserved for actual negotiations, but given the strength of De Gaulle's feeling, it is unlikely that France would agree to anything more than a West German government statement disavowing the use of force to change its borders and national control of nuclear weapons. The French feel that even these limited concessions should not be made without something in return from the Soviet Union.

West German Position on Berlin

In talks with President Kennedy in November, Chancellor Adenauer agreed to support further Allied exploratory talks with the USSR with a view to major negotiations over Berlin. In contrast to his long-standing position that any East-West accord on Berlin should come only within the context of an over-all solution of the German problem, Adenauer apparently now prefers a narrow approach limited to Berlin in order to avoid broader negotiations which might involve European security arrangements and limit West Germany's weapons capability. The new West German government's first policy statement declared that its fundamental foreign policy objectives would be:

1) the security of the Federal Republic;

2) the maintenance of the existing political, legal and economic ties between West Berlin and West Germany; and

3) continued adherence to the goal of German reunification, non-recognition of the East German regime and the eventual settlement of frontier questions in an all-German peace treaty. The coalition contract of the Christian Democratic and Free Democratic parties, which make up the new government, also explicitly rejected any loosening of ties with West Berlin or any recognition of the East German regime.

Adenauer's fondest hope has been that firm resolve and a strong military posture eventually would convince the Soviets that the West could not be intimidated, causing Moscow to back away from its demands and allow indefinite continuation of the *status quo*. In any event, Adenauer and most of Bonn's governmental leaders clearly give first priority to the maintenance of the independence and security of the Federal Republic, which they believe can only be assured by close military, as well as political, ties with the West. The Chancellor has strongly and consistently opposed any withdrawal of Allied forces from Germany or disengagement of the Federal Republic from NATO. Berlin, although very important, is secondary, and Adenauer is believed to be extremely reluctant to risk nuclear war over the city.

To facilitate agreement, Bonn officials have hinted that further technical-level contacts with East Germany—including the establishment of commissions for transportation, mail and trade matters—might be possible. Bonn also is willing to repeat its pledge not to use force to achieve reunification or modify existing boundaries, and will "stand by" its renunciation of ABC weapons—in anticipation that its needs can be met within NATO—although Adenauer opposes repeating the latter in connection with a Berlin solution.

In the past—especially during various periods of intense pressure on Berlin—Adenauer has considered extending *de facto* recognition to the East German regime, provided this would result in an effective *status quo* agreement. He reportedly expressed such views to the executive committee of the CDU Bundestag faction in March 1959, and in October 1960, reportedly stated his willingness to negotiate West Germany's then suspended interzonal trade agreement with East Germany at a governmental level high enough to imply such recognition if the East Germans would "guarantee" free access to and from West Berlin.

Generally speaking Berlin Mayor Brandt goes further than Adenauer in insisting that all ties between West Berlin and the Federal Republic be maintained, and has criticized the Chancellor for not being vigorous enough in maintaining them. Brandt opposes abandoning such symbols of Bonn-Berlin ties as the annual Bundestag meetings in West Berlin, and has assailed Adenauer's suggestion that certain non-essential agencies of the federal government might be removed from the city. Social Democratic Party (SPD) officials, including Brandt, are critical of the negotiating line favored by Adenauer and the US, arguing that no permanent Berlin solution is possible apart from reunification. Brandt also opposes the idea of a new Bonn-West Berlin "contract" to regulate the relations between the city and West Germany, warning that any change in the city's existing relations with the Federal Republic would require a constitutional amendment which the SPD can and will obstruct.

East German Policy Toward Berlin

Ulbricht's primary objective in any East-West negotiation is to gain at least *de facto* recognition. He won an important victory in this respect at the Geneva Foreign Minister's Conference of 1959, when East and West Germany were admitted on equal footing in an advisory capacity. Ulbricht defined his current demands on 23-26 November: "The negotiations ... will have to establish how—while account is taken of certain Western prestige interests—the troops stationed in West Berlin can gradually be reduced, how the sabotage and disruptive activities launched from West Berlin can be liquidated, and by what agreements with the GDR the use of the lines of communication from and to Berlin—all of which form part of the sovereign territory of the GDR—are to be settled. The Soviet government and the GDR government have declared their readiness to provide guarantees for the free city of West Berlin, provided the Western powers undertake to renounce any interference with the domestic affairs of the GDR and to respect the sovereignty of the GDR." He emphasized that East Berlin belongs *de jure* to the GDR and that lines of communication between West Berlin and West Germany are to be used only on the basis of "contractual" arrangements with

14

the GDR. Both demands are intended to enhance East German sovereignty, although the reference to "respect for," rather than "recognition of," East German sovereignty may permit some latitude.

The East Germans seek to weaken—eventually to eliminate—ties between West Berlin and West Germany, to reduce Bonn's stature and increase the West Berliners' sense of isolation. To date, their public statements have allowed for the maintenance of economic and cultural links between a "free city" of West Berlin and West Germany, on a "country-to-country basis," while demanding an end to all political ties and the elimination of West German government offices in the city. They appear to be moving on to new demands, however—probably encouraged by such developments as Bonn's decision not to convene meetings of the West German parliament in Berlin. On 14 December, East Berlin party boss Paul Verner demanded that the West Berlin Senate discontinue the practice of re-enacting West German laws for application in West Berlin.

Section II

Legal Basis for the Western Presence in Berlin

Basis for Occupation (Pertinent documents listed below*)

The four-power status of Berlin and the Western basis for occupying the city **as a whole** are derived from the four-power agreements of the European Advisory Commission (EAC) dated 12 September 1944-14 November 1944, amended 26 July 1945; the four-power statements of 5 June 1945; the Truman-Stalin letters of 15-16 June 1945; and the Potsdam agreements of 2 August 1945. The EAC agreements specifically defined zones of occupation in Germany and provided that Berlin was to be jointly administered. The 5 June "statement" signed by Marshal Zhukov specifically states: "The area of 'Greater Berlin' will be occupied by forces of each of the four Powers. An Inter-Allied governing Authority (*Kommandatura*) ... will be established to direct jointly its administration."

The Potsdam agreements state: "The Allied armies are in occupation of the whole Germany ..." and that "supreme authority in Germany is exercised, (by the four powers) each in his own zone of occupation, and also jointly, in matters affecting Germany as a whole ..."

On 14 June 1945 President Truman informed Stalin that American troops would withdraw from the Soviet Zone "in accordance with arrangement between respective commanders included in these arrangements simultaneous movement of the national garrisons into greater Berlin and **provisions of free access by air, road and rail from Frankfurt and Bremen to Berlin for US forces.**" In replying on 18 June 1945 Stalin asked for a postponement of US withdrawals and entrance into Berlin until July. No mention, however, was made by Stalin of future access to Berlin.

Access to Berlin

In addition to the Truman-Stalin exchange, which is the only document spelling out complete freedom of access to Berlin, there are separate agreements on road, rail, and air access. The three air corridors were agreed to by the Allied Control Council on 30 November 1945. An agreement was also reached by the Aviation Committee of the Air Directorate establishing the four-power Berlin Air Safety Center (BASC) on 12 December 1945, with minor revisions in 1946.

Rail access for Western military trains, together with a schedule of daily traffic, was agreed to on 7 September 1945 and approved by the

Control Council on 10 September 1945. An Autobahn route was agreed upon orally by General Clay and Marshal Zhukov on 29 June 1945.

There is no basic agreement concerning water access, although the British negotiated a separate agreement with the USSR in 1946.

There is, therefore, no specific document **signed by all four governments** providing for free and unrestricted access to Berlin. However, during the Berlin blockade the US, in a 6 July 1948 note to Moscow, stated that: "These agreements implied the right of free access to Berlin. This right has long been confirmed by usage."

*Pertinent Documents (included in Annex to original)

1. Allied Control Council CORC/P (45) 30, 7 Sept 1945

2. Allied Control Council CONL/P (45) 63, 28 Nov 1945

3. Allied Control Council CORC/P (45) 170, 22 Nov 1945

4. Allied Control Council CONL/M (45) 13, 30 Nov 1945

5. European Advisory Commission Agreement, 12 Sept 1944

6. European Advisory Commission Agreement, 14 Nov 1944

7. Potsdam Agreement, 2 Aug 1945

8. Allied Control Council Proclamation #2, 20 Sept 1945

9. US Note to the USSR, 6 Jul 1948

10. Truman-Stalin Letters, 15-16 Jun 1945

11. Allied Control Council DAIR/P (45) 67, 13 Dec 1945

Section III

The Berlin Wall

The wall separating East and West Berlin is actually a system of barriers and obstructions of many different types, rather than a single, definite feature. For 43 kilometers, or about 26-½ miles, it closely parallels the sector boundary but does not always coincide exactly. The wall, like the sector boundary, mainly follows roads, railroads, canals, or other dividing lines, such as the margins of parks and cemeteries. For about 28 kilometers, or 65 percent of its length, it traverses areas that are built up on one or both sides, whereas for the rest of the distance (15 kilometers: 35 percent) it extends through relatively open areas. The wall parallels railroads for some 8 kilometers and canals for about 10 kilometers. Structurally, it is most formidable in the densely populated central core of Berlin and somewhat less so in the less populated northern and southern areas.

Roughly one-third of the wall, mainly the central section, is composed of masonry alternating with the walls of sealed buildings, generally supported by secondary obstructions. Except for a stretch where the Spree constitutes a natural boundary, further fortified by barbed wire, masonry wall extends along the bulge in the central core of the city. Other sections are formed by multiple barbed wire fences which follow canals and railway embankments and other earlier barriers to east-west movement. Secondary obstructions of masonry wall, tank barriers, pavement blocks, and cleared strips back up the main wall. Lightly constructed fences seem to have been erected mainly to cut off visual contact. Communist officials of East Germany have announced that they will clear a continuous strip 100 meters in width along the East Berlin side of the wall. This will be costly and time-consuming, and involve obliterating cemeteries, churches, and historical landmarks. To date, the cleared-strip plan seems to have been implemented near the extreme northern and southern ends of the wall, where it involved little more than removing orchards, gardens, tool sheds, and the like. Only a few changes indicate clearing in the central core area.

The wall is strongest at the Brandenburg Gate, a point of great symbolic as well as geographic significance. Here the East Germans have piled prefabricated concrete slabs in layers forming a wall 7 feet high and 6 feet thick with steel-post reinforcement. Away from the Brandenburg Gate, the masonry wall is made of very large prefabricated concrete slabs one foot thick. Around sharp curves and awkward corners, smaller concrete blocks are used; they are also used in other places to increase the height of the wall.

Generally the masonry wall is topped by Y-shaped iron rods strung with barbed wire.

Most of the wall is about 8 feet high, but some stretches along Bernauer Strasse are 10 feet high; and the boundary wall of the French cemetery is even higher. Generally, where the sector boundary follows the building line instead of curb or street line, the buildings have been incorporated into the wall by sealing doors and windows.

At authorized crossing points, obstructions have been placed across the road forming a maze with relatively narrow openings that require vehicles to zigzag slowly around obstacles.

In places the masonry wall is backed up by tank barriers. The most publicized of these are between the Reichstag ruins and Potsdamer Platz. Here two rows of heavy steel tripods are cemented into the ground behind the wall. Tank barriers are also located at each end of the masonry wall and along Zimmerstrasse from Wilhelm Strasse to Linden Strasse.

The remainder of the wall is comprised of one or more wire fences, backed by watch towers at irregular intervals. At the northern end, for example, there are 3 fences 7-½ feet high. The first follows the sector boundary, the second is 10 feet inside, and the third is some 150 yards to the east. The ground between the first two fences is covered with wire obstacles, whereas the area between the second and third fences has been cleared and can be lighted at night. Watch towers spaced about 600 yards apart provide vantage points for the armed guards. Where the garden colony of Schoenholz formerly adjoined the boundary, everything has been leveled. The situation is the same on the southern end of the sector boundary where the garden colonies of Daheim, Spaethsfelde, Grueneck and Am Rehpfuhl have been changed to a no-man's-land.

Section IV

West Berlin
(186 square miles; population 2,200,000)

Impact of the Wall on West Berliners

The closure of the sector border on 13 August and the construction of the wall strongly affected the morale of the outwardly calm West Berliners. More worried than at any time in the past two years, they regard the wall as a major Communist success which has dealt a blow to the city's four-power status and tipped the balance in favor of the East. As a result, their usual self-confidence has been shaken.

As an immediate effect of the closure, West Berlin industry was deprived of about 60,000 East Berlin and East German "border crossers" or 6.5 percent of its 900,000-man labor force. Large industry and small industry were affected differently, of course; neither was able to compensate fully in a short time for the loss of skilled employees. Small enterprises, where the key personnel frequently were border crossers, suffered, as did freight handling and coal deliveries. Retail shops along the sector border faced bankruptcy.

The situation has been reflected only mildly in over-all economic statistics—because of the relatively short period of time which has elapsed and because of the efforts of West German industry to aid Berlin with continuing orders. Nonetheless, industrial orders have declined somewhat, and the business community is deeply concerned over the future. Personal savings deposits have declined steadily since June.

The border closure brought about an increase in the number of West Berlin residents leaving the city. Approximately 500 a week left before 13 August; after, the number rose to about 1,700. This efflux is partially compensated for by the movement—mostly from West Germany—to Berlin. This number rose slightly from about 800 before 13 August to about 900 since that date. Thus, the net population drain has been running around 800 persons a week".

City leaders, searching for some basis on which to build the future of their city, have suggested making it the cultural center of Germany, perhaps of all Europe, and a center for the training of persons from underdeveloped countries.

West Berlin's Legal Ties With Bonn (See Annexes 8 & C)

Although West Berlin has developed firm economic and political ties with West Germany over the past decade, the city's legal relationship with the Federal Republic remains complex and unique. West Berlin's legal status is in some ways similar to that of the West German states but remains limited by certain powers reserved to the three western Allies, whose forces officially occupy the city.

Since 1949 West Berlin has gradually become extensively integrated with West Germany in matters of economy, law, administration, and politics. West Berlin's relationship with the Federal Republic now is governed by the Western Allies' 1955 Declaration on Berlin. This document provides for a large measure of self-government by the Berliners and extensive economic and political integration with West Germany, but reserves certain key areas of responsibility to Allied control. The declaration did not change Berlin's status in international law as an occupied area. Neither the unilateral division of Greater Berlin by the Communists in 1948 nor the establishment of West German sovereignty in 1955 altered this status.

To avoid any action that might be interpreted by the USSR an nullifying the four-power responsibility for Berlin agreed on in 1944, Allied statements and declarations have consistently maintained that Greater Berlin has not become a state of the Federal Republic. The West Germans, on the other hand, have always considered Berlin legally one of their states—limited only by the special Allied responsibilities in Berlin. However, the common German-Allied interest in avoiding any situation lending itself to Soviet exploitation has thus far prevented this divergence of views from having much practical significance.

The Allies have actively encouraged the development of extensive political and economic relations between West Berlin and the Federal Republic. The most significant move in this regard was the approval in 1951 by the Allied authorities of a system in which Berlin may use "cover laws" to enact federal laws and regulations, merely by stating that the provisions of the federal law are also valid in Berlin rather than having the Berlin parliament re-enact the entire law.

Allied Responsibilities

Although all Berlin legislation, including that originating in the West German parliament, is still formally reviewed by the Western Allied commandants, a system of prior informal consultations has virtually eliminated the necessity for the Allies to amend or nullify such laws. Under this system, any federal bill containing a Berlin clause which might impinge on Allied rights or fields of special interest is discussed by Allied, Berlin and West German authorities when it is introduced into the Bundestag. This system has also promoted a close and cordial relationship between the Allies and the Germans and has minimized the chances for serious challenges to Allied authority in the city.

The degree of supervision exercised by the Allies has gradually been relaxed to the point where Berlin, with Allied consent, now may even amend occupation legislation. The 1955 Declaration on Berlin provided that the Allies would normally exercise powers only in such matters as (1) security, (2) disarmament and demilitarization, (3) relations with authorities abroad, (4) payment of occupation costs, and (5) authority over police to the extent necessary to ensure security.

As a result of continuing Allied responsibility for Berlin's security, West German defense legislation does not apply to Berlin, Berliners cannot be drafted into the West German armed forces, and West German Army units are not stationed in Berlin. Generally, however, Berlin is not precluded from participating in the fields reserved to the Allies as long as its actions do not conflict with existing Allied law. For example, despite the limitation of the 1955 declaration, the Federal Republic is allowed to represent Berlin abroad, and West Berlin is included in West German treaties which are made applicable by the same procedure used to effect federal German law in the city.

Berlin Role in Bonn Government

Despite legal restrictions insisted on by the Allies, Berlin takes an active and influential part in the federal government. The votes of Berlin's representatives in both houses of the West German parliament are not allowed to determine the passage or rejection of bills. Berlin delegates, however, participate in debates, introduce bills, and have full voting rights in committees. Berliners, moreover, hold high positions in the federal government and legislature: West Berlin Mayor Willy Brandt has served as president of the Bundesrat and was the chancellor candidate of the Social Democratic party in national elections last September; Heinrich Krone of Berlin is a minister without portfolio in the new Bonn government; and another Berliner, Ernst Lemmer, 1st minister for All-German affairs in the federal cabinet.

To stress Berlin's ties with the Federal Republic as well as to foster the idea that the city is Germany's national capital, the Bundestag and Bundesrat have regularly held annual meetings in Berlin, and two of the three meetings of the federal convention which elects the West German president have been held in Berlin. These meetings have come under increasing East German attack as part of a general bloc propaganda campaign against west Berlin's ties with West Germany. The federal government also has undertaken a special building program for government offices in Berlin, including reconstruction of the Reichstag building, burned in 1933. A Berlin residence for the federal president was completed in 1960.

Federal Agencies in Berlin

The development of close administrative, judicial, and fiscal relationships between Berlin and West Germany has led to widespread federal activity in the city. Preparations are under way to set up a new federal bank supervisory office in West Berlin early in 1962. Its establishment must, however, await a decision of the Federal Constitutional Court on objections to federal, as opposed to state, supervision of banking. The federal government is represented by a special commissioner for Berlin, Heinrich Vockel, who has under him a representative of each of the federal ministries, except defense. Federal agencies wield no executive powers over Berlin agencies, however, and in case of conflict with Allied policy, the authority of the Allied *Kommandatura* prevails.

Berlin is governed by a coalition of the Social Democratic party (SPD) and the Christian Democratic Union (CDU). As a result of the December 1958 city election, in which the SPD and CDU received 52.6 percent and 37.7 percent of the vote respectively, the West Berlin House of Delegates is comprised of 78 SPO and 55 CDU members. The Communists received only 1.9 percent of the vote and despite considerable effort and expenditure have no representation.

West Berlin Industry

West Berlin industry, despite its geographic isolation and mounting Soviet pressure against the city, shows no major sign of faltering. Since November 1958, 50,000 new jobs have been created. Of a total working force of nearly one million, 300,000 are employed in industry. Industrial sales rose almost 30 percent, from $1.9 billion to $2.5 billion during the period November 1958 to mid-1961. From August 1960 until August 1961, the city's production index rose by six percent, as compared to five percent for West Germany. There are more than 2,000 firms, including such world famous names as Telefunken, Siemens-Halske and Schering in West Berlin.

Electric and electronic products constitute the city's largest industry, accounting for 29 percent of its manufactures and 12 percent of the total West German electrical and electronics goods production. Food processing, textiles and machinery are among other leading industries. The physical reconstruction of Berlin also is a major industrial activity. The garment industry accounts for 46 percent of the total West German supply of women's clothing. Output of full length motion pictures has climbed to 40 a year.

Indices of West Berlin Industry

Production Index (1936 = 100)		Industrial Orders Index (1952 = 100)	
1952	51	1952	100
1953	62	1953	-
1954	76	1954	-
1955	94	1955	180
1956	107	1956	192
1957	114	1957	202
1958	119	1958	199
1959	133	1959	236
1960	153	1960	300
1961	166	1961	322
(Jan thru Oct)		(Jan thru Jun)	

Stockpiles

The knowledge that there exists a large stockpile which would stave off starvation in the event of another blockade is an important factor in bolstering West Berlin morale. Early in 1961, West Berlin was estimated to have on hand $200,000,000 worth of food, fuel and raw materials.

West Berlin officials estimated that as of 30 June 1961 reserves of hard coal, coke and brown coal briquettes were sufficient for a year and that supplies of storageable foodstuffs would last from four to twelve months. Fresh fruits and vegetables and whole milk are not stockpiled.

Enough construction materials, such as bricks, cement and lumber, have been accumulated to last a year. Petroleum stockpiles are inadequate, but additional storage facilities are being completed or are planned for early in 1962. A recent study by the West Berlin Senat indicated that—except for coal—the city gas and water works and other municipal enterprises had supplies for about six months. Based on their current levels of production, West Berlin industrial firms maintain an average of two months' supply, which, together with industrial materials maintained in stockpiles, would sustain plant activity for four to five months.

Table II

West Berlin Stockpiles
(as of 30 June 1961)

Fuels (in metric tons):

	Total Stocks	Percent of Program*
Coal, coke and briquettes	3,566,000	123
Firewood	22,600	100
Gasoline	27,039	-
Diesel Oil	31,035	-
*Program based on estimated needs for one year.		

Food (in metric tons):

	Total Stocks	Months Supply (Approx.)
Grain and flour	369,646	12
Cereals	52,473	12
Fats	28,324	6
Meat	46,200	6
Milk, dry whole	4,406	6
Coffee substitutes	6,132	12
Sugar	46,184	9

Dependence on West Germany

West Berlin's prosperity has been made possible only by extensive US and West German financial aid. For many years Bonn has made good the city's budget deficit and also has made large payments for social and insurance pensions. In 1960 the total West German contribution was about $370,000,000. This transfer of purchasing power enables West Berlin to cover its balance of payments deficit, which totaled $126 million in 1960. West Germany also assists Berlin through preferential taxes and shipping rates and promotes industrial orders for the city. Bonn recently put an additional $125 million at the disposal of West Berlin to help counteract the effects of the border closure.

West Berlin Trade

West Berlin has made remarkable progress in increasing exports and steadily reducing its import-export imbalance. In 1960 the city's total exports equaled 97 percent of imports. Some 86 percent of exports and about 90 percent of imports were accounted for in exchange with West Germany. Trade with the Communist bloc is limited, involving only 2 percent of exports and 3 percent of imports. East Germany supplies small quantities of fresh foods and agricultural products and a major portion of the brown-coal briquettes—a vital import since West Germany does not produce enough to meet its own and Berlin's needs. They are used extensively for heating Berlin's private dwellings. The bulk of West Berlin's food, hard coal, raw materials and various consumer goods are shipped from West Germany and other free world sources via the access routes through East Germany.

Berlin's leading exports are electrical, steel and chemical products and clothing. In recent years, West German markets have purchased about 65 percent of the city's total industrial output, including 73 percent of its production of the electrical equipment, the city's leading industry, and 70 percent of that of the clothing industry. The United States provides an increasing market for West Berlin exports, accounting for about $30,000,000 worth in 1960, as compared to $1,500,000 in 1950. The position of Asia and Africa—Berlin's fastest growing market in 1958—declined in 1960, while trade with European countries increased, reflecting a high level of demand throughout Europe and Berlin's difficulty in providing credits for under-developed countries.

West Berlin - West Germany Transportation (See Map)

West Berlin's dependence on its lifeline to west Germany is demonstrated by the fact that 9,860,345 tons of commercial freight were shipped to and from the city in 1960. About five times as much cargo moves into the city as out, with 36 percent of the incoming tonnage carried by water, 34 percent by highway, 27 percent by rail, and 1 percent by parcel post. Trucks carry 59 percent of Berlin's exports, against 23 percent for water, 14 percent for rail, 4 percent for parcel post, and a fraction of 1 percent for airlift.

Table III

Freight Traffic (Metric tons)

To Berlin		January-October 1961	12 Months 1960
Air		Negligible	Negligible
Road		2,630,705	2,913,200
Rail		2,030,664	2,249,344
IWT		2,351,117	2,985,098
	Total	7,012,486	8,147,642
From Berlin			
Air		1,088	1,141
Road		904,850	1,059,839
Rail		215,555	240,847
Water		355,265	410,876
	Total	1,475,670	1,712,703

Parcel Post (Rail car loads)

		January-October 1961	12 Months 1960
To Berlin		7,272	8,859
From Berlin		7,383	9,259
	Total	14,655	18,118

Passenger Traffic (Excluding Allied Traffic & German Rail Traffic)

	January-October 1961		12 Months 1960	
To Berlin		Passengers		Passengers
Air	16,584 planes	626,756	17,815 planes	688,250
Auto	561,356 cars	1,453,388	531,645 cars	1,384,494
Motor Cycle	11,953 cycles	18,739	12,982 cycles	20,824
Bus	26,782 buses	728,054	27,852 buses	757,715
Total		2,826,887		2,851,283
From Berlin				
Air*	16,584 planes	677,787	17,815 planes	842,785
Auto	571,684 cars	1,504,565	522,883 cars	1,390,438
Motor Cycle	12,729 cycles	20,269	13,934 cycles	22,660
Bus	26,693 buses	742,214	28,056 buses	770,095
Total		2,944,835		3,025,978
*Including fly-outs of refugees.				

Railroad Passenger Traffic (Excluding Allied Traffic)

Exact statistics on railroad passenger traffic between the German Federal Republic and West Berlin are not available because travelers may board or leave trains in East Germany enroute to Berlin, in West Berlin or in East Berlin and in some cases may pass in transit through East Germany to Poland and beyond. The following statistics reveal the number of travelers who crossed the interzonal borders by rail at the four interzonal crossing points between the German Federal Republic and East Germany during 1960 and the first 10 months of 1961.

	January-October 1961	12 Months 1960
Exits from Federal Republic	1,999,973	2,304,716
Entry into Federal Republic	1,909,685	2, 220,761

West Berlin SED

The Socialist Unity Party (SED) organization in West Berlin, headed by first secretary Gerhard Danelius, claims to be an autonomous branch of the East German SED. In fact, it is controlled by the East Berlin SED organization. Its members, now estimated at less than 5,000, are organized on a ward basis, with a local unit in each of West Berlin's 12 districts. A legal party, it has not shown significant strength in recent elections—in December 1958 it pulled 31,572 votes, or less than 2 percent of the total. In addition to the SED, the Communists have various auxiliary organizations in West Berlin, such as the Society for German-Soviet Friendship. All these organizations lack financial support because of the economies imposed by the parent East Berlin SED organization. They nevertheless retain a potential for sabotage and harassing actions of various kinds, although in the final analysis the threat of such actions comes from East Berlin and East Germany—rather than from inside West Berlin.

West Berlin City Transportation

Although the bus and street car systems were divided in 1949, the elevated (S-Bahn) and subway (U-Bahn) systems served both West and East Berlin until 13 August 1961.

With two exceptions, all S-Bahn lines now terminate at the last station before crossing the sector border. One S-Bahn line running from the northern West Berlin suburb of Tegel to the southern West Berlin suburb of Wannsee still runs through the East Berlin sector stopping only at Friedrichstrasse where anyone entering or leaving is subject to East German controls. The central West to East S-Bahn also enters East Berlin, stops at Friedrichstrasse and then returns to West Berlin. Passengers entering or leaving at Friedrichstrasse are subject to East German controls.

The S-Bahn is operated by a department of the East German Reichsbahn administration, and is guarded by the East German Transport Police (Trapos). It is generally the cheapest and fastest—and most dilapidated—of Berlin's transportation media. About 450,000 West Berliners used the S-Bahn daily before 13 August, after which a boycott, inspired by the trade unions, began. The number of riders then declined to about 50,000 but later climbed back to about 100,000. To break the boycott, the Communists have maintained and even improved S-Bahn service in West Berlin. The boycott has created considerable transportation problems for West Berlin since other media have not been able to fill the gap. Transportation authorities have grappled with the problem by lengthening subway trains, increasing schedules, and ordering additional busses, but for many West Berliners, travel time has doubled and even trebled.

The U-Bahn in West Berlin is run by the city-owned BVG (Berlin Transportation Company), which was founded in 1929 and split into East and West administrations in 1949. The West Berlin U-Bahn, which owns 718 cars, carried 137,000,000 passengers in 1958.

Only two of the four U-Bahn lines that formerly operated in both East and West Berlin still pass through East Berlin. The line from Tegel, in northern West Berlin, to Tempelhof transits East Berlin stopping only at Friedrichstrasse. The Gesundbrunner-Leinestrasse line passes through East Berlin without stopping.

The BVG also runs 29 street car lines with 990 motor and trailer cars and had 714 busses on 40 lines before 13 August. Since then, it has additionally ordered 100 busses, has leased 51 from private firms, and has had 45 placed at its disposal at no charge by West German cities.

Since the sector border closure, the East German authorities have forbidden their barges and sight-seeing boats to transit West Berlin on the Havel and Spree rivers and the system of canals and locks, and Soviet Zone freight trains no longer enter West Berlin from East Berlin, but only from the Soviet Zone.

The Exclave of Steinstuecken

About one-half mile south of the Zehlendorf District of the US sector, but belonging to it, is the exclave of Steinstuecken, which is entirely surrounded by the East German district of Potsdam. Its inhabitants commute to West Berlin via an East German road on which the VoPos maintain three control points. Passage is limited to Steinstuecken residents, or for those who are acknowledged to have a "second residence" in the exclave; the East Germans stopped issuing passes to others wanting to enter Steinstuecken after 13 August. Steinstuecken has been subject to intermittent Communist harassment—in 1951 East German police invaded the area and sought to annex it. A near-emergency situation has been reached as a result of pressure since 13 August 1961. The East Germans have fenced off the exclave, except for the one access road to West Berlin, and blocked normal entrance to houses facing the Zone.

Zehlendorf District authorities sought to construct new roads to provide access to all properties, but VoPos prevented them from bringing in construction workers as "second residents." Clergymen, undertakers, tradesmen, service personnel, and even trash collectors are denied entry. Firemen, a mailman, a doctor and an ambulance driver are the only non-residents permitted through. On the basis of a 1959 agreement, a West Berlin electric meter reader can enter the area, which is supplied with power by the Zone electric company.

Seven other tiny areas of forest or farmland also constitute exclaves of the western sectors, but for all practical purposes have been absorbed into neighboring areas of East Germany or East Berlin. Two of these exclaves belong to the US sector, and five to the British.

In addition to the exclaves of the Western sectors, a large area adjacent to the British sector belongs to "Greater Berlin"—i.e. to East Berlin. In September 1945 the British traded part of Staaken to the Soviets in exchange for Gatow airfield. Although technically this area forms part of the "Mitte" District of East Berlin, it is administered from Potsdam District and its border with West Berlin is treated as a zonal, not sector, border.

Section V

The Borders

West Berlin is surrounded by two borders—one of which separates it from the Soviet sector of East Berlin, and the, other separating it from East Germany.

A. The Sector Border

The border between East and West Berlin passes through the center of the city in an irregular jagged line following the ancient borough delineations which have not changed, despite the alterations through the years. As a result, the border may run through the center of a street, or bisect a building or plot of land. Prior to 13 August 1961 the streets that crossed this border were blocked to vehicular traffic or under surveillance by East German police. However, there was very little restriction of pedestrian traffic even though an occasional spot check was made. Vehicular traffic was checked. The elevated electric railroad (S-Bahn) and the underground electric railroad (U-Bahn) crossed the sector border at several points. Although there were facilities for inspection and control of passenger traffic, few restrictions were imposed.

Since 23 August, all but seven crossing points on this sector border have been closed. Of the crossing points remaining, one is reserved for Allied and foreign diplomatic personnel, 4 for West Berlin residents and 2 for West Germans. They are:

(1) Reserved for Allied occupation forces, members of diplomatic corps and foreign travelers.

    a. Friedrichstrasse

(2) Reserved for residents of West Berlin.

    a. Chausseestrasse

    b. Invalidenstrasse

    c. Oberbaumbruecke

    d. Sonnen Allee

(3) Reserved for residents of the German Federal Republic.

    a. Bornholmerstrasse

    b. Heinrich Heine Strasse

The West Berlin-East German Zonal-Border

The West Berlin-East German zonal border is controlled by Soviet and/or East German guards at seventeen control points. As of 12 August (later information not available) they were:

(1) Glienecke Bridge, on the road to Potsdam, where two Soviet soldiers and two Volkspolizei man a movable barrier.

(2) The Sakrow Ferry, where two Volkspolizei man a barrier. There is a constant Soviet patrol here.

(3) The Autobahn checkpoint at Babelsberg, where two to four Soviet soldiers and five Volkspolizei man a movable barrier and check Autobahn traffic.

(4) Fifty meters north of the US checkpoint at Dreilinden where two Volkspolizei stationed in a wooden shack check identification cards of travelers other than Allied official travelers. There is a constant patrol of two or three Soviet soldiers in this area.

(5) Stahnsdorferdamm, on the road to Klein Machnow. There is a barrier here where vehicular traffic is checked by one Soviet soldier and two Volkspolizei. Apparently there is no pedestrian traffic here.

(6) Machnower Strasse, on the road to Steinstuecken. A movable barrier 1s operated by two Volkspolizei who check pedestrians and bicyclists. No vehicles can pass here. Two Soviet soldiers patrol this area.

(7) Berliner Strasse, on the road to Teltow. The street is partially blocked by a fixed barrier, a barbed wire fence, a ditch and piled-up sand. One or more Volkspolizei control pedestrians and bicyclists here.

(8) Diedersdorferweg in Marienfelde. There are four ditches across this road as well as a screen of shrubbery. There is a barrier about 200 meters inside East Germany which is guarded by one Soviet soldier and two Volkspollzei. Apparently pedestrian traffic is permitted here.

(9) Sakrower Landstrasse, on the road to Sakrow. There is a barrier operated by Volkspolizei and a guard house 200 meters inside East Germany. In addition, the road is barred to vehicular traffic by a tree barrier, a ditch and a wooden fence.

(10) Krampnitzerweg. Vehicular traffic barred by a tree barrier and a ditch. A movable barrier for pedestrians is operated 200 meters inside East Germany by two Soviet soldiers and two Volkspolizei.

(11) Potsdamer Chaussee. Vehicular traffic here is barred by a ditch and a barbed wire fence. Two Volkspolizei in a guard house control pedestrian traffic.

(12) Heerstrasse, Highway 5 to Hamburg. A movable barrier is guarded by two Volkspolizei and two Soviet soldiers.

(13) Seegefelderweg, on the road to Falkensee. A barrier 20 meters inside East Germany is manned by two Soviet soldiers and one Volkspolizei. Vehicular traffic is barred by two ditches and a barbed wire fence.

(14) Schoenwalder Allee, on the road to Schoenwalde. Guarded by two Volkspollzei. Vehicular traffic barred by a ditch and screened by brush.

(15) Bergfeld Stadtweg, Frohnau. A barrier 200 meters inside East Germany guarded by Volkspolizei.

(16) Leninstrasse, leading to Glienecke. Closed to vehicular traffic. A fixed barrier guarded by one Soviet soldier and a Volkspolizei.

(17) Berlinerstrasse, to Glienecke. barrier, barbed wire and ditch. traffic. Blocked by a fixed barrier, barbed wire and ditch. Open to pedestrian traffic.

All access routes which are not controlled have been blocked and the entire border area is patrolled by East German police. Most of the border is marked by a fence and cleared areas and some sections contain watch towers. S-Bahn rail lines from West Berlin into East Germany have been blocked. Suburban East German travelers who formerly used the S-Bahn through West Berlin to East Berlin now must use the Berlin outer ring.

The Berlin Bypasses

A. **The Havel Canal** (Paretz-Niederneuendorf)

The Havel Canal, connecting the Upper Havel Waterway and the Oder River with the Lower Havel Waterway and the Elbe River is a means by which East German traffic may bypass West Berlin. The canal was completed in 1953 and is capable of handling barges of up to 750 tons. Two way traffic is possible although heavy silting sometimes limits two way traffic to barges of less than 500 tons.

B. **The Berlin Ring**

The Berlin ring is a standard gauge railroad which circles Berlin, thereby affording through trains a bypass of the center of the city. The outer ring was planned and some sections were completed before World War II. During 1948-1949 the uncompleted gaps were closed and about half of the entire route was double tracked. Since 13 August double tracking has been completed on the route from Birkenwerder on the northern outskirts of Berlin to Michendorf, southwest of Berlin, thereby completing the entire ring.

Section VI

The East Berlin Economy

East Berlin encompasses an area of 156 square miles and has 1,100,000 inhabitants, or 6.4 percent of the total population of East Germany. Industry provides employment for about one third of the 578,000-man work force. As a result of efforts to make it a "showplace" and to lessen the contrast with the Western sectors, living conditions probably are somewhat better than in the rest of the country. A key manufacturing center, it accounts for about 7 percent of East Germany's total industrial output, ranking 6th among the 14 administrative districts. East Berlin produces about 10 percent of the gross value of the country's metal processing industry output and is a major supplier of electric and electronic equipment to the Soviet bloc. It also provides a significant share of East German production of turbines, machine tools, high pressure boilers, antifriction bearings, rubber tires, and abrasives.

East German industry as a whole is heavily dependent on East Berlin industries, particularly for machinery and equipment. The four major East Berlin machine tool plants, for example, account for approximately half of the GDR's total production. The planned expansion of the East German electric power industry, moreover, will rely heavily on equipment produced in East Berlin. Finally, East Berlin is the most important center in the GDR for the manufacture of printing equipment, and ranks third in the output of ready-made clothing.

East German consumption levels generally are about 25 percent below those of West Germany, although this is less important now that the absolute level of East German consumption has passed the prewar level. Retail distribution gradually is being modernized; the East Germans have much less choice than the West Germans in purchasing consumer goods and consumer durables still are in very short supply. The supply of fresh fruits, vegetables and dairy products is irregular; there is still informal rationing of butter and potatoes. Before 13 August 1961 East Berliners were able to shop in the Western sectors, where the supply and choice of goods are much better. Some 50,000 East Berliners crossed daily to jobs in West Berlin and enjoyed a favorable rate of exchange for their earnings.

Section VII

Interzonal Trade

Interzonal trade between East and West Germany is conducted on the basis of a semi-barter agreement arranged through the TREUHAND-STELLE, a joint non-governmental agency. Trade in goods with the GDR represents 2 percent of the total West German exports and imports but it provides Bonn with a counter to possible East German moves to close access between the Federal Republic and West Berlin. For East Germany interzonal trade represents about 11 percent of its total volume of trade and provides important amounts of strategic items such as high grade steel products, machinery and transportation equipment, chemicals, coking coal, and some foodstuffs. When West Germany abrogated the interzonal trade agreement in September 1960, the East Germans realized the magnitude of their dependence on West Germany and launched a campaign to achieve "economic invulnerability" from western imports in general and West German imports in particular. Although interzonal trade will probably continue at a normal level in 1962, the achievement of "invulnerability" remains uppermost in the minds of the East German leaders and the GDR can be expected to continue dispersing its imports from West Germany to seek closer ties with the bloc.

A semi-barter trade agreement negotiated annually provides the basis for interzonal trade and establishes the amounts of permissible annual indebtedness between the two zones. Imbalances can be liquidated by deliveries of specified goods by the debtor country or by payment of currency. Total indebtedness is limited to 100 million DM on each account .

Goods exchanged between East and West Germany fall under two accounts. Sub-account I regulates exchange of steel, machinery, coal and coke for brown coal briquettes, petroleum products, and machinery. Sub-account II includes agricultural products, chemicals, textiles, some machinery and other goods not included in Sub-account I. East Germany has not only exceeded the credit margin under this account but is not able to transfer on the due date the money to pay its bills.

Section VIII

Access Routes and Controls

A. Air:

Flights between West Berlin and West Germany must pass through three corridors established by the occupying powers in 1945. The corridors are straight, 20 miles wide, and lead from a 20 mile "control zone" encompassing Berlin to Hamburg, Hanover and Frankfurt in the Federal Republic. The Western powers hold that there are no altitude limits within these corridors. The USSR, on the other hand, maintains that the Western powers have renounced any right to fly above 10,000 feet, and Moscow has objected to test flights of C-130 turboprop aircraft above this ceiling.

Within West Berlin three airports—Tempelhof, Tegel and Gatow—are used for military and commercial air traffic. Tempelhof, the largest, is most used for commercial operations. Located almost in the heart of the city, it has two 5,300 foot runways capable of accommodating C-124 and DC-7C type aircraft, is fully equipped for instrument flying, and has ample facilities for maintenance, freight and passenger handling and various operational offices. Tempelhof has a daily capacity of 720 planes.

Tegel, in the French Sector, opened for commercial traffic in January 1960. Equipped for instrument flying, it has 7,840 and 5,500-foot runways and is capable of handling medium-range jet aircraft, such as the Caravelle, It has a daily capacity of 500 planes. In the event of a blockade of surface transportation. Tegel would be of major importance. Gatow is a secondary field located in the British Sector. It is a military field. However. it has a permanently surfaced runway about 6,000 feet long, and a daily capacity of 280 planes.

Air corridor flights to Berlin are restricted to commercial-military planes of the occupation powers and subject to procedures and regulations agreed to by the quadripartite Berlin Air Safety Center, (BASC). The Western powers license air operations over Berlin and in the three corridors. Allied civil and US military flights are controlled by the US Air Force at Tempelhof. Military flights to Gatow and Tegel are controlled by the British and French military authorities.

Air France, British European Airways and Pan American fly into West Berlin. Together they made 17,815 flights in 1960, carrying 688,250 passengers into the city and 842,785—including 121,778 refugees—out. As of 1 November 1961 the three lines averaged 385 flights per week during 1961. Air France uses the Caravelle and the Super Constellation Aircraft, BEA the Vickers Viscount and Pan American the Douglas DC-6B.

B. **Roads**

Five roads are designated for interzonal and international traffic with East Germany and for traffic between West Berlin and the Federal Republic. All are thought to be in good condition. From north to south they are:

1. **Selmsdorf-Berlin**

This route enters East Germany north of Lubeck on highways 104 and 105. Highway 105 proceeds eastward to Wismar. Highway 104 proceeds in a southeasterly direction to Schwerin, where it connects with highway 106 running south to Ludwigslust and highway 5, the main Hamburg-Berlin route.

2. **Horst-Berlin**

This route enters East Germany on highway 5 and proceeds southeast through Ludwigslust, Nauen and Staaken to West Berlin.

3. **Marienborn-Berlin**

This is the four-lane autobahn which enters East Germany at Marienborn and extends eastward to Berlin, approximately 165 kilometers. It is the only authorized route for allied military and other official traffic. Personnel travel on documents issued by their allied military commanders or by the allied ambassadors in Bonn. Travel controls are exercised by Soviet guards at Marienborn, on the western end of the Autobahn, and at Babelsberg on the eastern end at the outskirts of Berlin, before entry into West Berlin. Allied freight carried by truck is not subject to inspection or control. During the last half of November 1961, permanent raffles and drop gates were erected at Babelsberg by the East Germans to facilitate traffic control.

4. **Wartha-Berlin**

This route, an autobahn, enters East Germany at Wartha and extends east to Gera, where it joins a north-south autobahn to Berlin.

5. **Hof-Berlin**

This route enters East Germany on highway 2 north of Hof and joins the main north-south autobahn to Berlin. It is the main Berlin-Munich autobahn; traffic is detoured over highway 2 because a principal bridge near the zonal boundary has not been restored.

All highways from the Federal Republic enter West Berlin at one of two points on the West Berlin-zonal border. The Selmsdorf-Berlin and Horst-Berlin routes enter West Berlin via East German highway number 5 at Staaken. The Marienborn, Wartha, and Hof routes enter West Berlin via the autobahn at the Babelsberg-Dreilinden checkpoint. Over 60% of all West German vehicles use the Helmstedt Autobahn. About 8,000 American passenger cars travel it annually. Freight traffic must pass East German customs control upon entering or leaving East Germany. Road tolls are assessed according to a schedule established by East German authorities. These tolls amounted to an estimated 41.7 million DM (West) in 1960.

C. **Railroads**:

There are seven East-West German interzonal crossing points for rail traffic. Five of them normally are used for freight. International passenger trains between Western Europe and East Germany, including Berlin, normally are routed over four of these crossing points. From north to south the seven crossing points are:

1. **Lubeck-Herrnburg**

This route serves the northern area of the German Federal Republic and East Germany and links with a ferry connection to Denmark and Sweden.

2. **Buchen-Schwanheide** (Hamburg-Berlin)

This is the principal route between Hamburg and Berlin and formerly extended about 245 kilometers from the interzonal crossing point, through West Berlin, to the main railroad station in East Berlin. At Nauen, in East Germany, it connects with the Berlin Outer Ring and by-passes West Berlin. The route is double-tracked from the interzonal crossing point to Wittenberge (110 km), and alternately double or single tracked from Wittenberge to the Berlin Outer Ring. There are 35 bridges, ranging in length from 10 to 70 meters, on this route. All are thought to contain demolition chambers.

3. **Vorsfelde-Oebisfelde**

This is a major route between the Ruhr and Berlin, and is used to route empty freight cars from West Berlin to the Federal Republic. The distance from Oebisfelde to the East Berlin main railroad station, passing through West Berlin, is about 170 kilometers. From Oebisfelde to the Berlin Outer Ring at Wustermark, the distance is 137 km. This route is largely single tracked from Oebisfelde to the Berlin outer Ring and multiple tracked into East Berlin. There are twenty-five bridges, ranging in length from less than ten meters to an 810 meter span across the Elbe River, on this route. All are thought to be chambered for demolition.

4. Helmstedt-Marienborn

All allied freight and passenger traffic and all West German freight traffic to West Berlin use this route. It also serves as the principal route for international rail traffic from Western Europe to Eastern Europe via Berlin, and for through passenger cars between Paris and the Hook of Holland and Moscow. The distance between Helmstedt and the East Berlin railroad passenger station, transiting West Berlin, is 196 kilometers. The distance from Helmstedt to Wildpark, where the route connects with the Berlin Outer Ring is 158 kilometers. The route is double tracked from Helmstedt to Beideritz, (56 km), and single tracked from Beideritz to Wildpark. There are about 45 bridges, the longest of which is a 680 meter span across the Elbe River. All are thought to be chambered for demolition.

As authorized by a 1945 quadripartite agreement, there are 13 freight trains, including all Allied military freight trains, from the Federal Republic to Berlin daily, with a maximum capacity of 800 tons per train. Allied freight, which is not subject to inspection or control, moves on the basis of a document known as a warrant. There has never been an agreement on outbound freight trains, which average about one per day. Empty freight trains returning to West Germany from West Berlin may be routed via Stendal through the interzonal crossing point at Oebisfelde.

There are ten pairs of West German passenger trains a day between West Berlin and the Federal Republic, plus two American and one British, in addition to two pairs of French trains a week. Allied trains to Berlin are pulled by East German locomotives and manned by East German personnel. As of 23 November 1961, USCINCEUR reported the following schedule for US Army Duty Trains:

Departure	Time	Arrival	Time
Bremerhaven	1948Z	Berlin	0512Z
Frankfurt	2014	Berlin	0652
Berlin	2040	Bremerhaven	0540
Berlin	1807	Frankfurt	0536

5. Bebra-Wartha

This route enters East Germany at Gerstungen, reenters the Federal Republic for a short distance north of Gerstungen and again enters East Germany near Wartha. The East German regime is constructing a by-pass for the Gerstungen-Wartha stretch near Eisenach. The distance from the interzonal border to the main railroad station in East Berlin via Erfurt and Leipzig, transiting West Berlin, is 350 kilometers. The distance from the interzonal border to Michendorf, where the route connects with the Berlin Outer Ring, is 310 kilometers. This route is double-tracked throughout, and electrified from Leipzig to Dessau. There are over 100 bridges, most of which are thought to be chambered for demolition.

6. Ludwigstadt-Probstzella

This is the principal route between Berlin and South Germany and provides a connection between Berlin and Munich and with Austria and Italy. It enters East Germany at Probstzella and proceeds to Berlin via Leipzig, transiting West Berlin, a distance of 323 kilometers. The distance from Probstzella to Michendorf, where the route joins the Berlin Outer Ring, is about 230 kilometers. It is single-tracked from Probstzella to Leipzig and double-tracked from Leipzig to Serlin.

7. Hof-Gutenfurst

This line, a principal route for international freight trains from Austria and Italy to Berlin and to the Scandinavian countries, enters East Germany at Gutenfurst and serves local passenger traffic.

All freight and passenger trains between the Federal Republic and West Berlin enter or leave West Berlin via Griebnitzsee and Drewitz in the Soviet zone. The Hamburg-Schwanheide, Vorsfelde-Oebisfelde, Helmstedt-Marienborn and the Bebra-Wartha lines enter West Berlin via Griebnitzsee, near Potsdam. The Ludwigstadt-Probstzella line enters via Drewitz in the south. Passenger trains on these lines stop at "Station Zoo" in West Berlin before crossing the intersector border and terminating at the Friedrichstrasse station in East Berlin. The Lubeck-Harrnburg and Hof-Gutenfurst: lines do not enter West Berlin.

Passenger traffic across the interzonal crossing points is subject to the same controls as highway traffic. However, in some instances customs and immigration control is exercised aboard the trains. International travelers to

East Germany may obtain entry or transit visas at the interzonal crossing points in East Germany or aboard the international trains in East Germany.

Freight traffic is subject to customs control upon entry into East Germany. Parcel post trains to and from West Berlin are subject to particularly careful control according to available reports.

D. **Inland Waterways**:

There are two inland waterway connections between the Federal Republic and East Germany. Both are linked to greater Berlin through a system of canals. The connecting waterways are the Elbe River and the Mittelland Canal.

1. The Elbe River connection is at Cumlossen about 45 kilometers downstream from Magdeburg, on the interzonal border. The Elbe flows from the Czechoslovak border 570 kilometers through East Germany, past Dresden and Madgeburg, and continues through the Federal Republic to Hamburg. Near Magdeburg it connects with the Elbe-Havel Canal which, in turn, links with the Lower Havel waterway system serving Berlin. In West Berlin the Lower Havel connects with the Teltow Canal, the Oder-Spree system and the Oder River at the Polish border. North of Berlin the Lower Havel connects with the Oder-Havel system, which also connects with the Oder River on the Polish border. The Havel Canal branches off the Oder-Havel system north of Berlin to join the Lower Havel system, thus by-passing West Berlin. The greater portion of this system is capable of handling barges of up to 750 tons, although there have been some indications that silting in the Havel Canal bypass may limit the capacity of that waterway to barges of less than 750 tons. Upstream from Hamburg to Magdeburg the Elbe River can handle barges of 1,000 to 1,350 tons.

2. The Mittelland Canal, the second connection, enters East Germany at Buchhorst and joins the Elbe near Magdeburg. The average transit line from the Ruhr to Berlin via the Mittelland system is 6 days for self-propelled craft and 12 days for barges under tow.

Freight is subject to customs control. All vessels are required to have operating permits issued by the Federal Republic and East German authorities. Prior to April 1961 West German barges were required to pay tolls which amounted to 23.6 million DM (West) in 1960. These tolls were abolished by a decree of the East German Council of Ministers on 20 April 1961. West German vessels may proceed to East Berlin via West Berlin and are subject to police supervision upon entering East Berlin. Vessels of East

German registry have been prohibited from transiting West Berlin since 13 August 1961 and are permitted to enter West Berlin only at the Henningsdorf checkpoint on the Havel River north of Berlin. Prior to 13 August 1961, 1700 East German vessels, carrying 320,000 tons of freight, transited West Berlin each month. East German vessels now use the Havel Canal to bypass West Berlin. East German barges from the West with cargoes destined for East Berlin proceed through the Havel and Oder-Havel Canals to the Oder River, up the Oder to the Oder-Spree Waterway and back to East Berlin via the Oder-Spree. This requires several additional days' time.

Soviet and Allied Military Forces

To match the firepower of the East Berlin border guards, West Berlin police on border patrol were issued American-made rifles and submachine guns on 23 October 1961—three days after the release of these weapons and gas grenades had been approved by the Allied Commandants. The Commandants also approved oral instructions to police to open fire (1) to protect fleeing refugees who reach West Berlin territory; (2) to return VoPo fire aimed into West Berlin and endangering police, civilians or military forces; (3) to repel VoPo encroachments; and (4) to prevent capture or damage of property in military or police custody.

Table IV

Western Strength in Berlin	
Force	Strength
United States Army	6,500
British Army	2,900
French Army	1,700
West Berlin Police	15,876

Allied Forces in West Germany

In the event of local hostilities the substantial Allied forces in West Germany probably are adequate for immediate defense purposes. (The comparative strengths of these forces appear in Table I.)

The West German armed forces, under the impetus of the current NATO buildup, are slowly approaching authorized strength. At present, they are at only 70 percent of that strength and their combat capabilities can be rated only as fair. The army is capable of providing an effective combat-ready force of eight fighting brigades from the eight NATO-committee divisions. Since mid-October 1961 Bonn bas recalled 5,000 reservists for one- to two-months' duty, twice extended by three months the terms of service personnel, agreed to increase arms purchases from the US, assembled F-l04 and G-9l aircraft for the first time in Germany, and approved seven NIKE sites in northern Germany. A law to extend conscription from twelve to eighteen months is to be introduced in the Bundestag early in 1962, when the Bundeswehr is expected to total 364,000. However, incomplete training and equipment will leave the West German military establishment substantially below full combat potential. The government has substantially increased its defense budget—according to one report by one billion dollars—and hopes to have twelve fully trained and equipped divisions assigned to NATO by July 1963, when total Federal Armed Forces strength will be approximately 375,000. Nine new air force squadrons—in addition to the eight already incorporated in NATO—are being formed. Production to fill part of the naval commitment to NATO lags because of shortfalls in the construction of conventional destroyers. The Defense Ministry is considering the construction of six missile firing destroyers.

The First French Army, headquartered at Baden-Baden, comprises two divisions in the Saar-Mosel and Palatinate-Wuerttemberg-Baden areas. Attrition and obsolescence of equipment and inadequate training has greatly reduced combat effectiveness. Paris has announced that it intends to fill out divisions in Germany—now at 80 percent of strength—by adding 10,000 men to the First Army. Another division, with its headquarters in France, has one brigade in Germany opposite the Swiss border. Paris has also recalled the 7th Light Armored Division and the 11th Light Infantry Division from Algeria to eastern France and has indicated that three additional divisions will be recalled to Europe in 1962. France has increased its air defense capabilities along the French-German border with the assignment to tactical units in 1961 of the first Mirage IIIs—a high-performance jet interceptor.

The British Army of the Rhine (BAOR), 50,000 men comprising five infantry and two armored brigade groups and the 3,000 man non-NATO Berlin garrison, would have to be increased by approximately 40,000 men to give it M-day status, according to NATO military authorities. Recent BAOR exercises revealed extensive deficiencies in manpower and conventional equipment and an unpreparedness to fight a non-atomic war. BAOR lacks support units and is dependent on 40,000 West German employees, whose loss in the event of hostilities would practically cancel combat logistic capabilities. British planning assumes a seven-days' warning in order to reinforce the BAOR with two brigade groups; but there are no UK forces currently earmarked as a strategic reserve—although moves are underway to assemble such a force by recalling reserves. Such troops would be partially trained. The BAOR probably could not be brought to wartime strength in fewer than 60 days.

Canadian forces consist of two excellently trained and equipped brigade groups, at 100 percent of strength. The Canadians are assigned to the British sector under the over-all command of the BAOR.

Belgian forces in West Germany are at about 75 percent of combat strength. Training and equipment are fair.

Table V

Allied Forces in West Germany					
Nationality	Army	Navy	Air Force		Total
			Manpower	Combat Aircraft	
West German	232,000	25,000	80,000	555	337,000
French	49,000	—	4,000	63	53,000
British	52,639	—	10,300	122	62,939
Canadian	5,800	—	2,500	—	8,300
Belgium	36,000	—	100	—	36,100
United States	237,000	700	343,000	357	271,700
Total	612,439	25,700	130,900	1,097	769,039

Communist Forces in East Germany

The comparative strengths of Soviet and East German forces in East Germany appear in Table III.

The Group of Soviet Forces, Germany (GSFG), consists of six armies made up of 10 tank and 10 motorized rifle divisions—at about 70-75 percent of strength. Support elements include: free rockets of up to 35 miles range, mounted on tracked amphibious chassis; and 150-mile, 350-mile, and possibly a few 700-mile SS missiles. The six Soviet armies are deployed tactically. The bulk of the motorized rifle divisions are forward in the armies on the western borders of East Germany, and the tank divisions of the tank armies are disposed on the flanks and in depth. These forces constitute a highly-trained, mobile, striking group capable of immediate deployment for combat operations.

The East German Army is organized into two military districts which, during war, could become tactical army headquarters. The units are disposed generally throughout the country. Its size has remained fairly constant, at 75,000 men, organized in four motorized rifle and two tank divisions similar to the most modern Soviet ones. It is well equipped, with no notable shortages except in heavy long-range artillery and reserve stocks of weapons. In training exercises, the East German Army has in the last few years displayed a high standard. In recent years, an extensive reserve program has been developed; and there are now about 250,000 trained reserves. The chief weakness of this army is its dependence on the Soviet Union for logistic support.

Soviet air forces immediately available for support of ground operations include 522 jet fighters and 120 jet light bombers of the 24th Tactical Air Army stationed in East Germany, and 252 jet fighters in the 37th Tactical Air Army in Poland. Readily available for reinforcement of the air forces in East Germany and Poland are 6 air armies in the western USSR and the air forces of the Soviet Southern Group of Forces in Hungary, plus bomber elements of naval aviation, with a total of 1,030 jet fighters, 490 light bombers, 1,216 medium bombers, and 87 heavy bombers.

The East German Air Forces consist of about 200 jet fighters organized into 6 fighter-interceptor regiments. Because of the relatively low level of pilot training and because only 24 of these aircraft are night fighters, the operational capability of these forces, particularly in night or all-weather flight operations, would be slight.

There are also 12 operational SAM sites protecting Berlin and key Soviet installations. Additional support to ground operations could be furnished by medium-range ballistic missiles deployed at Tauragesite and Mukachevo in the western border districts of the USSR, well within range of the target area.

The reinforcement of Soviet ground forces in East Germany could be most readily accomplished by 41 combat-ready line divisions now located in the 3 western border districts of the USSR and 2 in Poland. Disregarding the effects of any Allied interdiction effort, these divisions, using 8 major road and 6 rail routes from the Soviet Union to the West German border, could be introduced into the area of operations at the rate of 4 divisions per day, beginning on the third day after movement was initiated. Two of the divisions in the western border districts of the USSR are airborne units and could be deployed in East Germany within one or two days. The remainder of the divisions are tank and motorized rifle. Although they would not be employed in the limited action being assumed, the Czechoslovak Army of 14 divisions would probably be deployed along Czechoslovakia's northern and western frontiers and brought up to strength as a threat to tie down US forces in West Germany. The four divisions of the Soviet Southern Group of Forces in Hungary could also be a threat to the US southern flank, but these divisions might be required in Hungary to maintain the stability of the Communist regime there.

Enemy logistical requirements could be met from supplies currently stockpiled in the 14 major and numerous smaller depots in East Germany, which are believed sufficient to support the 20 divisions in GSFG for about 60 days of combat. Rail, road, air, and sea lines of communication from the Soviet Union into East Germany are adequate to move and support a force larger than the 6 East German and 63 Soviet line divisions mentioned above.

Soviet-East German basic capabilities, therefore, are as follows:

a. The East German Army could oppose a penetration of East Germany along the Helmstedt-Berlin Autobahn with 4 motorized rifle and 2 tank divisions, supported by 182 jet fighters of the East German Air Forces.

b. The Soviets could resist a penetration effort on the Helmstedt-Berlin axis by concentrating 4 motorized rifle and 3 tank divisions in the Helmstedt-Magdeburg area within 12 hours after starting movement. For this operation and defense of the remainder of the East German border, the Group of Soviet Forces, Germany, could use any or all of its 10 motorized rifle and 10 tank divisions, supported by missiles and by 522 jet fighters and 120 jet light bombers in East Germany, and by missiles and medium and heavy bombers from the Soviet Union.

c. The Soviets could reinforce their forces in East Germany with up to 43 divisions from Poland and western USSR within 12 days, as well as with additional fighters and light bombers.

d. Concurrently with these capabilities, the Soviets and East Germans could seize West Berlin at any time.

Tabel VI

1. Strength in East Berlin	
Force	Strength
Security Guard Regiment (MFS)	4, 500
1st and 2nd Border Brigades, Berlin	8,500
East German Army	—
Soviet Army	6,900
	2 motorized rifle regiments	
	1 tank regiment	
	5 independent brigades	
Total	19,900

2. Strength in East Germany			
	Soviet	East German	Totals
Army	320,000	85,000	405,000
Navy	500	11,000	11,500
Air Force			
Manpower	28,500	8,000	36,500
Aircraft	657	200	857
Other	—	50,000	50,000
Total	349,000	154,000	503,000

Annex A

Select Chronology On Berlin

-1958-

10 Nov   In a speech in Moscow, Khrushchev stated that the USSR intended to hand over to the East German regime "those functions in Berlin which are still with the Soviet organs." Khrushchev declared because of their "violation" of various aspects of the Potsdam Agreement, the Western Allies "have long ago abolished that legal basis on which their stay in Berlin rested." Charging that the Allies misused Berlin "which is the capital of the German Democratic Republic (GDR)" as a base for "subversive activities" against the GDR and the Warsaw Pact countries, Khrushchev called on the Allies to "form their own relations with the GDR and come to an agreement with it themselves if they are interested in certain questions connected with Berlin ... " He also committed the USSR to give military support to the GDR in the event that the Western Powers engaged in "provocation" to defend their access rights to Berlin. Khrushchev further stated that "the Soviet Union has been proposing and proposes to tackle this matter [signing of a German peace treaty] without delay."

27 Nov   The USSR sent a note to the three Western Powers in which it stated that "the Soviet Government finds it possible for the question of Western Berlin to be settled for the time being by making Western Berlin an independent, demilitarized free city." The USSR laid down an apparent ultimatum stating that if the Western Powers did not agree to negotiate the details of a "free-city" status for West Berlin within six months, there would be "no topic left for talks on the Berlin question by the former occupying powers," that the East Germans would be empowered to control Allied access to the city, and the Soviet Union would refuse further contact with the Allies there. By specifically confining its proposals to West Berlin. Moscow showed that it considered East Berlin as East German territory. By demanding that both German states participate in any agreements concerning the creation of a "free-city" of West Berlin, the USSR indicated that recognition of the GDR was an immediate goal.

-1959-

10 Jan   In reply to the Western notes of 31 December, the Soviet Union sent notes to 27 other countries that fought Germany in World War II proposing that a 28-nation conference be held within two months in Prague or Warsaw to negotiate a peace treaty with Germany as a step toward settling the West Berlin problem. Accompanying the notes was a draft peace treaty to be signed by both German states.

24 Jan   At a news conference in Moscow, Mikoyan said that the main factor in the Berlin crisis is not the Soviet deadline but to get talks started between East and West and "to end the occupation status of West Berlin." Negotiations "could be prolonged for a few days or even a few months" if they were conducted "in the spirit of finding a settlement" and if the Soviet Union could "see there is goodwill on the part of the Western Powers."

7 Feb   Khrushchev, in a speech at Tula, stated for the first time that the USSR was ready to sign a separate peace treaty with East Germany by which the GDR would "acquire all the rights and will be bound by all the obligations of a sovereign state." "Therefore, no encroachment whatever on the territory of the GDR, in whose center Berlin lies, can be permitted, either by land, air, or water. Any violation of the sovereignty of the GDR will meet with a vigorous rebuff, irrespective of whether it will happen on water, on land, or in the air. All this should be considered by the gentlemen imperialists." The USSR, he said, has no concessions to make on the German question.

9 Mar   In Berlin, Khrushchev reaffirmed Soviet willingness to have the UN participate in guaranteeing the status of West Berlin as a "free city," adding that there would be no objection to a minimum garrison composed of US, British, French and Soviet forces as well as neutral troops to enforce the guarantee, but with no right to interfere in the "internal" affairs of the city. He repeated this formula the following day, insisting on Soviet participation if the West remained, but without mentioning neutrals.

9 May   Soviet Foreign Minister Gromyko, arriving in Geneva, called for a liquidation of the occupation forces in Berlin and for an early summit conference, which could make "necessary" decisions. East German Foreign Minister Bolz called for recognition of East Germany.

Khrushchev told a group of West German editors visiting Moscow that the Soviet Union could wipe the western Allies off the face of the earth.

10 May   Gromyko asked for full participation of both East and West Germany in the conference. The western foreign ministers said that a dispute on this question could prevent the conference from opening on time.

11 May   The Geneva conference opened after a delay caused by the Soviet proposal that East and West German delegations be admitted as full participants. Both sides claimed victory in the compromise seating arrangement which permitted both German delegations to be seated near, but not at, the conference table.

10 June   Gromyko offered a proposal for an interim agreement on Berlin. The West could "temporarily" maintain certain occupation rights for one year. During this period the two German states would set up a committee to discuss and work out measures on unification and peace treaty. If the Germans failed to reach agreement after one year, the USSR would sign a treaty with East Germany. The Western Powers were to reduce forces in Berlin to "symbolic contingents," restrict hostile propaganda, liquidate subversive organizations in Berlin, and agree not to station atomic or rocket weapons in West Berlin. If these were agreed upon, then the USSR would preserve communications to Berlin in present form. The interim agreement was to be guaranteed by four powers, and, secondly, by the East German government. The guarantees were to be based on a protocol already submitted (apparently for free city). The arrangement was to be supervised by a four power body.

19 June   Gromyko renewed his proposal for an interim settlement on Berlin but extended the 12 month deadline to 18 months with the foreign ministers to meet at the end of this interim agreement. The Big Four foreign ministers agreed to recess the conference until 13 July. The Western foreign ministers issued a statement charging that the latest Soviet proposals would reserve "freedom of unilateral action" to the USSR at the end of the specified period. The Soviet proposals were basically the same as those offered on 10 June. The western statement declared the Soviets hoped to induce the West to acquiesce in the liquidation of Western rights in

Berlin and Western responsibility for maintaining the freedom of the city. It referred to the recess as an opportunity for the USSR to reconsider its position and for the West to examine the situation in the light of Khrushchev's 19 June speech in which he said that the Soviet Union would never sign an agreement perpetuating the occupation status of West Berlin. Khrushchev called on the foreign ministers to renew their efforts to reach an interim settlement, and asserted that the Soviets have never issued an ultimatum on the Berlin situation. He repeated his willingness to go to any number of summit meetings to achieve a solution to East-West problems, and reaffirmed his intention to sign a separate peace treaty if there were no agreement on an all-German treaty within a specified period.

9 July   Soviet Deputy Foreign Minister Zorin told the West German Ambassador in Moscow that the USSR would accept a compromise time limit of two years, during which the West could remain in Berlin but under new agreements superseding those on which Allied rights are presently based, and that an all-German committee would attempt to negotiate a permanent settlement. Zorin stated that the USSR would not challenge Western rights in West Berlin at the end of this period if agreement had not been reached by the Germans. He observed that a separate peace treaty with East Germany would be a very serious step and that Moscow would resort to this alternative only after all attempts to reach a negotiated settlement had failed.

23 July   Khrushchev made a statement in a speech at Dnepropetrovsk that "the time has come" for the heads of government to tackle "complex unsettled international issues."

5 Aug   In a press conference in Moscow, Khrushchev adopted a posture of statesmanlike moderation and restraint, stressing the prospects for establishing a "climate of confidence and mutual understanding" between the US and the USSR and underscoring the "immense importance" of the state of US-Soviet relations for maintaining peace. He contended that there are no territorial disputes or "insoluble contradictions" standing in the way of "improved relations" and renewed his pledge that the status of Berlin would not be changed while negotiations are in progress. He added, however, that he did not consider the talks with Eisenhower a substitute for a conference of heads of government which the USSR still considered "useful and necessary."

27 Sept   The joint communiqué signed by Eisenhower and Khrushchev at the close of the Camp David Talks emphasized that the question of general disarmament was "the most important one facing the world today," stated that an exchange of views had taken place "on the question of Germany including the question of a peace treaty with Germany," and that, on the subject of Berlin, an understanding had been reached "subject to the approval of the other parties directly concerned, that negotiations would be opened with a view to achieving a solution which would be in accordance with the interests of all concerned and in the interest of the maintenance of peace."

21 Dec   The Western powers in similar notes to Moscow proposed the holding of a summit meeting in Paris on 27 April 1960.

25 Dec   Khrushchev's prompt and cordial acceptance of the Western proposal of 21 December for a four-power summit meeting in Paris carefully refrained from injecting any controversial issues. He expressed "profound satisfaction" that the powers had found it desirable to discuss "major international problems" at summit meetings which "should be held from time to time in countries participating in such conferences." His offer of alternative dates for the meeting was carefully phrased to avoid any appearance of pressure. His reference to the "four-power" meeting suggested that he did not intend to press for full participation by the two German states. On the other hand, in private talks with the Western ambassadors when delivering the 25 December letters, Gromyko raised the question of bringing in the Germans.

26 Dec   An official of the East German council of ministers said that Khrushchev and Ulbricht had worked out a "Berlin strategy" to be carried out in successive phases, according to a usually reliable source. In the first phase—the first summit meeting—Khrushchev would introduce a plan for the neutralization of West Berlin and follow this up with a proposal to eliminate all traces of the Federal Republic. In the second phase, the Communists would maintain pressure against West Berlin following the summit meeting to create suspense. In the third, the plan for neutralization would again be introduced, and Khrushchev would propose a four-power administration—including the USSR—in West Berlin. The Communists would be patient, in the expectation that it was only a

matter of time until the Western powers became "tired." The East German official further stated that bloc strategy was to some extent based on the assumption that a Democrat would be elected to follow President Eisenhower.

-1960-

25 Apr   In a major address at Baku, Khrushchev combined a rigid restatement of the maximum Soviet demands on Germany and Berlin with his most sweeping portrayal of the consequences of a separate peace treaty for the Western position in Berlin since he first threatened to conclude such a treaty. He totally rejected any summit discussion of reported Western proposals for an all-German plebiscite on reunification and a peace treaty. While his statements did not add any new elements to the established Soviet position on Berlin, he had not previously personally spoken of a separate peace treaty ending Western Allied air access to Berlin and of meeting force with force since his speech of 17 February 1959.

9 May   The Soviet Ambassador gave De Gaulle a proposal for an Interim Agreement on Berlin, "to prepare conditions for the ultimate transformation of West Berlin into a free city and the adoption of measures leading to the preparation of future peace settlement …

A. This temporary agreement would be for two years; to include approximately the same list of questions as discussed at Geneva. The agreement should envisage: (1) Reduction of effective strength of forces of three powers, to take place progressively in several stages; (2) No nuclear weapons or missile installations in West Berlin; (3) Measures to prohibit the use of West Berlin as a base of subversive activity and hostile propaganda; (4) The agreement would take account of the declaration of the Soviet Union and the GDR concerning the maintenance of communications of West Berlin with the outside world; (5) The engagements concerning the GDR could take a form which would not Signify diplomatic recognition of the GDR by West; (6) Supervision of agreement by four-power committee.

B. The Four Powers would make a declaration inviting the two German states to take advantage ot the interim period to attempt to arrive at a common point of view on the German question. Contact could be established between the two German states by creation of an all-German committee or some other form.

C. If the German states refuse to engage in conversations or if it becomes clearly evident that they are not able to come to an understanding, the four-powers will sign a peace treaty with the two German states, or with one of them, as they would judge it desirable. Moreover, measures will be taken in order to transform West Berlin into a free city. As for a statute for a free City, USSR would prefer to elaborate this in common with the three-powers. The Soviet Union states that it also favors participation of the UN in the guarantees for a free city.

20 May   Khrushchev made a speech in East Berlin in which he stated that the USSR had a moral right to sign a separate peace treaty with East Germany that would end Western rights in Berlin and give the GDR full control of access to the city. No unilateral action would be taken, however, until efforts were made at a summit meeting within "six to eight months" to reach agreement on a treaty with both German states. He offered qualified guarantee of *status quo* on condition that the Western powers would be willing to avoid "any unilateral steps" which would prevent a meeting in six to eight months. East German leaders were visibly distressed by Khrushchev's speech.

-1961-

9 Mar   In his conversation with Ambassador Thompson, Khrushchev showed some flexibility in his discussion of the Berlin problem, and asserted that the USSR would provide any guarantees necessary to preserve the internal situation in West Berlin and assure the US that its prestige would not suffer as a result of a settlement. He reiterated his intention to sign a peace treaty with the GDR with a clause providing for a free city of West Berlin if the West did not agree to a peace treaty with both German states, but he set no deadline for action.

24 Apr   Khrushchev told West German Ambassador Kroll that he had originally planned to raise the Berlin question during the first part of 1961, but that he realized President Kennedy needed more time. While emphasizing his determination to solve the Berlin and German Question during 1961, Khrushchev stated that the bloc had set no precise deadline and could wait until the West German elections and "possibly" until the Soviet party congress before convening a bloc peace conference to sign a separate treaty with

East Germany. Such restraint, however, would depend on no "unexpected" Western moves such as a Bundestag meeting in Berlin. As to the consequences of a separate treaty, Khrushchev stated that the Western powers would have to make arrangements with East Germany to maintain their communications to Berlin and that he would advise Ulbricht to abolish the air corridors. In response to Kroll's statement that this could bring about an international crisis, Khrushchev said he was convinced that the West would not risk a general nuclear war over Berlin. He said he expected that the West would resort to economic sanctions and possibly a break in diplomatic relations but that the USSR could cope with such measures.

4 June   The *aide memoire* delivered at the conclusion of the President's talks in Vienna with Khrushchev, summarized the standard Soviet position on Germany. While not foreshadowing a precipitate Soviet move on Berlin, it made clear that Moscow is not prepared to offer any concessions to break the existing impasse and, in effect, left the next step up to the West. The memorandum proposes a decision "without delay" to convene a peace conference to conclude a treaty with both German states, or to sign separate but similar treaties between the bloc and East Germany and between the West and the Federal Republic. The treaty would establish a free city and, as part of the guarantee for it, the West and Soviets would maintain token forces in West Berlin:. Neutral forces could also be introduced. If the West is reluctant to agree to a peace conference, the memorandum proposed an interim decision "for a specified period of time." All four-powers would then appeal to the "two German states" to negotiate a peace settlement and reunification within a period of "not more than six months." If these bilateral German talks tall, Moscow proposes to sign a separate treaty with East Germany, transferring access control to the GDR, formally defining West Berlin as a free city, with access to it "by land, water or air" dependent upon negotiations with the East Germans.

15 June   Khrushchev used his report on the Vienna meeting to emphasize his determination to carry through with his announced policy on Berlin and Germany. For the first time. he committed himself publicly to sign a separate treaty and transfer access controls to the East Germans if no East-West settlement is reached "this year." His exposition of the Soviet positions on other aspects of the German and Berlin issues followed closely the *aide memoire* handed to the US at the conclusion of the Vienna talks.

17 July   Soviet Ambassador Menshikov told White House staffer W.W. Rostow that it is "absolutely firm and predictable" that the USSR would convene a peace conference during the second half of November to sign a separate peace treaty with the East Germans. Menshikov said that invitations would be sent at some future date and asked whether he was correct in assuming that the US would not attend. He told Rostow that for the first time he believes war to be possible, though not inevitable; he expressed the hope that there would be US-USSR negotiations before it became inevitable. Asking, "Why do you wish to be in Berlin as conquerors," Menshikov said that, given a separate treaty, the East Germans will not interfere with Western access if "offensive activities" in West Berlin are halted and if the West—without necessarily extending *de jure* recognition to the GDR—is prepared to deal with the Ulbricht regime.

12 Aug   Effective upon publication, the East German Ministry of Interior issued a decree which limited interzonal pedestrian and vehicular traffic to 13 crossing points—Kopenhagenerstrasse, Wollankstrasse, Bornholmerstrasse, Chausseestrasse, Brandenburger Tor, Friedrichstrasse, Heinrich Heine Platz, Oberbaumbruecke, Puschkin Allee, Elsenstrasse, Sonnen Allee and Rudowerstrasse— sealing off the remaining 74. All roads leading from West Berlin into the Soviet Zone were sealed except for the Helmstedt Autobahn and the main highway to Hamburg, according to West Berlin police. Allied personnel, other foreign nationals and West Berliners were to be permitted to cross into East Berlin—and did so without difficulty during the first 24 hours after promulgation of the decree—although West Berliners were required to show identity cards issued by West Berlin city authorities. West Germans seeking to enter East Berlin henceforth were to be required to apply at one of four East Berlin police control posts for "one-day passes."

13 Aug   The Brandenburg Gate crossing point was closed.

22 Aug   The East German Ministry of Interior further restricted access to East Berlin by West Germans, West Berliners, and Allied diplomatic and military personnel. Foreign nationals, members of the diplomatic corps, and personnel of the Western occupation forces were limited to use of the Friedrichstrasse checkpoint; West Germans, to the Bornholmerstrasse and Heinrich Heine Strasse

points; West Berliners, to Chausseestrasse, Oberbaumbruecke, Sonnenallee, and Invalidenstrasse. West Berlin citizens were required to obtain an East German permit, at a cost of one West German mark, to enter East Berlin. The Ministry of Interior announcement stated that the new regulations—like those of 13 August—will stay in effect "until the conclusion of a peace treaty."

6 Oct   At his meeting with the President, Gromyko read from a prepared text. He stressed that the Soviet government attaches great importance to the conclusion of the peace treaty; if the US does not agree, the Soviets will sign a separate treaty, but they do not wish it to further aggravate US-Soviet relations. Therefore, prior to a separate treaty, they are prepared to work out jointly a free city status for West Berlin and to reach an understanding on other questions relating to "normalization of the situation" in West Berlin. The Soviets proceed on the premise that such understanding: (1) would be reflected in a Soviet-GDR treaty (2) that it would be formalized in special documents appended to the peace treaty. Gromyko said that the Soviet government believes that the best thing is to see a way out on the basis of a compromise. Even though a separate Berlin agreement would benefit the US, the USSR is prepared to have such a separate agreement. As to the timing of a treaty, the Soviet government sees no fatal date. Negotiations must not be artificially protracted. The Soviet government believes that agreement on a free city would provide strict guarantees with regard to the observance of the City's status and non-interference in its internal affairs. These guarantees would be in the form of Four-Power contingents, neutral or UN troops stationed in Berlin for specified periods of time. The Soviet government does not intend to restrict West Berlin's ties with the outside world or access to West Berlin by land, water, or air. But the Soviet Union does propose that the procedure for the exercise of such ties and the use of communications lines across the GDR be the same as that applied in the case of any other state. Gromyko said the Soviet Union could not agree to any West German claims to West Berlin; West Germany has no relation to West Berlin. Future ties between Bonn and West Berlin must be on the same basis as ties between any other sovereign state and the city. If the US declines to sign a treaty, then—in addition to the solution of West Berlin problem—an understanding will have to be reached on other questions important to European peace and security; (1) the legal formalization of existing German borders, and (2) the non-transfer to two Germanies of nuclear and rocket weapons, as well

as the prohibition of the manufacture of such weapons in the two states. Gromyko stated that the Soviet government places the utmost emphasis on these questions.

17 Oct   Khrushchev's report to the 22nd Party Congress contained a generally moderate and routine restatement of established Soviet foreign and domestic policies. His formal and specific withdrawal of the year-end deadline for signing a German peace treaty probably was intended to meet Western objections to negotiating under pressure of threats of unilateral action. His positive assessment of Gromyko's recent talks with US and British leaders and his reaffirmation of the USSR's readiness to seek a "mutually acceptable and agreed settlement through talks" were also aimed at opening the way for formal negotiations on Berlin and Germany. He specified, however, that a German settlement cannot be "postponed endlessly" and repeated that a German peace treaty will be signed with or without the Western powers.

27 Oct   Foreign Minister Gromyko's uncompromising stand in his talk with Ambassador Thompson suggests that the USSR considers its prestige has been challenged by recent events in Berlin. Gromyko read a formal protest which warned that if American actions continue, "they will be regarded as an act of provocative armed invasion of GDR territory, and the German Democratic Republic will be given necessary support for purposes of ending such actions." During the ensuing conversation with the Ambassador, Gromyko made no effort to respond to suggestions that the discussions on the issue could continue in Moscow or Berlin. The Soviet protest also went beyond the current issue of identification documents for US personnel in civilian clothes to assert in effect that East German police have the authority to permit or deny all passage across the sector border. Ambassador Thompson's preliminary conclusion is that the USSR considers it has a good issue and will be prepared to use force. Despite the tense situation in Berlin. Khrushchev in his third speech at the party congress made a point of reiterating his previous statement withdrawing a deadline for a German treaty and urging a "businesslike and fair solution of the problem." He also endorsed further US-Soviet exploratory talks in order "to prepare fruitful negotiations" although he coupled this with a warning against use of talks merely to delay a settlement. He concluded his remarks on Germany and

Berlin by stating: "Such is our stand, we have adhered to it so far, and we abide by it firmly." According to a TASS summary Khrushchev did not touch directly on the current events in Berlin. He claimed that the West wanted the USSR to act as "traffic police" in Berlin but that the Soviet Union could not be forced to act against its "vital interests." He also emphasized that it was "high time" the West realized that it could not negotiate with the Soviet Union on the basis of "positions of strength."

15 Nov   The NATO Council agreed that the basic objectives of its policy in regard to Berlin are: (1) the maintenance of the presence and security of the three Western garrisons in West Berlin, (2) the maintenance of the freedom and viability of West Berlin, (3) the maintenance of freedom of access to West Berlin. The Council also agreed that under present circumstances, contacts with Moscow should be resumed "at an early moment."

29 Nov   In its first policy statement, the new West German government presented three fundamental principles— 1) the security of the Federal Republic; 2) the maintenance of the existing political, legal and economic ties between West Berlin and the Federal Republic, including free civilian access; and 3) the maintenance of a joint policy with regard to reunification, non-recognition of GDR regime and eventual settlement of frontier questions in an all-German peace treaty—which "in no event could be abandoned."

Annex B
Major Documents Establishing Berlin's Legal Status

1. **Protocol on the Zones of Occupation in Germany and the Administration of Greater Berlin**, concluded by representatives of the United States, Britain, and the Soviet Union in September 1944, established the status of Greater Berlin as a separate and special occupied area under three-power control (France was added as a fourth power in July 1945) and provided for a governing authority (*Kommandatura*) to direct the city's administration. (The unilateral division of the city by the Soviet authorities in 1948 suspended the four-power administration, leaving West Berlin under tripartite western administration but did not change four-power responsibility for Berlin.)

2. **Article 23 of the Basic Law (Constitution) of the Federal Republic of German (1949)** included "Greater Berlin" as a state (land) of West Germany.

3. **Military Governors' Letter of 12 May 1949** stipulated that Berlin should not be governed by the Federal Republic and could be represented in the federal parliament only on a non-voting basis.

4. **Three-Power Statement of the Principles Governing the Relationship Between the *Kommandatura* and Greater Berlin (14 May 1949)** declared Berlin should not be included as a state in the initial organization of the Federal Republic.

5. **Berlin Constitution (1950)** included Berlin as a state of the Federal Republic, contrary to the 1949 Statement of Principles, and stated that the West German constitution and laws are binding on Berlin. (The Western military commandants suspended these provisions of the Berlin Constitution and established the requirement that any federal law to have effect in West Berlin must first be adopted separately by the Berlin parliament.)

6. **Convention on Relations Between the Three Powers and the Federal Republic (1954)**. The Western Allies recognized the close relationship between West Berlin and West Germany by stating their intention to consult with the Federal Republic in regard to the exercise of Allied rights and responsibilities in Berlin.

7. **Declaration on Berlin (5 May 1955)** superseded the 1949 Statement of Principles and Is the basic document governing Allied-German relations in Berlin. It provided for a large measure of self-government for West Berlin and for extensive economic and political integration with West Germany while reserving certain key areas of responsibility to Allied control. Berlin's status in international law as an occupied area was not changed.

Annex C

Extracts from Articles of West German Constitution
Pertaining to Berlin

Article 23

For the time being, this Basic Law applies in the territory of the Länder Baden, Bavaria, Bremen, Greater Berlin, Hamburg, Hesse, Lower-Saxony, North Rhine-Westphalia, Rhineland-Palatinate, Schleswig-Holstein, Wuerttemberg-Baden and Wuerttemberg-Hohenzollern. In other parts of Germany it is to be put into force on their accession.

Article 127

Within one year of the promulgation of this Basic Law the Federal Government may, with the consent of the governments of the Länder concerned, extend to the Lander Baden, Greater Berlin, Rhineland-Palatinate and Wurttemberg-Hohenzollern the legislation of the Bizonal Economic Administration, insofar as it continues to be in force as federal law under Articles 124 or 125.

Article 144

(1) This Basic Law requires adoption by the representative assemblies in two-thirds of the German Länder in which it is for the time being to apply.

(2) Insofar as the application of this Basic Law is subject to restrictions in any Land listed in Article 23 or in any part of such Land, the Land or the part thereof has the right to send representatives to the Bundestag in accordance with Article 38 and to the Bundesrat in accordance with Article 50.

Article 145

(1) The Parliamentary Council determines in public session, with participation of the representatives of Greater Berlin, the adoption of this Basic Law and signs and promulgates it.

(2) This Basic Law comes into force at the end of the day of promulgation.

(3) It is to be published in the Federal Gazette.

Annex D

West German Agencies in Berlin

(17,000 employees as of April 1961. Source: *Die Bundesrepublik*, 1958/9)

The Plenipotentiary of the Federal Republic in Berlin — Dr. Vockel

Branches:

Federal Ministers of:

>Foreign Affairs
>
>Interior
>
>Justice
>
>Finance
>
>Economics
>
>Food, Agriculture and Forestry
>
>Labour
>
>Transport
>
>Federal-owned Property
>
>Housing
>
>Refugees
>
>All-German Affairs

Federal Public Accounting Court

Further Federal Offices

Federal Statistical Office

Institute of the Federal Health Office

Institute for Water, Earth and Air Hygiene

Max-von-Pettenkofer Institute

Main Archives

German Archaeological Institute

External Branch of the Institute for Space Research

Federal Office for the Acceptance of Foreign Refugees

German Patent Office

Federal Building Directorate

Federal Debt Administration

Welfare Institute of the Federation and the Länder, Berlin Liaison Office

Federal Printing Office

Federal Commissioner for the Handling of Payments to the Conversion Fund

Refugees Transit Centre

Federal Cartel Office

Federal Railways (various administrative offices)

Technical Telecommunications Office

Postal Technical Office

Federal Supervisory Office for Insurance and Building Society Funds

Berlin Institute of the Physical-Technical Federal-Institute

Federal Institute for Material Testing

Federal Insurance Institute for Employees

Federal Insurance Office

Import and Supply Depot for Grain and Fodder

Import and Supply Depot for Fats

Import and Supply Depot for Meats

Biological Federal Institute for Agriculture and Forestry

Federal Research Institute for Grain Products

Federal Research Institute for the Meat Trade

Courts

Division of Supreme Court for Criminal Appeals

Federal Administrative Court

Supreme Federal Prosecutor - Federal Administrative Court

Federal Disciplinary Court

Annex E

The United States Mission in Berlin

In 1954, when West Germany gained sovereignty, the functions formerly exercised by the US High Commissioner devolved upon the US Ambassador in Bonn who retained his role as chief of the Mission in Berlin. Actual leadership in Berlin is shared by the US Commandant, with the rank of deputy chief of Mission, and the assistant chief of mission, the top US diplomatic official in the city. Effective 1 December 1961 the US Commandant, now also entitled Commanding General Berlin, reports to the Commander-in-Chief, US forces Europe. The Berlin Garrison, now designated as the Berlin Brigade, is subordinate to the Commandant. In addition, General Lucius Clay was appointed as President Kennedy's personal representative in Berlin in August, 1961.

Annex F

Documents Required by the East German Regime for Entering East Berlin, Transiting The GDR Or Entering The GDR

To Enter East Berlin

A. **West Germans** are required to secure 24-hour permits (*Aufenthaltsgenehmigung*) from East German police at certain specified crossing points on the city sector border (degree of 9 September 1960). According to the terms under which Bonn agreed to reactivate the interzonal trade agreement on 29 December 1960, the East Germans undertook to facilitate the issuance of these permits. In practice, Bonn has implicitly recognized the right of the GDR to issue such permits.

B. **West Berliners** have been required since 23 August to secure East German permits to enter East Berlin. Most West Berliners have refused to comply with this requirement, or are unable to enter East Berlin to secure them, and have not visited the Soviet sector; those who continue to hold jobs in East Berlin or find it necessary to go to the Soviet sector pick up the permits at the crossing points. The GDR is seeking to establish permit-issuing offices in West Berlin.

C. **US, French and British military** personnel in uniform at present are not required to show documentation. Nevertheless, in the past, in response to East German attempts to force the showing of documentation the British have flashed their identity cards: the US and French have refused.

D. **US, French and British civilian members** of the occupying forces or diplomatic missions in West Berlin and military personnel out of uniform are required by the East Germans to show identification—AGO cards have been accepted although efforts have been made by the East Germans to insist on passports, in some cases successfully. Military personnel on foot and not in uniform have long been permitted to show their identification but personnel, both military and civilian, not in uniform but traveling in US licensed vehicles have not shown credentials. In October, the East Germans began demanding identification from such individuals and at present, Allied officials not in uniform are not permitted to enter the Soviet sector except on official business.

US and French military personnel in uniform refuse to show documentation to East German police. In the past, British personnel in uniform have flashed their identity cards. US Mission personnel traveling on the S-Bahn are authorized to show their AGO cards; to date, East German guards have usually accepted this identification. At present, all personnel, military and civilian, of all three powers are permitted to travel to the Soviet sector only on official business. Civilian personnel traveling on US and French military sightseeing buses do not show identification; British have on at least one occasion shown passports. At present, no military buses are entering the Soviet sector.

E. **Officials and private Citizens other** than those of the three Western occupying powers are required to show passports but visas have not been required. This applies even to the members of the military missions accredited to the pre-1948 *Kommandatura*.

To Enter or Transit East Germany

A. **West Germans** transiting the GDR to Berlin are required to present their identity cards (*Kannkarte*) but do not have to show passports. To visit in East Germany they are required to have "residence permits" (*Aufenthaltsgenehmigung*) issued by local authorities in the area visited. At the zonal crossing points, West Germans are subject to customs controls and, if driving automobiles, pay vehicle taxes.

B. **West Berliners** desiring to enter East Germany are required to present identity documents (*Ausweis*) issued by the West Berlin Senat and have to secure "residence permits" issued by local East German authorities.

Since 15 September 1960 the GDR, and later other bloc countries, have refused to recognize the use of West German passports by West Berliners for travel within the bloc but have accepted West Berlin identity documents and issued GDR visas on separate sheets of paper.

West Berliners transiting East Germany to West Germany are required to show identity documents.

C. **Allied military and civilian officials** transiting the GDR on the Autobahn present Russian translations of travel orders issued by "competent authorities" to Soviet officials at the two checkpoints; the latter stamp the documents and return them. "Competent authorities" are defined as the three Western commandants in Berlin, the commanders-in-chief of the US, French and British forces in Europe, and the ambassadors of the three Western powers in Bonn. While traveling on the Autobahn, US and French personnel not in uniform have refused to show identification to East German police but the British have done so on occasion.

D. **Allied military trains** on the Helmstedt-Berlin route travel under the four-power occupation rights and train commanders show Russian translations of travel orders for the train and for all passengers, Russian translations of individual travel orders, and AGO cards or passports to Soviet officials at the Marienborn checkpoint.

E. **Military convoys on the Autobahn** also travel under four-power occupation rights and do not acknowledge East German jurisdiction. The convoy commanders present the convoy manifest to Soviet officials at both checkpoints, showing the names and rank of all personnel and descriptions of all vehicles. Soviet and Allied authorities make a head count of personnel and Soviet guards check vehicles against the manifest but are not permitted to climb onto the vehicles to carry out their inspection.

F. **Military Liaison Mission** personnel are accredited to the Commander-in-Chief, GSFG and are given permits to travel in non-restricted areas of the GDR by his office. Vehicles also receive permits from the Commander-in-Chief's office. Not all personnel attached to the missions receive travel permits.

G. **Other Categories**:

1. **All private citizens** other than West Germans are required to show passports and obtain visas. US citizens are advised not to enter the GDR or, if they must do so, not to accept a visa stamp in the passport.

2. **Officials from non-bloc countries** (other than the three Western occupying powers) are required to show passports and obtain visas.

Annex G

Currency Controls

West Berliners and West Germans entering or leaving East Berlin and East Germany are not permitted to bring East German currency. Currency must be exchanged at the high legal rate at designated points along the sector border or at certain East German banks. Identification is required. Such travelers must keep a record of all exchanges and are subject to heavy penalties if caught trying to take East marks with them when they leave. The regime is eager to secure hard western currencies.

Soviet and East German Ground Forces

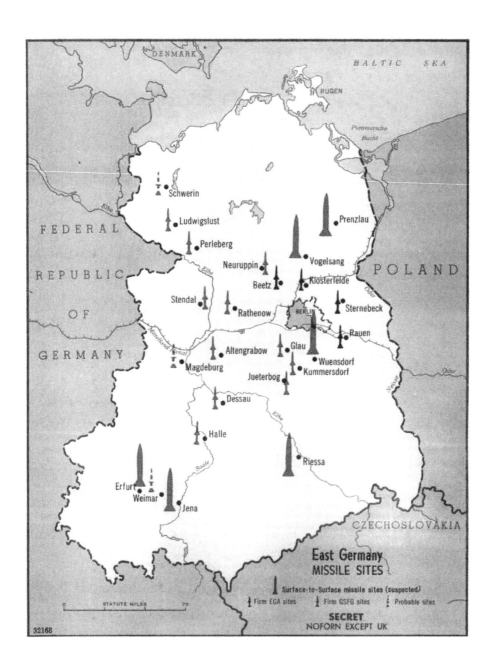

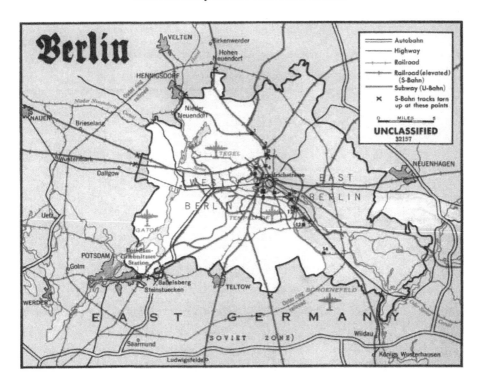

Authorized Border Crossing Points

Members of Diplomatic Corps and Occupation Forces Only	Original Crossing Points of 13 August Now Closed
8. Friedrichstrasse	1. Kopenhagenerstrasse
West Germans Only 3. Bornholmerstrasse 9. Heinrich Heine Strasse	2. Wollankstrasse 4. Brunnenstrasse 7. Brandenburger Tor (Gate) 11. Pushkin Allee
West Berliners Only 5. Chausseestrasse 6. Invalidenstrasse 10. Oberbaumbruecke 13. Sonnen Allee	12. Eisenstrasse 14. Rudowerstrasse

Authorized East Germans and East Berliners presumably can cross at any border points still open.

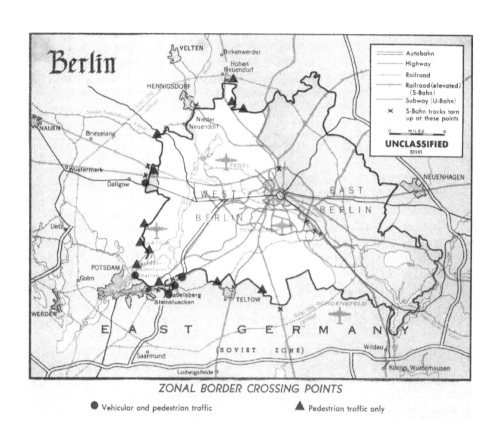

ZONAL BORDER CROSSING POINTS

● Vehicular and pedestrian traffic   ▲ Pedestrian traffic only

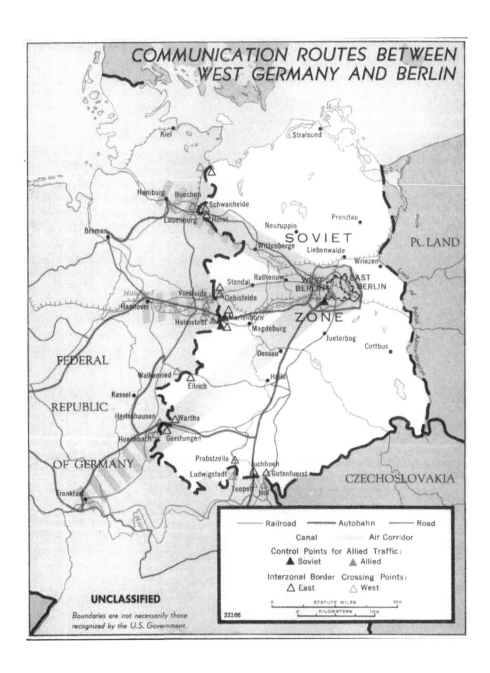

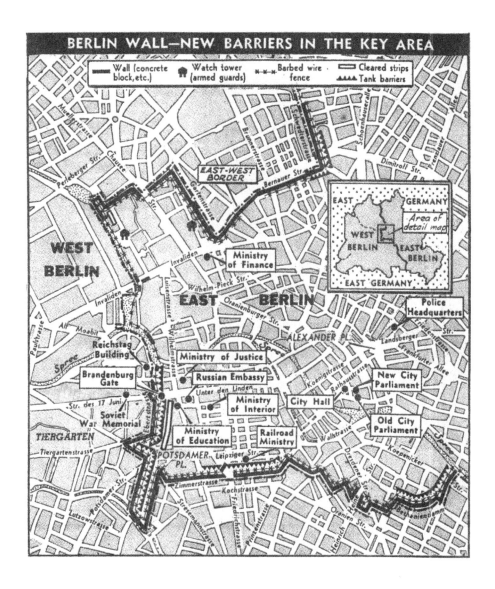

Refugee Flights From
East Germany and East Berlin

1949

Monthly Totals		Total for the year = 129,245
January		
February		
March		
April		
May		
June		
July		
August		
September	17,260	
October	18,563	7 Oct: Establishment of the so-called "GDR"
November	14,344	
December	7,078	
Total	57,245	

1950

Monthly Totals		Total for the year = 197,788
January	13,479	
February	12,401	8 Feb: Establishment of the Ministry for State Security and the State Security Service
March	15,443	
April	14,696	
May	17,580	
June	21,207	
July	21,253	
August	20,421	
September	18,089	
October	17,693	15 Oct: "Elections" for the People's Chamber
November	14,967	
December	10,659	15 Dec: "Law for Defense of the Peace" passed by the People's Chamber
Total	197,888	

1951

Monthly Totals		Total for the year = 165,648
January	12,289	
February	11,583	
March	12,514	
April	13,892	
May	12,928	
June	14,177	
July	15,385	
August	17,389	
September	16,184	1 Sept: Reorganization of the university system
October	14,848	
November	11,817	
December	12,642	4-19 Dec: German Question before the UN
Total	165,648	

1952

Monthly Totals		Total for the year = 182,393
January	7,227	
February	10,596	6 Feb: The Bundestag passes a law for an All-German Election
March	18,420	
April	9,307	
May	9,793	26 May: Security measures along the Zonal boundary
June	16,883	
July	15,190	12 Jul: "The building of Socialism" proclaimed
August	18,045	7 Aug: Establishment of the Society for Sports and Technology (a paramilitary formation)
September	23,331	
October	19,475	
November	17,156	
December	16,970	
Total	182,393	

1953

Monthly Totals		Total for the year = 331,390
January	22,396	
February	31,613	25 Feb: Restrictions placed on interzonal tourist travel
March	58,605	6 Mar: Stalin dies
April	36,695	
May	35,484	May: Climax of the Church struggle
June	40,381	9 Jun: "New Course;" 16-17 Jun: uprising
July	17,260	Jul: Arrests and political purges
August	14,682	
September	19,267	
October	22,032	
November	19,913	21 Nov: New regulations for Interzonal Traffic
December	13,062	
Total	331,390	

1954

Monthly Totals		Total for the year = 184,198
January	15,060	
February	11,655	18 Feb: Conclusion of the Berlin Foreign Ministers Conference
March	18,054	27 Mar: "Sovereignty" declaration of the "GDR"
April	17,611	
May	14,816	
June	15,380	
July	16,606	
August	17,051	
September	17,276	
October	15,526	27 Oct: "Elections" for the People's Chamber
November	13,755	13 Nov: Beginning of propaganda for "youth consecration"
December	11,408	
Total	184,198	

1955

Monthly Totals		Total for the year = 252,870
January	14,350	
February	12,474	
March	15,754	
April	18,076	
May	19,550	15 May: Warsaw Pact signed
June	20,252	
July	19,493	18-23 Jul: Geneva Summit Conference; 24 Jul: Khrushchev emphasized "achievements of the GDR"
August	25,690	
September	28,183	
October	32,874	Oct/Nov: Geneva Foreign Ministers Conference
November	25,963	
December	20,211	
Total	252,870	

1956

Monthly Totals		Total for the year = 279,189
January	26,711	18 Jan: The Law establishing the "National People's Army" passed
February	22,526	25 Feb: The Anti-Stalin campaign in the USSR
March	21,001	
April	26,718	
May	23,121	
June	22,098	
July	23,124	
August	27,522	
September	25,647	
October	25,985	Oct/Nov: Polish "October" and Hungarian uprising
November	20,208	
December	14,478	
Total	279,139	

1957

Monthly Totals		Total for the year = 261,622
January	19,373	30 Jan: Proposal for a "German Confederation"
February	16,754	
March	19,476	7 Mar: Show-trials of advocates of "Revisionism"
April	19,334	
May	20,388	29 May: Bans on travel of students to West Germany
June	18,469	
July	24,280	
August	27,590	
September	27,029	
October	26,630	13 Oct: Currency reform imposed without warning
November	23,682	
December	18,617	Law calling for further restrictions on travel to West
Total	261,622	

1958

Monthly Totals		Total for the year = 204,092
January	21,343	
February	15,646	
March	15,796	
April	15,872	
May	15,500	
June	14,232	
July	19,283	10 Jul: Fifth SED Congress adopts Programs to expedite "Socialist Transformation"
August	21,595	
September	21,107	
October	19,297	
November	13,873	27 Nov: Soviet ultimatum on Berlin
December	10,548	
Total	204,092	

1959

Monthly Totals		Total for the year = 143,917
January	13,142	10 Jan: Soviet peace treaty draft proposed
February	10,072	
March	10,391	
April	15,764	
May	12,290	10 May: Beginning of Geneva Foreign Ministers Conference
June	10,718	
July	12,107	
August	13,610	5 Aug: End of Geneva Foreign Ministers Conference
September	13,960	
October	12,824	
November	9,754	
December	9,285	2 Dec: New School Law (Polytechnical education)
Total	143,917	

1960

Monthly Totals		Total for the year = 199,188
January	9,905	
February	9,803	
March	13,442	
April	17,183	April: Forced collectivization campaign
May	20,285	17 May: Paris Summit Conference wrecked
June	17,888	
July	16,543	
August	21,465	
September	20,698	12 Sept: Formation of State Council with Ulbricht as chairman
October	21,150	
November	16,427	
December	14,399	
Total	199,188	

1961

Monthly Totals		Total for first six months = 103,159
January	16,697	
February	13,576	
March	16,094	
April	19,803	12 April: Labor Code declared by State Council
May	17,791	May: Serious and prolonged food supply crises
June	19,198	Jun: International tensions sharpened as a result of Soviet Policy
July	30,415	
August	47,433	13 Aug: Berlin borders closed
September	14,700	
October	5,366	
November	3,412	
December		
Total	204,485	

West German Ministry of Refugees, 1961

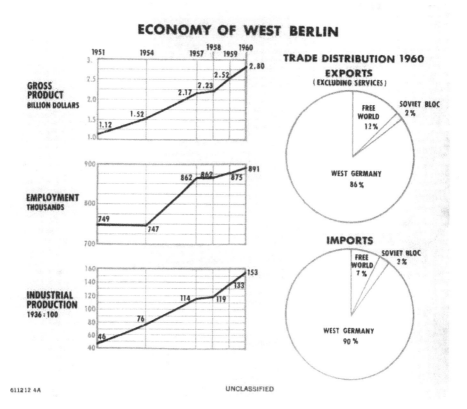

ECONOMY OF WEST BERLIN

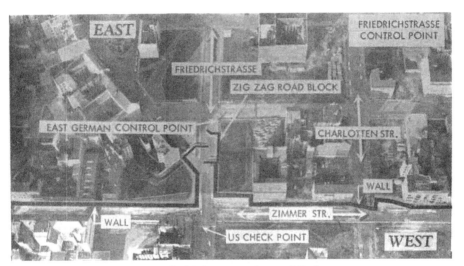

Friedrichstrasse Control Point

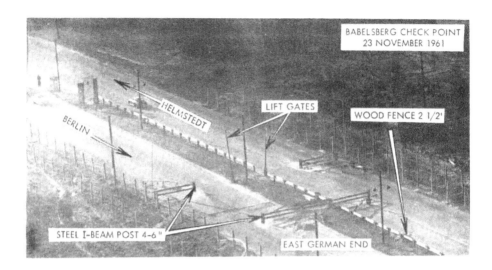

Babelsberg Checkpoint

Annex H

Schoenefeld Airport, south of Berlin, is one of the most important airfields in East Germany and the Berlin terminal for civil and military aircraft of the USSR and all the Satellites except Albania. Western airlines do not fly regularly to Schoenefeld, although specially chartered flights have landed there.

Construction to expand the airfield into a major terminal, equipped for all types of commercial aircraft, began early in 1959. An 11,000-foot runway, capable of handling the largest Soviet planes, was completed in the summer of 1961. It connects with a 6,600-foot concrete-asphalt runway, Which is being lengthened to 6,800 feet. In addition, there are two 2,700-foot runways, and two more runways are to be finished by 1965. The airfield is well-equipped with navigational/ landing aids—airport control, D/F, beach approach system, approach control, ILS, GCA, and a broadcast station in Berlin—and obstruction, rotating runway and approach lights. Long-line telephone and teletype services, and complete aerological service are provided. The field has adequate fire fighting and snow removal equipment.

Two underground fuel storage dumps, with an estimated capacity of 800,000 gallons, are located near the southeast edge of the field and are served by a railroad spur. An average of 4 tank cars of fuel arrive each day. These will be augmented by a new storage facility about 10 miles east of the field at Kablow, connected by pipeline.

The field has terminal and administration buildings, workshops, a motor transport section, power plant, and warehouses, and is capable of providing aircraft field maintenance. Two large hangars with maintenance shops are located at the south-east end of the field. A new 6-bay hanger is about 75 percent completed. In addition, there are barracks and dependents' quarters, mess, VIP hotel accommodations, and medical and recreational facilities.

Access routes to the airport, now only adequate, are being improved. There are good roads to Berlin, and a branch of the Berlin/Mittenwalde railroad services the airport with a station at Schoenefeld. A new S-Bahn line to connect East Berlin and the southeast portion of the airport via East Berlin/Wuhlheide and East Berlin/Adlershof-Gruenau lines is due for completion in the spring of 1962. A short double-tracked spur will branch off from the Adlershof-Gruenau line and terminate west of the airport. It probably will carry POL to the storage center. A single line which already connects the western part of the airport with the POL facilities will be improved. The S-Bahn line will be paralleled by a new 4-lane highway.

Schoenefeld's relatively large area and its location away from the heavily populated central part of Berlin make it potentially superior to West Berlin's airports as a base for jet operations. This, coupled with the fact that use of West Berlin airports is restricted to civil airlines of the Western occupation powers, may make the prospect of using Schoenefeld increasingly attractive to non-Allied airlines. The East Germans, backed by the USSR, are likely to intensify their efforts to attract airlines, such as the Scandinavian Airlines System (SAS), which do not use West Berlin's airports. International usage requires that government-to-government air agreements be concluded before the inauguration of regularly scheduled civil flights. The East Germans will not be able to capitalize fully on Schoenefeld until its expansion has been completed and international recognition of the regime achieved.

background

BERLIN

Department of State Publication 7257

European and British Commonwealth Series 64

Released August 1961

Office of Public Services

Bureau Of Public Affairs

Compiler's Preface to

Background Berlin

This reprint combines the draft version, which has a "Foreword" by Dean Rusk dated 2 August 1961, with the print edition (**Department of State Publication** 7257), which has a "Foreword" by Dean Rusk dated 16 August 1961.

The booklet was distributed with a number of covers, in both a terse and a verbose version. The terse version was limited to the main text without the annexes, and occasionally without the photographs. This is the verbose version.

The draft copy of the text for this Department of State booklet on Berlin carried the working title "State Department White Paper on Berlin." What is of particular interest is that the "White Paper" was only "Approved For Release" by the CIA on 24 April 2003:

Approved For Release 2003/04/24 : CIA RDP80BO1676R000800100057-3

while the published version had been circulated freely by the USIS at embassies around the globe, beginning in August 1961.

The base text is the "White Paper." This reprint shows the differences between it and the published version in-line, by marking the original text that was ~~deleted~~ from the "White Paper" with a ~~strikethrough~~, and the text that was substituted for it in the published version in a sans serif font.

Some of the differences are editorial, for example: ~~U.S.~~ United States, or ~~plain~~ clear, or ~~in~~ within, or ~~five~~ 5 percent.

Some of the differences are questions of political semantics, for example the word ~~"summit"~~ is placed in quote marks throughout the "White Paper," while in the printed version it appears as summit.

Some of the differences mark a change to a less verbally aggressive stance toward East Germany and the Soviet Union. For example: the Soviets and their German ~~puppets~~, or "With Soviet backing, these German Communists set out systematically to destroy all opposition. ~~These German Communists, with Soviet backing, systematically set out to harass,~~

muzzle, intimidate, subdue, and destroy all opposition., or the Communists began Nazi-like maneuvers to capture control of the entire city from within."

Some differences show a sense of caution at making assumptions that might be called to question. For example: "These talks and others at high level led to a Big Four "summit" meeting in Paris on May 15, 1960. That conference was never formally convened, although all the principals were on hand. Khrushchev used the U-2 incident to break it up. Some thought his real reason was his discovery prior to the conference that the Western Allies would not bow to his demands."

Some of the differences reflect the impact of events that took place between 2 and 13 August. All the paragraphs concerning the flow of refugees from East Germany to West Berlin are changed from the present tense to the past tense, and a whole section entitled "Closing of the Escape Hatch" has been added.

The rhetoric of the closing section was particularly heavily edited. In the "White Paper," the discussion of the threat to Berlin ends with: "Those Communist military displays were an ominous hint of the probable eventual fate of West Berlin if it were stripped of military defenses." In the published version, that sentence remains, and the threat is embellished with an additional sentence: "**The hint became even plainer in August 1961, when the East German regime deployed large military forces, including tanks, in East Berlin.**"

The booklets have been repaginated to fit the format of this book (6X9 inches). The original page size was 5.5X8 inches. Only blatant typographical errors have been corrected. The *emphasis* is that of the original.

The quality of the photographs is limited by the quality of the available originals.

Three Presidents of the United States on Berlin

"We cannot and will not permit the Communists to drive us out of Berlin, either gradually or by force. For the fulfillment of our pledge to that city is essential to the morale and security of West Germany, to the unity of Western Europe, and to the faith of the entire free world."

President John F. Kennedy
(Radio-television report to the Nation, July 25, 1961)

"The world must know that we will fight for Berlin. We will never permit that city to fall under Communist influence. We are defending the freedom of Paris and New York when we stand up for freedom in Berlin."

President John F. Kennedy
(Statement for special issue of *Berliner Illustrierte,* 1961)

"We have no intention of forgetting our rights or of deserting a free people. Soviet rulers should remember that free men have, before this, died for so-called 'scraps of paper' which represented duty and honor and freedom. ... We cannot try to purchase peace by forsaking two million free people of Berlin. ... We will not retreat one inch from our duty."

President Dwight D. Eisenhower
(Radio-television report to the American people, March 16, 1959)

"I made the decision ten days ago to stay in Berlin ... *I insist we will stay in Berlin—come what may."*

President Harry S. Truman
(From his diary, July 19, 1948)

Contents

Annexes

Foreword

For the third time in just over 13 years, the Soviets have launched a major threat to the freedom of West Berlin. We and our Western Allies are pledged to protect that freedom. I am confident that we and our Allies and the stalwart people of West Berlin will meet this challenge, ~~united in our strength, and calm in our knowledge that our duty is plain~~. This pamphlet sets forth some of the basic facts about Berlin, the repeated assaults on its freedom, and our obligations. It outlines also our patient and persistent efforts to resolve the issues involved by peaceful means ~~and the obstacles placed in the way of a peaceful settlement by the Soviet Union~~. I believe that it will provide useful background for ~~the informed~~ all citizens. Public understanding of the necessity for both firmness and ~~the full uses of the processes of~~ diplomacy will contribute to the prospects for peace.

DEAN RUSK

Secretary of State
August ~~2~~ 18, 1961

A Few Basic Facts

Berlin lies more than 100 miles behind the Iron Curtain ~~in~~ within the Soviet-occupied ~~eastern~~ zone of Germany. It is not, however, part of that zone. It is a separate political entity for which the four major allies of the war against Nazi tyranny are jointly responsible. Its special status stems from the fact that it was the capital not only of Hitler's Third Reich but of the German nation formed in the latter half of the 19th century. In essence, the four major allies agreed to hold Berlin, as the traditional capital, in trust for a democratic and united Germany.

~~In the~~ *The* Federal Republic of Germany, comprising the former occupation zones of the Western Allies, ~~political democracy has been fully established. The 53,000,000 people of Western Germany~~ is a democratic state. Its 53 Million people enjoy self-determination at all levels. Through their freely elected Federal Government, they have taken their place in the community of free nations.

By contrast, the ~~16,000,000~~ 16 million inhabitants of the eastern zone are ruled by the Soviet Union through its Communist creature, the East German regime which calls itself the "German Democratic Republic." *That regime is neither democratic nor a republic.* It was not chosen by the people it controls and has never been freely endorsed by them. It was imposed by duress and is maintained by all the oppressive apparatus of a police state backed by the military forces of the Soviet Union.

Berlin contains four sectors. The 2,250,000 inhabitants of its three western sectors live under a municipal government which they have freely chosen. The eastern sector has some 1,100,000 inhabitants. In 1948, in violation of their commitments, the Soviets separated it from the rest of the city. Subsequently, in further violation of their commitments, they permitted their German agents to declare it the capital of the East German regime. Thus the people of ~~East Berlin~~ the GDR, like those of the eastern zone of Germany, are ruled by a regime they did not choose.

The government of West Berlin is the only freely elected government behind either the Iron or the Bamboo ~~Curtains~~. Repeatedly the Soviets and their German ~~puppets~~ agents have sought to blot out this island of freedom. Their methods have ranged from the brazen to the devious, but their purpose has always been clear ~~except to the uniformed or naive~~.

~~Khrushchev has called Free Berlin "a cancerous tumor" and "a bone stuck in out throat." He has publicly declared his resolve "to eradicate this splinter from the heart of Europe."~~

Every President of the United States since the Second World War has deemed the defense of Free Berlin ~~critically important~~ critical to the security of the United States and of the entire free world. The United Kingdom, France, and the United States stand pledged to defend West Berlin by whatever means may be necessary. ~~So do the governments of Great Britain and France.~~ All the ~~other 12~~ members of the North Atlantic Treaty Organization ~~NATO~~ stand pledged to support them in ~~meeting this~~ discharging that obligation.

These solemn commitments were not undertaken lightly. If the reasons why they were undertaken and must be honored are not self-evident, they become so when one reviews the history of the last 16 years.

The Allied Trusteeship

The nations which bore the major burden of liberating Europe, including Germany, from the aggressive Nazi tyranny were ~~agreed~~ determined that Germany should never again be permitted to become a threat to peace. To that end they agreed on the total defeat and destruction of the Nazi regime and occupation of all Germany by Allied military forces. ~~Long~~ Well before the Nazi surrender, the U.S.S.R., the ~~U.K.~~ United Kingdom, and the ~~U.S.~~ United States agreed on the areas their respective military forces would occupy and temporarily administer. The basic document was signed in London on September 12, 1944, by representatives of the three powers. It specifically set aside Greater Berlin as a separate area to be occupied and administered jointly by all three. It made crystal clear that Greater Berlin was not a part of any zone of occupation. Later—on July 26, 1945—France was admitted to partnership in the occupation, with a zone in Western Germany and a sector and joint responsibilities in Berlin. Stalin had acceded to this reluctantly, with the condition that the French zone and sector be carved out of those previously assigned to Britain and the United States.

Meanwhile, at the Potsdam Conference, July 17–August 2, 1945, the Heads of Government of the U.S.S.R., the ~~U.K.~~ United Kingdom, and the ~~U.S.~~ United States agreed on certain more specific measures to be applied in Germany. These included reparations and the eradication of the National Socialist Party and of all Nazi institutions and propaganda. They included also positive measures to prepare for the "eventual reconstruction of German political life on a democratic basis and for eventual peaceful cooperation in international life by Germany."

Under the Potsdam Agreement (or Protocol), ~~more popularly known as the Potsdam Agreement,~~ local government was to be developed immediately on democratic principles through elective councils. As soon as practicable, elections were to be held for regional, provincial, and state (Land) governments. At all these levels, the occupation authorities were pledged to encourage *all democratic political parties* by granting them rights of assembly and public discussion.

Agreement to Reestablish Germany as One Nation

For the time being, Germany was not to have a central government. But it was to be treated as a single economic unit and "certain essential central German administrative departments, headed by State Secretaries" were to be established in the fields of finance, transport, communication, foreign trade, and industry. These were to act under the supervision of the Allied Control Council, the central governing body for the four occupation zones.

~~The Potsdam Conference agreed in principle to the ultimate transfer to the Soviet Union of the city of Koenigsberg and adjacent areas. Pending a peace treaty, it assigned to Polish administration the prewar German territories lying east of the Oder and Western Neisse Rivers. During the was, the major allies had leaned, in one degree or another, toward the division of Germany into several separate states. But in~~ In declaring that Germany was to be treated as a single economic unit, the Potsdam Agreement clearly indicated that Germany, ~~after~~ with some readjustment of its boundaries, was to be reestablished as one nation.[1] In setting "eventual peaceful cooperation in international life" as a goal, ~~the Potsdam Protocol~~ it spoke of "Germany," not of two or more Germanies.

~~In other words, by this time the western Allies had succeeded in rising above their bitter indignation and moral revulsion over the inhuman atrocities perpetrated by the Nazi regime and the loss of life and property inflicted upon their peoples by Hitler's military forces. They looked to the future and their joint responsibilities for creating international conditions which would promote social and economic progress in political freedom to be enjoyed by all peoples of the world. Accordingly, they decided that the splintering into separate states of a people such as the Germans could only contribute to the~~

---

[1] The Potsdam Conference agreed in principle to the ultimate transfer to the Soviet Union of the city of Koenigsberg and adjacent areas. Pending a peace treaty, it assigned to Polish administration the prewar German territories lying east of the Oder and Western Neisse Rivers.

creation of new frustrations and instability, which would threaten world peace anew.

Ruins of the Kaiser Wilhelm Memorial Church in *West Berlin, which was destroyed in* World *War II. Berliners have* preserved *this remnant of the church as a reminder to coming generations of the cost of aggressive* war.

Whatever may have been his reason, Stalin advocated at this time a single Germany. In his "Proclamation to the People" of May 8, 1945, he had declared that "the Soviet Union ... does not intend to dismember or destroy

Germany." It was not until later, when their hopes of communizing all of Germany waned, that the Soviets opposed the reunification of Germany.

Thus the major allies became trustees for a reformed Germany—trustees for all the peoples who had fought against or suffered from ~~Nazi~~ the aggressions and ~~other crimes~~ atrocities of the Nazi regime. Not least, they were trustees for the people of Germany. The reformed Germany to which they committed themselves was to be peaceable, self-governing through democratic political processes, and eventually united.

At the heart of this trusteeship was Berlin, the traditional national capital. Although geographically it lay deep within the Soviet occupation zone—indeed much closer to the Oder-Neisse line than to the western boundary of the Soviet zone—not even Stalin ~~was presumptuous enough to suggest~~ suggested that it should be under exclusive Soviet custody. *He agreed that Berlin was the joint responsibility of all four of the major allies and that it should be administered as a unit.* Such were the main terms of the trusteeship to which the major allies—the U.S.S.R. as well as the three Western Powers—bound themselves.

The Right of Access to Berlin

The Western Powers obviously could not perform their duties and exercise their rights in Berlin without the right to transport troops and supplies from their own zones of occupation. Their right of free access to Berlin was thus plainly inherent in their right to be in Berlin. This was confirmed by Stalin in his reply of June 18, 1945, to President Truman's cable of June 14 concerning the withdrawal of American troops from the Soviet occupation zone and their entry into Berlin. Mr. Truman stipulated, among other things, "free access by air, road, and rail from Frankfort and Bremen to Berlin for United States forces." Stalin promised to take "all necessary measures" in accordance with the plan stated by Mr. Truman.

Ten days later representatives of the Soviet Union, the United Kingdom, and the United States agreed on arrangements for use by the Western Powers of specific roads, rail lines, and air lanes between the western occupation zones and Berlin. These arrangements were further defined by actions of the Allied control machinery in Berlin and, in due course, extended to the French. With these guarantees, United States troops entered Berlin on July 1, 1945.

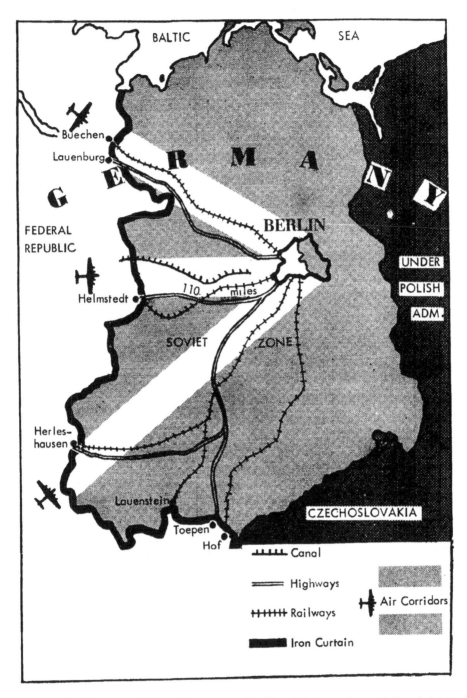

The Western rights of access to Berlin plainly embraced the right to transport food and other supplies for the civilian population of Berlin. And the right of the people of Berlin to receive goods from, and export goods to, the western zones and beyond was plainly inherent in the special political status accorded to Berlin. It was further buttressed by the Potsdam Agreement that Germany should be treated as an economic unit. In point of fact, in September 1945, the Soviet Commander, Marshal Zhukov, insisted on a step which made Berlin *more* dependent on shipments from the West than it otherwise would have been. He notified his opposite numbers that the Soviet zone could no longer supply the food which normally had gone to Berlin. The Western Powers were thus compelled to assume instantly the responsibility for feeding the inhabitants of the city's western sectors.

~~Soviet Conduct Before the Blockade~~
Early Communist Maneuvers

~~Soviet troops captured Berlin and held it for approximately ten weeks before troops of the western Allies were admitted. The Western Armies did not attempt to capture Berlin. The~~ The Western armies could have captured Berlin or at least joined in capturing it. But the Supreme Allied Commander, General Eisenhower believed that ~~his forces~~ they could be more usefully employed against the major German forces elsewhere ~~in ending the German military resistance and forcing unconditional surrender~~. As a result, the Soviets captured Berlin, but when ~~the Germans~~ Germany surrendered, the Western armies held much more, and the Soviets much less than the areas assigned to them by the Four Power occupation agreement ~~reached many months earlier~~ of September 1944. ~~The~~ In return for their admission to Berlin, on July 1, 1945, *the British and American forces relinquished to the Russians three historic German provinces and part of a fourth with a total population of more than 8,000,000—nearly half the area and half the people of the eastern zone.*

About 70 percent of the buildings in Berlin had been destroyed or severely damaged by Allied bombs and shells. During their 10 weeks of sole occupation, the Soviet authorities systematically removed most of the still usable machinery and equipment ~~which had survived the war~~. Their spoils included machines and tools from the larger plants, generators from power stations, most of the buses, undamaged streetcars and subway trains, and 52 automatic telephone exchanges with a capacity of 250,000 lines. This systematic Soviet looting added much to the burden of the Western Allies in restoring order and sustaining life in their sectors of Berlin.

The Soviets took advantage of their capture of Berlin to appoint a provisional government of the city and its subdivisions. They took special care to plant reliable agents in the police.

The Communist Election Failure

The Western Allies, however, successfully insisted on the right of the people of Berlin to elect their own government. In preparation for this the Soviet authorities tried to force a merger of the non-Communist Social Democratic Party (SPD) with the Communist Party (KPD) into the Socialist Unity Party (SED). They succeeded in the eastern zone of Germany, where they held full power. But in Berlin, under joint Allied control, they failed. Even so, they probably expected the Communists to do well in the city elections. Several districts of Berlin had been Communist strongholds during the Weimar Republic, and the Communists appointed to key city and subdivision posts by the Soviets could reasonably be expected to deliver votes.

The Berlin elections were held October 20, 1946. The result: Social Democratic Party (SPD), 48.7 % percent; Christian Democratic Party (CDU), 22.2 percent; Socialist Unity Party (SED), 19.8 percent; Liberal Democratic Party (LDP), 9.3 percent. Thus the Communists won less than one-fifth of the vote and only one-fifth of the seats in the city parliament, which proceeded to elect a Social Democrat as mayor. In April 1947 he was repudiated by the parliament because he had signed a promise to cooperate with the SED.

He resigned, and on June 24, 1947, parliament elected Social Democrat Ernst Reuter as Mayor. The Soviets "vetoed" Reuter's election. Until December 1948 a Deputy Mayor conducted the city's affairs.

The Soviets also systematically obstructed the efforts of the legally elected city government to control the city police, as authorized by the *Kommandatura* (the Allied governing body for Berlin). Instead, Soviet agents in the police took orders only from Soviet officials. Eventually the city government, with Western support, established control over the police in the western sectors. But in the Soviet sector, the Communist police officials defied to the end the orders of the *Kommandatura* and the Berlin Government.

The elections of October 20, 1946, were the last, as well as the first, city-wide elections held in post-war Berlin. The Soviets could not prevent self-determination in the western sectors. But never again did they allow the inhabitants of the Soviet sector to choose their government.

Imposition of Communist Control on East Germany

Meanwhile, in the eastern zone of Germany and by its conduct in the Allied Control Council for Germany, the Soviet Union had been making

~~crystal~~ clear its determination to ~~sterilize~~ vitiate most of the positive principles of the Potsdam Protocol. Instead of encouraging, or even permitting, reconstruction of German political life on the democratic basis of free choice, it riveted Communist control on government at all levels. It began by appointing seasoned German Communists to key posts. Most of them had spent the Nazi period in the Soviet Union and now returned to Germany with the Soviet armies. ~~Others had weathered the war in the underground or in concentration camps.~~

Among them was one Walter Ulbricht. He had received intensive training in Communist dogma at the Lenin Institute in Moscow from 1926 to 1929. He had gone back to the Soviet Union in 1937 or 1938 and remained there during the war. He was reported to be a Soviet citizen. In 1945 he returned to Germany as a Colonel in the Soviet Army. He soon emerged as the chief Soviet agent in eastern Germany.

~~These German Communists, with Soviet backing, systematically set out to harass, muzzle, intimidate, subdue, and destroy all opposition.~~ With Soviet backing, these German Communists set out systematically to destroy all opposition. A favorite political device was the single ticket chosen by the Communists. By compelling the ~~The largest non-communist party in the Soviet Zone,~~ the Social Democratic Party ~~was brought to heel by compelling it~~ to merge with the Communist Party~~.~~ in the Socialist Unity Party, the Communists forged their basic political instrument. ~~Within the resultant Socialist Unity Party, the Communists rapidly established domination.~~ Several other political parties were, and still are, allowed to exist for show purposes but are in fact under tight Communist rein. To intimidate and subdue their opponents, the Communists employed all the practices of a police state.

Simultaneously, by similar tactics the Soviets and their local Communist agents were imposing their control on Poland, Rumania, Hungary, Bulgaria, and Albania, in flagrant violation of the pledges of free elections made by Stalin in the Yalta declarations on Poland and on liberated Europe.

In the western zones of Germany, by contrast, the basic right of self-determination was not only permitted but fostered. ~~All non-Nazi parties and candidates, including Communists, were allowed to compete on even terms, as the~~ The political life of Germany was reconstructed on a democratic basis, beginning with local elections and rising, by stages, to state (Land) elections. All non-Nazi parties and candidates, including the Communists, were allowed to compete on even terms. Despite ~~complete~~ unhampered freedom of activity, the Communists were so unsuccessful in West German elections that they eventually failed to obtain even the ~~five~~ 5 percent of the popular vote necessary for seats in parliament.

The Soviets also blocked or evaded execution of the provisions of the Potsdam Protocol for treating Germany as an economic unit and for allowing reconstruction and self-support. In December 1945, they vetoed a proposal to open zonal borders to travel by Germans. When the Western Powers asked them to place manufactures from East Germany in a common pool to meet the costs of essential imports, in accordance with the Potsdam Agreement, they did not deny the agreement but failed to comply with it. Meanwhile, they had looted the eastern zone and refused to account for what they had taken. They also commandeered and shipped eastward almost the entire agricultural yield of their zone.

Economic Merger of the Western Zones

~~In the late spring and early summer of 1946, the disagreements within the Allied Control Council were taken up at the session of the Council of Foreign Ministers of the four occupation powers. Secretary of State James F. Byrnes pointed out that, contrary to the Potsdam Agreement, Germany was being administered "in four closed compartments with the movements of people, trade, and ideas between the zones more narrowly restricted than between most independent countries." Consequently, he stated, none of the zones was self-supporting and Germany was threatened with economic paralysis. He~~ proposed ...

A year after the surrender, the German economy still lay in semi-chaos. None of the zones was self-supporting. The United States renewed the effort to implement the Potsdam agreement that Germany was to be treated as an economic unit. It proposed prompt establishment of central German administrative agencies, free trade between zones, and a balanced program of imports and exports. The British agreed at once. The French agreed on condition that the Saar be excluded ~~from the jurisdiction of the proposed German agencies. The Soviets, using~~ Using the French condition as a pretext, the Soviets rejected the entire proposal.

On September 6, 1946, Secretary of State James F. Byrnes made a ~~major policy~~ speech at Stuttgart in which he said bluntly that the Allied Control Council was "neither governing Germany nor allowing Germany to govern itself." He explained the impending economic merger of the British and American zones and laid down a positive economic program for all of Germany. This included drastic fiscal reform to prevent ruinous inflation, organization of transportation, communications, and postal service throughout the country without regard to zonal barriers, and a central administrative department for agriculture to improve production and distribution of food. He also stressed the importance of permitting Germany to increase industrial production and organize the most effective use of her raw materials, granting that she must share her coal and iron with the liberated countries of Europe.

View of Lenin Allee in East Berlin

That fall the British and American zones were merged for economic purposes. France held back, hoping that differences with the Soviets could be resolved ~~at the fourth session of the Council of Foreign Ministers scheduled for March, 1947, in Moscow. The hope proved vain.~~ But the Soviets remained obdurate. At ~~They remained obdurate at~~ the fifth session of the Council of Foreign Ministers of the four occupation powers, held ~~at London~~ in November and December, 1947. ~~The Soviets proposed at the conference a strongly centralized German government. It was a fair inference that they expected to gain control of all Germany.~~ The Western delegates concluded that agreement with the Soviets could be reached "only under conditions which would not only enslave the German people but would seriously retard the recovery of all Europe."

Soviet Imperialist Aims vs. West European Rehabilitation

Soviet objectives in Europe had become increasingly plain. *The first was to rivet Communist regimes on all the areas of eastern and central Europe which the Red armies had occupied during and at the end of the war. The second and larger objective was to extend Communist domination over the independent nations of western and southern Europe.* The Soviets were actively supporting an aggression against Greece, euphemistically called a "civil war." They were strongly pressing Turkey for concessions which would jeopardize its independence and open the way for further Soviet expansion into the Mediterranean area and beyond. In western Europe they were banking on economic stagnation and political paralysis to set the stage for Communist take-overs.

In March 1947, the United States moved to curb Soviet expansion by extending economic and military aid to Greece and Turkey and setting forth proclaiming a general policy of such aid to other nations resisting covert overt or overt covert aggression. This quickly became known as the Truman Doctrine.

The United States had already made large contributions to relief, rehabilitation, and reconstruction in Europe. Through UNRRA (The United Nations Relief and Rehabilitation Administration) it had helped eastern Europe and the Soviet Union, as well as western Europe. It had made a large loan to Great Britain and emergency loans and grants to various other nations. But these had proved insufficient to reinvigorate the economies of the Western European nations. A larger, sustained effort was obviously necessary.

In June 1947, in a speech at Harvard, Secretary of State George C. Marshall set in motion what became a great cooperative European recovery program known as the Marshall Plan.

The central conflict of purpose was set forth in Secretary Marshall's report to the Nation in December 1947:

> The issue is really clear-cut, and I fear there can be no settlement until the coming months demonstrate whether or not the civilization of western Europe will prove vigorous enough to rise above the destructive effects of the war and restore a healthy society. Officials of the Soviet Union and

leaders of the Communist Parties openly predict that this restoration will not take place. We on the other hand are confident in the rehabilitation of Western European civilization with its freedoms.

The nations of western Europe responded to the Marshall plan with enthusiasm and vigor.

The next years saw the economic recovery of western Europe, including the western zones of Germany. At the same time, West Germany began a political reconstruction on a democratic basis.

~~Fortunately for the future of civilization, the Soviets were unable to prevent the economic recovery of Western Europe, including the western zones of Germany. Likewise, they were unable to prevent the political reconstruction of Western Germany on a democratic basis.~~ On March 6, 1948, with the concurrence of Belgium, the Netherlands, and Luxembourg, the Western Allies agreed to fuse their zones economically and politically. They agreed also on a new Occupation Statute which, while reserving essential powers to the Allies, enabled West Germans to participate in the community of free peoples through a Federal government of their own choosing. On June 18, the Western military governors announced a reform basic to West Germany's economic recovery: the substitution of a sound currency, the Deutschemark (or D-Mark), for the inflated Reichsmark.

The Soviets responded to those constructive measures by a series of ~~violations of their~~ aggressive steps, in violation of solemn commitments, culminating in a total blockade of West Berlin.

The Blockade and the Airlift

On March 20, 1948, the Soviets walked out of the Allied Control Council for Germany. On April 1, they imposed rail and road restrictions on Allied traffic to Berlin. On June 16, they walked out of the Berlin *Kommandatura*. On June 23, German Communists staged riots around the Berlin City Hall, situated in the Soviet sector. Many of them were carried to the scene in Soviet trucks. This was the day currency reforms were introduced in Berlin. The Western Allies had not previously extended to Berlin the West German currency reform of June 18. They were willing to retain the old Reichsmark in Berlin, provided that they shared control over the amounts issued. The Soviets refused to share this control. Instead, they introduced a new currency of their own in ~~both the soviet~~ their zone and sector. The Allies promptly introduced the new D-Mark into the western sectors of the city.

*Berlin children cheer the arrival of a C-54 airlift plane
during the Berlin blockade of 1948*

On June 24 the Soviets totally severed all land and water routes between Berlin and the western zones of Germany. Their undisguised intent was to force the Western Allies out of Berlin and starve the people of the city into the Communist fold.

In response to this bald aggression against their rights and the freedom of the people of Berlin, the Western Allies would have been fully justified in using force, to whatever degree necessary to reopen and maintain surface routes to Berlin. Instead, they chose to supply Berlin by air.

For the next ~~eleven~~ 11 months every pound of food and coal, and all else necessary to keep alive the people of West Berlin and supply the forces of the Western Allies in Berlin, was transported by air. In a total of 277,728 flights, American, British, and French airmen brought in 2,343,301 tons of food and supplies. At the peak of the Airlift, planes were landing in West Berlin at the rate of one every 45 seconds.

Why didn't the Soviets try to stop the Airlift? Initially they probably did not dream that it was possible for Western Berlin and the Allied forces in it to be sustained by air. A little later they probably thought that the fog and snows of winter would bring the Airlift to a halt. Perhaps most influential was the fact that they could not seriously interfere with the Airlift without shooting down Allied planes, a course obviously too dangerous to risk. ~~That they knew better than to risk.~~

The Airlift had its casualties, nevertheless—72 men, including 31 Americans, lost their lives in accidents. Their names are perpetuated on a soaring monument in front of Tempelhof Airport. A Berlin foundation, "Airlift Gratitude," provides scholarships for the children of these fallen heroes. In due course, they may, if they wish, attend the Free University of Berlin as guests of the Free Berlin government.

That university was born under the Airlift, when many teachers and students from the old University of Berlin, situated in the Soviet sector, chose freedom in the western sectors. It held its first classes by candlelight in nine cold rooms in an old building. The Free University of Berlin, with more than 12,000 students, has become one of the world's great institutions of higher education. ~~Today~~ Last year one-fourth of its students came from East Germany and East Berlin.

The Heroic Stand of the West Berliners

The Airlift is an indelible chapter in the history of the ~~history of the~~ defense of freedom. So is the fortitude of the people of Berlin during the blockade. They subsisted on a slim diet. The Communists offered them food if they would register in East Berlin, but all but a few thousand spurned the offer. During the winter, as fuel was scarce, they were usually miserably cold. For months electric current was on only ~~three~~ 3 hours in 24. The Berliners proved themselves worthy of the fraternity of free peoples. Admiration for their courage and endurance helped greatly in rehabilitating the name of the German people in the eyes of the world.

The ~~common~~ experience of the blockade forged a lasting bond of friendship among Berliners, Americans, and their allies. Every noon the ringing of the Freedom Bell from the tower of the West Berlin City Hall serves as a reminder of their common cause. The Freedom Bell was a gift from the American people—millions of them, including schoolchildren, voluntarily contributed to the fund to make and install it. It was inspired by the Liberty Bell enshrined in Independence Hall, Philadelphia, which in 1776 pealed the tidings of the American Declaration of Independence, with its immortal truths "that all men are created equal, that they are endowed by their Creator with certain unalienable Rights, that among these are Life, Liberty and the pursuit of Happiness," and that governments derive "their just powers from the consent of the governed."

Unhappily, during the Airlift the inhabitants of the eastern sector lost most of the limited freedom they had briefly enjoyed. In addition, the Communists began ~~Nazi-like~~ maneuvers to capture control of the entire city from within. Repeatedly, on Soviet orders, they rioted around City Hall, still located in East Berlin. They even forced their way inside the building and injured some of the West Berlin deputies, including women. On November 30, 1948, the Soviets formally split the city. The vast majority of legally elected deputies withdrew to West Berlin. A new "rump" municipal government was set up in East Berlin, with the promise of free elections. Those elections were never held. Moreover, in violation of a specific pledge given earlier, the Soviets prohibited East Berliners from voting in the citywide elections of December 5, 1948. Barred from returning to City Hall in the Soviet sector, the new parliament set up headquarters in West Berlin and elected Ernst Reuter as Mayor. Legally he was Mayor of the entire city. Actually, of course, he could exercise authority only in its western sectors.

In the spring of 1949 the Soviet Union tacitly admitted failure in its first great effort to oust the Western Powers and swallow all of Berlin. Soviet–U.S. diplomatic conversations in New York led to a Four-Power agreement on May 4, 1949,[2] providing in part:

> All the restrictions imposed since March 1, 1948, by the Government of the Union of Soviet Socialist Republics on communications, transportation, and trade between Berlin and the Western zones of Germany and between the Eastern zone and the Western zones will be removed on May 12, 1949.

This article was implemented on May 9 by Order No. 56 of the Soviet Military Government and Commander in Chief of the Soviet occupation forces in Germany. It was reaffirmed, strengthened, and amplified the following month by the Council of Foreign Ministers meeting in Paris.

The Soviet Union did not faithfully adhere to its renewed pledges. In January 1950, it began a "creeping blockade," designed to wreck the now recovering economy of West Berlin. With persistent interference with transport and deliveries, it, combined a violent propaganda campaign intended to frighten the West Berliners. These were only the first of a long series of harassments.

---

[2] It is perhaps not insignificant that the North Atlantic defense pact had been signed April 4— exactly 1 month previously.

Statement by Vice President Lyndon B. Johnson
Upon His Return to Washington From Berlin, August 21, 1961

My first duty on returning to Washington from our mission to Bonn and Berlin is to present a report to the President on the results of our journey.

May I, at this time, express my thanks to General Lucius Clay and Ambassador Charles Bohlen for their generous and devoted service at every stage of our mission.

I have returned from my conferences with Chancellor Adenauer and Mayor Brandt with even greater confidence in the distinction and responsibility of free German leadership, and with the conviction that the bonds between this country and West Germany and West Berlin, already very strong, have been made even stronger and more enduring.

I would be remiss in my duty if I did not take this first public opportunity to tell the American people of the inspiring and unforgettable welcome accorded us by the citizens of the Federal Republic and West Berlin. The reception given to the American troops which were sent to West Berlin as reinforcements for freedom by direction of President Kennedy was most heartwarming. Our troops know that they carry the honor of America with them as they begin their important task of helping to protect this outpost of peace and freedom. That trust could not be committed to safer or stronger hands.

It is impossible to give an adequate picture, in these few words, of the courage and the dedication to freedom which sustain the people of West Berlin in these difficult days. They are being tested and harassed by Communist power; but their heroic conduct in this emergency has become one of the major assets of the free world. I have returned with feelings of unlimited gratitude to the people of West Berlin and West Germany and with feelings of unlimited compassion for the suffering now being endured by the people of East Berlin and East Germany and their relatives and friends in the West. No one who has seen and talked with the refugees from East Germany, as I have done, can fail to realize what a profound human tragedy is involved. That realization must heighten the urgency with which we consider our own responsibilities, and the responsibilities of our allies, in dealing with the issues raised by the Berlin crisis.

When I left Washington on Friday night, I ventured the hope that our journey to West Germany and West Berlin would prove to be a mission for peace that would remove anxieties between friends and strengthen the securities of freedom. It was in that spirit that our mission was undertaken, and it was in that same spirit that we were received and welcomed by everyone in Bonn and in Berlin. The Communist threat to Berlin is very real and is but a part of the continuing struggle between the world of freedom and the world of coercion. As a result of our mission I believe that we will be better able to meet whatever the future may bring because of the greater unity of purpose and the reaffirmation of common policies achieved in our recent discussions.

Remarks Made by President Kennedy on August 21, 1961, Following Vice President Johnson's Return From His Trip to Berlin

The Vice President has given me a report on his remarkably successful and important trip to West Germany and West Berlin. His report emphasizes the confidence and trust which the people of West Berlin have in this country and in its commitments, and it places a heavy responsibility upon all of us to meet that responsibility.

I want to express my thanks to him for this most important service he has rendered to our country, and to General Clay who accompanied him, who was the Commandant in Berlin during the airlift in the late forties—and Mr. Bohlen from the State Department. The Secretary of State Mr. Rusk and I are most gratified by their visit, and we are aware, and the Vice President has emphasized this, that we are going to pass through difficult weeks and months in the time ahead in maintaining the freedom of 'West Berlin, but maintain it we will.

Aug. 20, 1961. During his visit to West Berlin, Vice President Lyndon B. Johnson greets Col. Glover S. Johns Jr., commanding officer of the First Battle Group, 18th Army, U.S. Infantry.

Berlin After the Blockade

With the end of the blockade, Free Berliners set about. energetically to rebuild their city and revive its industries. They completed the task of clearing away war ruins and rubble and of restoring public parks and gardens. They re-equipped factories and power plants and built new ones. (An immense new electric power plant, its giant generators flown in piece by piece during the blockade, made West Berlin independent of Communist-controlled sources of power.)

Distance and related handicaps made it hard for Free Berlin's industries to compete with West German and foreign firms. In 1955 the Communists added to these handicaps by increasing drastically tolls on highway traffic between West Germany and Berlin. But through driving initiative, hard work, and Marshall plan aid—which, directly and indirectly, totaled almost ~~one~~ $1 billion ~~dollars~~— Free Berlin's industrial output rapidly grew. New office buildings, apartment houses, and hotels sprang up. Stores and shops began to bulge with all the goods that the advanced technology and manufacturing techniques of the West can provide. ~~In recent years,~~

~~Berlin's industrial growth has been assisted by subsidies from the Federal German Republic.~~

Free Berlin has again become Germany's greatest industrial city and the greatest metropolis between Paris and Moscow. Since the end of the blockade, approximately 320,000 new jobs have been created in Free Berlin. ~~Every day more than 50,000 East Berliners come to work in Free Berlin (About 7,000 West Berliners work in East Berlin.)~~

Night scene of the bustling Kurfuerstendamm,
one of West Berlin's principal shopping streets.

Although somewhat below that of West Germany, the average standard of living in Free Berlin is far above that of any city anywhere in the Communist world. Incidentally, more than 200,000 West Berliners own automobiles. In the last few years, the Soviets and their German puppets have striven to make East Berlin a showplace. Despite their efforts, East Berlin remains a drab place compared to Free Berlin.

The high standard of living in Free Berlin is not confined to material things. Free Berlin has become a great cultural center, where one may enjoy not only the best in German culture but samplings of the culture of other Western nations.

Most important of all, the people of West Berlin read what they please, think and speak as they please, and vote as they please.

~~East Berliners and East Germans like to visit Free Berlin. In 1960 they bought 560,000 tickets to West Berlin theaters and opera, and 10,000,000 to West Berlin movie houses. They borrowed 250,000 books from Free Berlin Libraries.~~

The Political Reconstruction of West Germany

The blockade of Berlin did not halt the political reconstruction of West Germany. On September 1, 1948, the West German Parliamentary Council convened in Bonn, under the chairmanship of Dr. Konrad Adenauer, anti-Nazi former Mayor of Cologne, to draft a provisional constitution (or Basic Law, as it is called). The Council completed its work in May 1949. On August 14, 1949, the people of West Germany voted in the first free general election Germany had known since 1932. On September 21, the Federal Republic of Germany came into being with Dr. Adenauer, leader of the Christian Democratic Party, as its Chancellor.

The Soviets Set Up an East German Puppet Regime

On October 7, 1949, the Soviet authorities set up their puppet regime in the eastern zone of Germany.

~~In 1951 the United Nations set up a special commission to determine whether the conditions were suitable for the holding of free elections throughout Germany. This U.N. Commission was unable to complete its task because it was barred from the Soviet zone of Germany and Soviet sector of Berlin.~~

With Soviet support and in further violation of the Four Power agreements, the imposed East German regime proclaimed the Soviet sector of Berlin to be its capital.

In the spring of 1950, the Soviet Union began arming East German forces, at first under the guise of "People's Police." The Western Allies protested, but to no avail. By the end of 1953, East Germany, with only ~~17,000,000~~ 17 million people, had 140,000 military personnel, including three mechanized divisions and an air force, plus 100,000 armed police. *This was more than a year before the establishment of an armed force by the*

Federal Republic, which had only 150,000 regular police for a population three times that of East Germany.

In a series of steps in 1954 and 1955 the Soviets purported to grant their East German puppet full sovereignty. Among other things, they transferred to it control of the borders with the Federal Republic and West Berlin and over German traffic between the two areas. The Western Powers emphatically reminded the Soviet Union that these arrangements did not alter its obligations under its prior and overriding agreements with them regarding Germany, including Berlin.

In 1951 the United Nations set up a special commission to determine whether conditions were suitable for the holding of free elections throughout Germany. This U.N. commission was unable to complete its task because it was barred from the Soviet zone of Germany and Soviet sector of Berlin.

As the East German puppet regime was unlawfully created and does not rest on the consent of the governed, but is kept in power by the apparatus of a police state backed by military forces of the Soviet Union, the Western nations have refused to recognize it. So have all other non-Communist nations.

What a great majority of the East Germans and East Berliners think of their Communist masters has been manifested in many ways. One telling testimonial was the spontaneous strike against new Communist work "norms" which boiled up in East Berlin on June 17, 1953. Almost simultaneously, spontaneous strikes and demonstrations occurred in East German cities. The East German puppet regime was unable to subdue these uprisings with its own police and troops. It had to call for Soviet armed forces. It was saved by Soviet tanks.

Most significantly, these strikes, which became popular uprisings, were led by construction and factory workers and other wage-earners the very people whom the Communists claim particularly to represent. *They were a revolt of the proletariat against the "dictatorship of the proletariat."*

Another telling, and continuing, testimonial was **is** the massive migration of East Germans and East Berliners to freedom in the West. After the experience of 1953, the Soviets and their German agents decided not to exploit the East German workers quite so ruthlessly. Some foodstuffs have been almost chronically in short supply. In the early summer of 1961 strict rationing of several important foods was re-introduced. Nevertheless, average living levels in East Germany and East Berlin have risen appreciably, although they remain far below those of West Germany and West Berlin.

That material improvement did not, however, stay the exodus of East Germans and East Berliners.

East Berlin, June 1953, Workers march through the Brandenburg Gate into *West Berlin during the revolt against the East German Communist government.*

"People Who Vote With Their Feet"

In the last 16 years an estimated 3,300,000 Germans have fled East Germany and East Berlin. More than 2,500,000 of these have left since records began to be kept in West Berlin and the Federal German Republic in 1949. Since 1953 the ~~The~~ border between East Germany and the Federal Republic ~~is~~ has been dangerous for a refugee to try to cross. The Communists guard it with barbed wire, watch towers with sharpshooters, and a "death strip" of plowed earth. ~~Once~~ However, until August 1961 a refugee ~~reaches~~ who reached East Berlin~~, however,~~ could ~~he can~~ cross to West Berlin on foot or by subway or the elevated line—provided he acted ~~acts~~ like a commuter and carried ~~carries~~ no tell-tale luggage. Consequently, a large majority of the refugees from East Germany have escaped via West

129

Berlin, whence most have been transported by air to refugee camps in the German Federal ~~German~~ Republic. In these centers arrangements are made for their housing and employment in West Germany.

Over the years, the ~~The~~ German Communists ~~have~~ applied increasingly strict measures to curb this trek to freedom. A. refugee caught in the act was made ~~is~~ liable to imprisonment. So were ~~are~~ his close relatives if they ~~remain~~ remained behind. Contrary to Communist propaganda, the German Federal ~~German~~ Republic, the government of Free Berlin, and the Western Powers did ~~have~~ not encouraged the exodus. In fact, high officials of the Federal Republic often appealed to the population of the Soviet zone to remain there as long as possible ~~they possibly can~~. They do not want to see East Germany depleted of its most stalwart elements. Above all, they do not want to give the Soviets an excuse to move non-German workers into East Germany. (Communist rule ~~has~~ combined with the West Berlin "escape hatch" to give East Germany a unique distinction in the world of today: a shrinking population.)

Nevertheless, the flow of refugees ~~has~~ continued. The rate varied ~~varies~~ but in recent years averaged about 4,000 a week. ~~In July, 1961, with a revival of Soviet pressures on Free Berlin and the threat to seal off this portal to freedom, the rate approximately doubled.~~[3] The refugees have included a high percentage of East German physicians and men and women of various other professions but *most have been ~~are~~ workers fleeing "the paradise of the workers."* Significantly also, a majority have been young people—approximately 50 percent under 25 years of age. They were ~~nine~~ 9 years or younger when the Soviets and their German puppets began to try to make them into Communists. (Incidentally, the German lass who won the Miss Universe contest at Miami in July 1961, had fled East Germany only a year earlier. She is an electronics engineer.)

The continuing westward trek of East Germans and East Berliners who decided to "vote with their feet" was an eloquent judgment on Communist rule.

---

[3] ~~Almost certainly it would have risen still more if the frantic East German regime had not clamped new restrictions on travel from East Germany into East Berlin. The East German regime also instituted measures to reduce the number of East Berliners working in West Berlin.~~

Hungry crowds line up before the Wilmersdorf City Hall in West Berlin to receive U.S. emergency food rations during the 1953 anti-Communist uprisings.

The Federal Republic Comes of Age

During the ~~nineteen fifties~~ 1950's, the German Federal Republic took its place as a partner in the world of self-governing peoples. On May 26, 1952, the three Western Powers signed Contractual Agreements ending the occupation status of West Germany, to take effect when the Federal Republic was integrated into the western European defense community. They reserved

131

only the rights necessary to fulfill their obligations in regard to Berlin, the unification of Germany, and a final peace settlement. They retained the right to station armed forces in Germany for "defense of the free world, of which the Federal Republic and Berlin form part." On May 27, 1952, they pledged themselves again to maintain armed forces in Berlin "as long as their responsibilities require it" and reaffirmed their previous declaration that they would "treat any attack against Berlin from any quarter as an attack upon their forces and themselves."

On October 3, 1954, the Federal Republic was admitted to full partnership in the Western European Union (Brussels Treaty) and NATO. It accepted limits on both armaments and independent military action. On its behalf Chancellor Adenauer voluntarily undertook not to manufacture atomic, biological, or chemical weapons. He also undertook not to produce long-range missiles, guided missiles, strategic bombers, and larger war-ships, except with the approval of the Council of Western European Union by a two-thirds vote. The Federal Republic placed all of its military forces under NATO command—the only NATO member to have done so.

Soviet propagandists attempt to promote the myth that the Soviet Union fears a rearmed German Federal Republic. In doing so, the Soviet leaders seek to play on sentiments still remaining from the Nazi experience. However, the fact is that, by deliberate policy of the Federal Republic, legitimate German security requirements are completely tied in with the 15-country NATO alliance and its intricate international staff and command system, in which the United States plays a major role and which is wholly defensive in its nature and objectives. Moreover, the Federal Republic is a strong supporter of the movement toward European integration through the European Common Market, the European Atomic Energy Community, and the European Coal and Steel Community, which are well on the road toward creating a united Europe. These Atlantic and European institutions leave no room for genuine fears of a new German supernationalism, particularly if Germany is permitted to reunite in peace and freedom. The Soviet leaders know this full well.

Through wise policies, driving initiative, and hard work, West Germany's economic recovery surged forward. Its rate of increase in gross national product became one of the highest in the world.

For twelve 12 years now West Germany has been a fully-functioning political democracy, with regular free elections at all levels from local to national, free speech, and all the other rights and safeguards for individual liberty essential to a self-governing society.

In these same ~~twelve~~ 12 years, East Germany has moved just as rapidly in the opposite direction: toward increasing regimentation, collectivization, and progressive strangulation of individual liberties.

Refugees from communism in East Germany crowd into a reception center in West Berlin just before the Communists closed the border in August 1961.

Free Berlin and Free Germany

As West Berlin remains under joint Allied trusteeship, it is not part of the German Federal Republic. But naturally the association between these two self-governing areas is close. The Federal Republic contributes ~~maintains various offices in Berlin. It gives financial support~~ to the economy and cultural life of Free Berlin. Free Berlin has representatives in the Federal Parliament in Bonn, although they do not vote.

Modern freeway, one of the many new thoroughfares in West Berlin.

The Quest For a German Peace Settlement

After Stalin's death and the Korean truce in 1953, the Western Allies resumed their efforts to obtain a peace settlement for Germany as a whole. Another meeting of the foreign ministers, convened in Berlin January 25, 1954, proved fruitless. The Soviets made plain their resolve to keep East Germany in captivity and to permit its unification with West Germany only under conditions which would favor the extension of Communist control over all of Germany.

The Austrian ~~State Treaty (more popularly~~ peace treaty, formally known as the Austrian State ~~peace~~ Treaty), to which the Soviets finally acceded in May 1955, rekindled hope. And at the summit conference in Geneva in July 1955, the Heads of Government of the Big Four agreed, in a directive to their foreign ministers, that "the settlement of the German question and the reunification of Germany by means of free elections shall be carried out in conformity with the national interests of the German people and the interests of European security."

At the subsequent foreign ministers meeting, convened in October 1955, the Western Powers submitted proposals in full harmony with that directive. The Soviets insisted that unification be effected only by agreement. between "two German states."—the freely constituted Federal Republic, then with some 50,000,000 inhabitants, and the puppet East German state with about 17,000,000. The fruitless conference adjourned on November 16.

In 1956 and 1957, President Eisenhower and other Western leaders sought further clarification of Soviet views. Moscow's responses were rigid: But in 1957, Premier Bulganin of the U.S.S.R. sought to persuade the Federal Republic to negotiate directly with the East German regime, first on trade, then on loose confederation. As the latter proposal, publicly advanced by the East German puppet President, made no provision for central authority or free elections, the Federal Republic rejected it. In this decision Chancellor Adenauer was fully supported by the leader of the opposition, the Social Democrat, Erich Ollenhauer.

In July 1957, the Western Powers, including the Federal Republic, tried again to reopen negotiations, coupling the reunification of Germany with European security arrangements which offered far-reaching assurances to the Soviet Union. Again they found themselves up against a stone wall.

In December 1957, the Soviet Union called for a new "summit" conference. After consultation with NATO members President Eisenhower agreed to participate, provided that the groundwork was laid through diplomatic channels and the foreign ministers. But the exchanges which followed yielded no progress.

The Second Major Assault on Free Berlin

Late in 1958, the Soviet Union launched its second major assault on the freedom of West Berlin. The attack began with a speech by Khrushchev on November 10, another on November 26, and a note to the Western Powers on November 27, 1958. In that note the Soviet Union said that it considered null and void all of its agreements with the Western Allies as to Berlin and demanded the withdrawal of Western military forces from the city. It proposed to make West Berlin a demilitarized "free city." As to the reunification of Germany, it proposed that "the two German states" enter into negotiations looking toward a confederation (without free elections in the eastern zone).

The Soviet note set a deadline of 6 months. It said that if the Western Allies had not acceded to its demands by then, the Soviet Union would sign a peace treaty with the "German Democratic Republic" and turn over to it control of all access routes to Berlin.

The ~~arrogant and peace-disturbing~~ Soviet note, like so many other documents emanating from Moscow, was replete with omissions and distortions ~~and omissions of fact~~.[4]

A few fundamental points may be noted here: *The. Soviet Union cannot take away the rights and obligations of the Western Powers to remain in and protect Free Berlin.* Those rights and obligations were not conferred by the Soviet Union but are rooted in the Nazi surrender. They include the right of access to Berlin. Likewise, the Soviet Union cannot unilaterally annul ~~or modify~~ its agreements with the Western Allies as to Berlin, including its guarantees of access to the city. Those agreements can be altered only by consent of all Four Powers. ~~The Soviet Union cannot legally divest itself of these commitments or transfer them to anyone else without approval of the Western Powers.~~

In its reply of December 31, 1958, the United States rejected the Soviet demands and said that it could not embark on discussions with the Soviet Union "under menace ~~or~~ **of** ultimatum." It nevertheless inquired if the Soviet Union were ready to enter into discussions among the Four Powers on the question of Berlin "in the wider framework of negotiations for a solution of the German problem as well as that of European security." Similar replies were sent by the United Kingdom and France.

On January 10, 1959, the Soviet Union proposed the calling of a peace conference and "summit" talks on Berlin and Germany, with participation by the "German Democratic Republic" and the Federal Republic of Germany. It did not mention, although it did not withdraw, the 6-month deadline.

Construing this as an implicit retreat from duress, the Western Powers on February 16 informed the Soviet Government that they were prepared to take part in a Four Power Conference of Foreign Ministers to deal with the problem of Germany in all its aspects. They consented that German "advisers" be invited.

The Soviets eventually agreed. The Foreign Ministers Conference opened in Geneva on May 11, 1959. Representatives of the Federal Republic and of the East German regime were permitted to be present as advisers ~~seated as advisers at tables separated by two pencils' width from the main table at which sat the representatives of the four negotiating powers~~.

---

[4] Corrections of some of the more obvious of these may be found in a pamphlet, Department of State publication 6757, released in January 1959, and entitled *The Soviet Note on Berlin: An Analysis.* As the Communists have continued to propagate these same distortions and to ignore the same significant facts, reading of this pamphlet is still recommended.

Mr. Johnson Speaks to the People of West Berlin

"I have come to Berlin by direction of President Kennedy.

"He wants you to know—and I want you to know—that the pledge he has given to the freedom of West Berlin and to the rights of Western access to Berlin is firm. To the survival and to the creative future of this city we Americans have pledged, in effect, what our ancestors pledged in forming the United States: '… our Lives, our Fortunes and our sacred Honor.'

"I come here at a moment of tension and danger—in your lives, the lives of my countrymen, and the common life of the free world.

"A barrier of barbed wire has been thrown across your city. It has broken for you—and more important, for your brethren to the east— vital human and communal ties, ties that reach back into the lives of families and friends and into the long life of this great city."

The Western Peace Plan

On May 14, 1959, the Western Allies put forward a comprehensive peace plan which reached far to accommodate Soviet interests and views. It was a phased plan which did not insist on immediate free elections in East Germany but provided time for a mixed German committee to draft an electoral law and work out plans for increased trade and other contacts between the two parts of Germany. Interlocked with a series of steps toward the reunification of Germany were provisions for measures against surprise attack and for progressive reductions in military forces both in an area of Europe and by overall ceilings on Soviet and U.S. military personnel.

This far-reaching plan, to be applied by stages, was designed to consolidate peace in Europe, east and west. The Soviets rejected it out of hand.

The Soviet Plan

The Soviet plan, presented on May 15, called for:

1. Separate peace treaties with the "two German states," the negotiation of reunification to be left to them, with no time limit, thus no assurance that Germany would ever be reunited or that free elections would ever be permitted in East Germany.

2. Pending German reunification, West Berlin to become a "free, demilitarized city," thus "occupation" by the Western Powers to end.

3. The NATO powers to withdraw their forces and dismantle all military bases on "foreign territory." The Soviets, in return, to withdraw their forces from East Germany, Poland, and Hungary.

The first point ~~above should be labeled, as Secretary of State Christian A. Herter observed at the time, the "Soviet Treaty for the Permanent Partition of German." When~~ when combined with the third~~, however, it~~ became a plan to weaken the security of West Germany, and indeed of all Free Europe, thus opening the way for eventual extension of the Communist domain.

The withdrawal of military forces from, and dismantling of military bases on, "foreign territory" is a staple item in Communist "peace" and "disarmament" proposals. It means the expulsion of American military power from the Eurasian continent and adjacent, islands and the dissolution of NATO and the other alliances which restrain Communist expansion by military means. These alliances were brought into being by Communist threats and aggressions, notably the take-over in Czechoslovakia, the Berlin Blockade, and the attack in Korea. All are defensive, freely entered into by their members, and in strict conformity with the United Nations Charter. The participation of the United States is what gives them sufficient strength to deter or cope with major aggression. And the presence of American military forces at various key points on and near the Eurasian continent is the visible proof, to friend and foe alike, that we will honor our obligations.

In return for the withdrawal of Allied forces from West Germany and of American forces from all of Europe to the United States, more than 3,000 miles across the ocean, the Soviets offered to withdraw their forces a few hundred miles, whence they could return quickly. This was not a peace proposal but a design for conquest, by making the free nations of Europe vulnerable to Communist threats and eventually to outright attack.

The Plan For a "Demilitarized Free City"

The term "demilitarized free city" is appealing. As West Berlin is already a free city, the key word is "demilitarized."

No one could seriously argue that the small contingents of Western troops in West Berlin, which in July 1961 numbered only 11,000, are a threat to peace. They are surrounded by 22 or more Soviet divisions plus the armed forces of the East German regime. In 16 years they have not been responsible for a single provocative incident. They are kept there as proof and warning that the Western Allies will protect the freedom of West Berlin, come what may.

West Berlin has no troops of its own. And, as it is not part of the Federal Republic, no West German troops are stationed there. By contrast,

East German armed forces are stationed in East Berlin. In the Communist May Day celebrations in 1959, 1960, and 1961 calling for the demilitarization of West Berlin, these East German forces, including tanks, were ostentatiously paraded in East Berlin. Those Communist military displays were an ominous hint of the probable eventual fate of West Berlin if it were stripped of military defenses. The hint became even plainer in August 1961, when the East German regime deployed large military forces, including tanks, in East Berlin.

At various times the Soviets have suggested or hinted at certain modifications of their proposal to demilitarize West Berlin. Khrushchev has said that he "would even agree to the United States, Great Britain, France and the U.S.S.R. or neutral countries maintaining some sort of minimum forces in West Berlin." He has suggested also the possibility of a United Nations guarantee.

If the Soviets really want to see the freedom of West Berlin preserved, why do they insist on a change in the present arrangement, which guarantees that freedom while preserving the peace? Khrushchev says that, since many years have elapsed since the Nazi surrender, it is time to do away with the occupation agreements. He likes to call the position of Berlin "abnormal."

If the position of Berlin is abnormal, it is because the situation in Germany is abnormal. The Soviets Those agreements could have been dispensed with years ago if the Soviets had complied with them. If they had done so, or would do so now, there would be no Berlin problem and no German problem. But they still prevent by force both the unification of Germany, which would automatically settle the Berlin question, and a free expression of will by the people of East Germany and East Berlin on that or anything else.

In fact, by the standard of all who believe in self-determination, the situation throughout Eastern Europe, the Soviet Union, and the whole Communist orbit is "abnormal." By that Standard Free Berlin is, as its Mayor, Willy Brandt, has remarked, the only "normal" city situated anywhere within the Communist world.

The 'Western Powers have made it clear plain that they are not wedded to any particular form of protection for the freedom of West Berlin, provided that it does not weaken the protection which now keeps West Berlin free. Suggestions that this task be turned over to the United Nations must be considered in the light of Khrushchev's assault on the U.N. Secretary-General, Dag Hammarskjold, and his demand for a three-headed secretariat, or "troika," in which each of the three would have a veto. That plan, if adopted, would paralyze the executive functions of the U.N. Secretariat.

139

In gauging Khrushchev's real intentions regarding West Berlin, one should observe that the Soviet note of November 27, 1958, stated that "the most correct and natural" solution would be to absorb West Berlin into the "German Democratic Republic." Soviet Foreign Minister Andrei Gromyko reiterated on May 30:

> If we are to speak frankly, the Soviet Government considers the creation of a Free City far from being an ideal solution of the West Berlin question. The most equitable approach to this question would be, of course, the extension to West Berlin of the full sovereignty of the German Democratic Republic. I think that the German Democratic Republic, whose capital the division of the city continues to mutilate, could with the fullest Justification demand such a solution of the question.

The Soviet plan to make West Berlin a "demilitarized free city" is thus obviously intended as a temporary way station on the road to "the most correct and natural" solution. If Khrushchev himself has left any doubt about that, Walter Ulbricht,[5] the number-one No. 1 East German Communist, has not. Ulbricht's statements, several of which appear as annex VI, at times have the brutal candor of Hitler's *Mein Kampf.*

Khrushchev's War Threat

Since November 1958, Khrushchev has repeatedly warned that if the Western Allies did not settle the Berlin and German questions on terms satisfactory to him he would sign a separate peace treaty with the East German regime and turn over to it control of the access routes to Berlin.

Nobody can prevent Moscow from signing a "peace treaty" with this or any other of its puppets. Such an act This would be simply a ventriloquist stunt.

The threat to peace begins with the Communist contention, contrary to international law, that such that a "peace treaty" between Moscow and the East German regime would annul all Western rights pertaining to Berlin. The threat to destroy those rights implies action to prevent their

---

[5] Ulbricht received intensive training in Communist doctrine at the Lenin Institute in Moscow from 1926 to 1928. In 1937 or 1938, he returned to the Soviet Union and remained there during the war. He returned to Germany in 1945 as a colonel in the Soviet Army. The Soviet authorities installed him and other well-trained Communists in key positions in East Germany. He is reported to have held Soviet citizenship for several years.

exercise. The Western Allies can accept neither the legality nor the potential practical consequences of that position. For example, as free access is indispensable to the survival in freedom of West Berlin, it is the inescapable duty of the Western Allies to see that free access is not blocked, interrupted, or whittled away. Yet the East German regime, which according to Khrushchev would control all access routes on conclusion of a "peace treaty," is a member of the Warsaw military pact, of which the Soviet Union is the architect and chief member. *This, in essence, is what makes Khrushchev's declared intention a grave threat to peace.* ~~What makes it grave is the Soviet threat to go to war if the Western Allies exercise their indubitable duty to prevent those rights from being extinguished.~~

~~Thus, when examined, Khrushchev's threat to make a separate peace treaty with the East German regime is an aggressive move backed by the threat of war.~~

~~It has been widely conjectured that the East Germans would not immediately try to restrict Western access, but would do so only gradually, a bit at a time. Such "salami" tactics would appear to be shrewd from the Communist viewpoint, as they might present difficulties to the Western Allies in deciding when to resist. But Ulbricht has indicated that he would like to apply at least one severe limitation at once: that he would try to close Tempelhof Airfield in West Berlin, compelling all air traffic to and from Berlin to use a field under East German control. This would close the main road to freedom for East Germans.~~

Impasse and Another Approach to the Summit

In mid-June, 1959, the Soviets brought the Foreign Ministers Conference in Geneva to a crisis. The conference recessed June 20, resumed July 13, and adjourned without tangible progress on August 5. Meanwhile, President Eisenhower invited Khrushchev to the United States. They conferred at some length during the Soviet leader's visit, which lasted from September 15 to September 27, 1959, and carried him from coast to coast. Khrushchev suspended his threat to sign a separate peace treaty with the East Germans. These talks and others at high level led to a Big Four "summit" meeting in Paris on May 15, 1960. That conference was never formally convened, although all the principals were on hand. Khrushchev used the U-2 incident to break it up. ~~Some thought his real reason was his discovery prior to the conference that the Western Allies would not bow to his demands.~~

The blowup at the "summit" and the 1960 national elections in the ~~U.S.~~ United States brought a pause in discussions with Moscow. Khrushchev did not remain silent or inactive, however. Among other things, he attended the U.N. General Assembly in New York from September 20 to October 13.[6]

After the elections, conversations between Washington and Moscow were resumed through various channels. Certain small frictions between Moscow and Washington were eased, ~~and Khrushchev indicated that he was willing to give the new U.S. President, John F. Kennedy, time to settle into his job before pressing serious negotiations.~~

The Third Assault

Khrushchev did not wait long, however. He indicated during the winter and early spring months that he still regarded Berlin and Germany as urgent questions. Meanwhile he was promoting or aggravating trouble in Laos and elsewhere and making bellicose speeches.

President Kennedy decided, and Khrushchev concurred, that a direct exchange of views ~~talks between them~~, without attempting negotiations, might be useful. These talks were held June 3-4, 1961, in Vienna. They were, in President Kennedy's word, "somber." [stopped here]

A Soviet *aide memoire* on Germany and Berlin, delivered June 4, marked the formal beginning of the third great assault on the freedom of Berlin. The Western Allies replied on July ~~18~~ 17. The text of the U.S. reply (see Annex II) is self-explanatory.

The circumstances and tone of the third assault, together with Khrushchev's belligerent words at Vienna and elsewhere, suggest that in manufacturing another crisis over West Berlin the Soviets have far-reaching aims.

Closing of the Escape Hatch

The third assault on the freedom of West Berlin produced reactions which Khrushchev perhaps did not anticipate. President Kennedy recommended and the U.S. Congress promptly authorized a substantial expansion and strengthening of the American armed forces. Corresponding steps were taken by other NATO members. Among these and other reactions, not least significant was a sudden rise in the outflow of East Germans and East Berliners. In July 1961, more than 30,000 found refuge in the West, nearly twice the previous monthly average.

---

[6] It was on this trip that he launched his savage attack on the Secretary-General and became the first man in the history of the United Nations to express displeasure by taking off a shoe and pounding it on the table.

The East German authorities instituted new measures to stem the flow. They restricted travel from East Germany to East Berlin. In Berlin, through more frequent checks and interrogations, they stopped and turned back some of the refugees trying to escape across the sector border. They took steps to force some 50,000 East Berliners working In West Berlin to give up their jobs. They supported these and related steps with an intensive propaganda campaign, which ranged from branding refugees as "traitors" to inventing a "polio epidemic" in West Germany.

Day after day, the efforts of the East German authorities became more frantic. They probably succeeded in blocking the flight of many thousands who were seeking freedom. But they did not stop the exodus. More than 22,000 refugees arrived in West Berlin in the first 12 days of August.

On August 13, 1961, the communists took the desperate step of sealing the Berlin sector border against East Germans and East Berliners. Shortly after midnight a communiqué was published by the Warsaw Pact nations, the Soviet Union and its European satellites, calling for such action. It was accompanied by a decree of the "German Democratic Republic" prohibiting East Germans and East Berliners from entering West Berlin. East German troops and armed police, with armored cars and tanks, were deployed along the entire sector border. They put up barbed wire barriers. A few days later they began building a wall of cement blocks. Other East German troops were deployed on the edges of the city. These in turn were backed by a ring of troops from three Soviet divisions, including one tank division. These large-scale supporting deployments were obviously intended to inhibit a popular arising such as had occurred in East Berlin and East Germany in 1953 and in Hungary in 1956.

Thus was the escape hatch from the East German prison slammed shut and locked. And thus once again was it demonstrated that the Communists can maintain their rule only by force. The closing of the sector border and the deployment of East German troops in East Berlin were further violations of Soviet pledges. The Western Allies protested (see annexes VIII and IX), but with no immediate result.

Modern architecture of the Hansa Viertel, which was completely destroyed daring the war, typifies West Berlin's reconstruction

The Allied Trusteeship—What the Record Shows

The record shows that the Western Allies have been faithful to the trusteeship they assumed in 1945. They have fostered the reconstruction of Germany as a peaceable, self-governing nation. They have fostered and protected free institutions in West Berlin. ~~Where they could prevail, they have performed what they promised.~~

The record shows that the Soviet Union, which joined in the same pledges, has dishonored them by a long series of nonfeasances, misfeasances, and malfeasances. It shows that the Soviet Union has violated, flagrantly and repeatedly, its wartime and postwar agreements on the occupation and rehabilitation of Germany and on the special status of Berlin. ~~(In the limited space of this pamphlet only some of the major ones could be noted.)~~

~~The Soviet Union~~ It has prevented the reunification of Germany. It has denied~~, and prohibited~~ democratic self-government and self-determination to the people of ~~in~~ East Germany and East Berlin, instead imposing on them and maintaining by force a police-state regime. It armed that regime. In these and many other ways it broke its agreements.[7] ~~It repeatedly sought to extinguish freedom in West Berlin.~~

---

[7] For a list of major Soviet violations of its agreements concerning Germany and Berlin, see annex X.

The Soviet Union separated East Berlin from the rest of the city. It permitted its East German puppet to proclaim Berlin as its capital. It permitted its East German puppet to parade, and finally to station, troops and tanks in East Berlin. It has now sealed the sector border against East Germans and East Berliners wishing to go to West Berlin. In these and many other ways it has broken its clear-cut agreements with its war-time allies as to the special status of Greater Berlin.

Not content with inflicting its will on the peoples of East Germany and East Berlin, the Soviet Union has repeatedly tried to force or suffocate the people of West Berlin into submission to Communist tyranny.

What the Free Berliners Want

No one who believes in self-determination could be deaf to the clearly expressed wish of the people of Free Berlin. They have made it unmistakably clear plain that they want the Western Allies to stay as guardians and are adamantly opposed to any weakening in the protection they now enjoy.

East German soldiers with armored cars and high pressure water trucks bar passage through the Brandenburg Gate on the East-West border in Berlin, August 1961

The status of Berlin was a key issue in the West Berlin elections of December 1958, held just after Khrushchev issued his ultimatum. The candidates of the SED (Communist Party) advocated a change. All other candidates of all other parties opposed any change. The Communists were as free as the others to advocate their cause. (Indeed, West Berlin police and firemen broke up anti-Communist demonstrations against Communist political rallies.) Ninety-six percent of the electorate voted. The Communists received only 1.9 percent of the vote cast. Such was the verdict of a people who know what communism means because they are surrounded by it.

The Free World's Stake in Berlin

West Berlin is a lighthouse of freedom in a dark totalitarian sea. It demonstrates the It is a showcase for the material superiorities of a free society which allows and encourages individual initiative. More important, it is a shining model of political, intellectual, and spiritual freedom in which individual liberties are assured and the people choose those who govern them.

Khrushchev and his followers profess to want "peaceful coexistence" and "peaceful competition." For more than a decade Berlin has been a test tube of peaceful competition. Hundreds of thousands of visitors have seen at first hand the result—that the difference between West and East Berlin is the difference between day and night.

For the peoples of East Berlin and East Germany, the special status of Berlin holds the hope of their eventual reunion with the people of the Federal Republic in a united democratic German nation. For many of them, until mid-August 1961, West Berlin was a venthole in the prison wall—a place they could visit, now and then for a life-sustaining breath of free air.[8] For those of them who could no longer endure Communist tyranny it was, until then, the escape hatch to freedom.

For all the peoples held in captivity in the vast detention camp which is behind the Iron Curtain in Eastern Europe, West Berlin is a beacon of hope—a hope nourished since 1948 by the ability of the Western Powers and the Berliners to maintain its freedom.

For the peoples of East Berlin an East Germany, the special status of Berlin holds the hope of their eventual reunion with the people of the Federal Republic in a united democratic German nation. Meanwhile, for such of them as are able to visit it, Free Berlin provides a life-sustaining breath of oxygen.

---

[8] In 1960, East Berliners and East Germans borrowed 250,000 books from West Berlin libraries and bought 560,000 tickets to West Berlin theaters and operas and 10 million admissions to West Berlin movie houses.

~~For the people of East Berlin and East Germany who can lo longer endure Communist tyranny, Free Berlin is the escape hatch to freedom.~~

Of all this, Khrushchev and his German Communist puppets are painfully aware. That is why West Berlin is to Khrushchev ~~them~~ a "cancerous tumor" and a "bone stuck in our throat." That is why he has publicly declared his resolve "to eradicate this splinter from the heart of Europe."

For the Western Allies, Free Berlin is the symbol, the evidence, and the acid test of their unity, strength, and determination. It has become in a real sense the keystone of the defensive arch of NATO. Were the Western Allies to permit the freedom of West Berlin to be lost, whether by direct assault or by erosion, they would be false to their pledges. Who would trust their word again? And if they, who are the backbone of the security of the free world, should falter and fall apart, what hope would remain for freedom anywhere?

~~Americans are proud of the role of their own struggle for independence and the great ideas enunciated by its leaders in inspiring other peoples to throw off the yokes of despotism and imperialism. They believe that the American Revolution was the beginning of a "new order of the ages." (The words "novus ordo seclorum" are inscribed on the Great Seal of the United States.) They believe with Abraham Lincoln that it was "meant for all mankind." (Check accuracy of quote) In the 19th and early 20th centuries they rejoiced in the liberation of peoples and growth of democratic self-government in Latin American and Europe. In the last 15 years they have rejoiced in the emancipation of the peoples of Asia and Africa and their rise to "the separate and equal station to which the Laws of Nature and of Nature's God entitle them." They believe that these same idea which have swept over so much of the earth — of self-determination, personal liberty, and individual dignity — are rooted in the nature of man and will eventually sweep over and bury the spurious doctrine of the inevitable triumph of Communism.~~

Berlin is a focal point in a worldwide struggle. ~~Meanwhile, however, freedom must be protected from destruction by force.~~ The central issue in that, struggle is, in ~~In~~ the words of Secretary of State Dean Rusk: ~~"The central issue of the crisis is~~ the announced determination to impose a world of coercion upon those not already subjected to it. ... At stake is the survival and growth of the world of free choice and ... free cooperation."

147

That central issue, he pointed out, "is posed between the Sino-Soviet empire and all the rest, whether allied or neutral; and it, is now posed in every continent."[9]

All peoples throughout the globe who enjoy or aspire to freedom, including the captive peoples of the Communist empires, have a vital interest in the preservation of freedom—of self-determination in West Berlin. ~~Berlin is a focal point in the struggle between the world of coercion and the world of free choice.~~ In defending Free Berlin we defend not only Bonn, Paris, London, Oslo, Ottawa, Washington, Kansas City, Boise, but,—in fact, every citizen in the North Atlantic community. Equally we defend New Delhi, Kuala Lumpur, Tokyo, Lagos, Tunis, Cairo, Rio de Janeiro, Montevideo, and every other city and village and people who wish to be free.[10]

Everyone who treasures freedom ~~All peoples throughout the globe who enjoy or aspire to freedom, including the captive peoples in the Communist empires, have a vital stake in the freedom of West Berlin. They~~ can join the stout-hearted Free Berliners in saying to Khrushchev and his Communist satraps ~~proconsuls~~ what two emissaries of a free city of ancient Greece said to a Persian satrap ~~tyrant, Xerxes~~ who asked them why they did not submit to the Persian tyrant Xerxes. They replied, according to Herodotus: "You have experience of half the matter; but the other half is beyond your knowledge. The life of a slave you understand; but, never having tasted liberty, you can never know whether it be sweet or not. But ah! had you known what freedom is, you would bid us fight for it, not with the spear only, but with the battle-axe."

---

[9] Address at the National Press Club, Washington, D.C., July 10, 1961.

[10] It is pertinent to note that approximately 20 of the independent nations belonging to the United Nations are less populous than West Berlin and that more than 50 have a gross national product smaller than West Berlin's.

An elderly East German couple, seeking to join the millions of East Germans who have fled to freedom in the West, are turned back by Communist guards at the West Berlin border.

Annex I

Soviet *Aide Memoire* of June 4, 1961[11]

Official translation

1. The years-long delay in arriving at a peace settlement with Germany has largely predetermined the dangerous course of events in Europe in the post-war period. The major decisions of the Allies on the eradication of militarism in Germany, which once were considered by the Governments of the United States and the U.S.S.R. as the guarantee of stable peace, have been implemented only partially and now are actually not being observed in the greater part of German territory. Of the Governments of the two German States that were formed after the war, it is only the Government of the German Democratic Republic that recognizes and adheres to those agreements. The Government of the Federal Republic of Germany openly proclaims its negative attitude to those agreements, cultivates saber-rattling militarism and advocates the review of the German frontiers and the results of the Second World War. It tries to establish a powerful military base for its aggressive plans, to kindle a dangerous hotbed of conflicts on German soil, and to set the former Allies in the anti-Hitler coalition against each other.

The Western Powers have allowed the Federal Republic of Germany to start accumulating armaments and setting up an army, which are clearly in excess of defense needs. The NATO Powers took new, dangerous steps when they gave the Federal Republic of Germany permission to build warships of up to 6 thousand tons displacement and also to use the territory of the United Kingdom, France and Italy for military bases as the Federal Republic of Germany.

2. The Soviet Government is earnestly striving towards removing the sources of tension between the United States and the U.S.S.R. and to proceed to constructive, friendly cooperation. The conclusion of a German peace treaty would allow the two countries to come much closer to the attainment of this goal. The U.S.S.R. and the United States fought together against Hitlerite Germany. Their common duty is to conclude a German peace treaty and thereby create a reliable guarantee that German soil will never again give birth to forces that could plunge the world into a new and even morn devastating war. If the desire of the Soviet Union to consolidate peace and to prevent the unleashing of a new world war in Europe does not run counter to the intentions of the United States Government, then it will not be difficult to reach agreement

---

[11] Handed to President Kennedy by Premier Khrushchev during their meeting at Vienna June 3-4.

3. Proceeding from a realistic evaluation of the situation, the Soviet Government stands for the immediate conclusion of a peace treaty with Germany. The question of a peace treaty is one that concerns the national security of the U.S.S.R. and of many other States. The time has already passed for allowing the situation in Germany to remain unchanged. All the conditions for the conclusion of a peace treaty matured a long time ago and this treaty must be concluded. The point is who will conclude it and when, and whether this will entail unnecessary costs.

4. The Soviet Government is not pursuing the goal of harming the interests of the United States or other Western Powers in Europe. It does not propose to change anything either in Germany or in West Berlin in favor of any one State or group of States. The U.S.S.R. deems it necessary in the interests of consolidating peace formally to recognize the situation which has developed in Europe after the war, to legalize and to consolidate the inviolability of the existing German borders, to normalize the situation in West Berlin on the basis of reasonable consideration for the interests of all the parties concerned.

In the interests of achieving agreement on a peace treaty the Soviet Union does not insist on the immediate withdrawal of the Federal Republic of Germany from NATO. Both German States could for a certain period, even after the conclusion of a peace treaty, remain in the military alliances to which they now belong.

The Soviet proposal does not tie the conclusion of a peace treaty to the recognition of the German Democratic Republic or the Federal Republic of Germany by all the parties to this treaty. It is up to each Government to decide whether or not to recognize this or that State.

If the United States is not prepared to sign a joint peace treaty with the two German States, a peaceful settlement could be achieved on the basis of two treaties. In that case the States that participated in the anti-Hitlerite coalition would sign a peace treaty with two German States or with one German State, at their own discretion. These treaties need not be completely identical in wording but they must contain the same kind of provisions on the most important points of a peaceful settlement.

5. The conclusion of a German peace treaty would also solve the problem of normalizing the situation in West Berlin. Deprived of a stable international status, West Berlin at present is a place where the Bonn revanchist circles continually Maintain extreme tension and organize all kinds of provocations very dangerous to the cause of peace. We are duty-bound to prevent a development where intensification of West German militarism could lead to irreparable consequences due to the unsettled situation in West Berlin.

At present, the Soviet Government does not see a better way to solve the West Berlin problem than by transforming it into a demilitarized free city. The implementation of the proposal to turn West Berlin into a free city, with the interests of all parties duly taken into consideration, would normalize the situation in West Berlin. The occupation regime now being maintained has already outlived itself and has lost all connection with the purposes for which it was established, as well as with the Allied agreements concerning Germany that established the basis for its existence. The occupation rights will naturally be terminated upon the conclusion of a German peace treaty, whether it is signed with both German States or only with the German Democratic Republic, within whose territory West Berlin is located.

The position of the Soviet Government is that the free city of West Berlin should have unobstructed contacts with the outside world and that its internal regulations should be determined by the freely expressed will of its population. The United States as well as other countries would naturally have every possibility to maintain and develop their relations with the free city. In short, West Berlin, as the Soviet Government sees it, should be strictly neutral. Of course, the use of Berlin as a base for provocative activities, hostile to the U.S.S.R., the G.D.R. or any other State, cannot be permitted in the future, nor can Berlin be allowed to remain a dangerous hotbed of tension and international conflicts.

The U.S.S.R. proposes that the most reliable guarantees be established against interference in the affairs of the free city on the part of any State. Token troop contingents of the United States, the United Kingdom, France and the U.S.S.R could be stationed in West Berlin as guarantors of the free city. The U.S.S.R. would have no objections, either, to the stationing in West Berlin, for the same purpose, of military contingents from neutral States under the aegis of the U.N. The status of free city could be duly registered by the United Nations and consolidated by the authority of that international organization. The Soviet side is prepared to discuss any other measures that would guarantee the freedom and independence of West Berlin as a free demilitarized city.

All this considered, the settlement of the West Berlin problem should naturally take into account the necessity of respecting and strictly observing the sovereign rights of the German Democratic Republic, which, as is well known, has declared its readiness to adhere to such an agreement and respect it.

6. The Soviet Government proposes that a peace conference be called immediately, without delay, that a German peace treaty be concluded, and that the problem of West Berlin as a free city be solved in this way. If for any

motives the Governments of the United States or other Western Powers are not ready for this at the present time, an interim decision could be adopted for a specified period of time.

The Four Powers would appeal to the German States to come to an agreement in any form acceptable to them on problems relating to a peace settlement with Germany and its reunification. The Four Powers would declare in advance that they would recognize any agreement achieved by the Germans.

In the event of a favorable outcome of the negotiations between the G.D.R. and the F.R.G. a single German peace treaty would be agreed upon and signed. If the two German States fail to reach agreement on the above-mentioned issues, steps would be taken to conclude a peace treaty with the two German States or with one of them, at the discretion of the States concerned.

To avoid delaying a peace settlement it is essential to fix a time limit within which the Germans should seek possible ways for agreements on problems within their internal competence. The Soviet Government considers that not more than 6 months are needed for such negotiations. This period is quite sufficient for the G.D.R. and F.R.G. to establish contacts and to negotiate, since an understanding of the necessity of putting an end to the vestiges of the Second World War in Europe has matured during the sixteen post-war years.

7. The Soviet Government is prepared to consider any constructive proposals of the United States Government on a German peace treaty and on normalizing the situation in West Berlin. The Soviet Government will show a maximum of good will in order that the question of a German peace treaty may be settled by mutual agreement between the U.S.S.R., the United States, and other States concerned. The signing of a German peace treaty by all the members of the anti-Hitlerite coalition and the settlement of the question of a neutral status for West Berlin on this basis would create better conditions for trust among States and for the solution of such important international problems as disarmament and others. But, if the United States does not show that it realizes the necessity of concluding a peace treaty, we shall deplore it because we shall be obliged to sign a peace treaty, which it would be impossible and dangerous to delay, not with all the States but only with those that wish to sign it.

The peace treaty would specifically define the status of West Berlin as a free city and the Soviet Union, just as the other parties to the treaty, would of course observe It strictly; measures would also be taken to ensure that this status be respected by other countries as well. At the same time, this would mean putting an end to the occupation regime in West Berlin with all its implications. In particular, questions of using the means of communication by land, water or air within the territory of the G.D.R. would have to be settled solely by appropriate agreements with the G.D.R. That is but natural, since control over such means of communication is an inalienable right of every sovereign State.

8. The conclusion of a German treaty would be an important step towards the final post-war settlement in Europe for which the Soviet Union is persistently striving.

Annex II
U.S. Note of July 17, 1961[12]

The United States Government has given careful consideration to the Soviet Government's *aide memoire* received on June 4, 1961, in Vienna. It has consulted with Its British and French Allies and has found itself in full agreement with them. It has also consulted the Government of the Federal Republic of Germany, and the other member Governments of the North Atlantic Treaty Organization.

The United States Government fully concurs with the Soviet Government that a peace settlement is long overdue. It is clear from the public record of efforts on the part of the Western Powers to reach agreement with the Soviet Union on the terms of such a peace settlement that it is the Soviet Union which has blocked all progress. The United States first suggested in 1946 that a special commission be appointed to draft a German peace treaty. It has continued its efforts throughout all the intervening years but without avail because of Soviet efforts to obtain special advantages for itself and the Soviet bloc in any such settlement at the expense of a lasting peace.

The United States Government would like to be able to believe the Soviet Government's statement that it sincerely desires to remove the sources of tension between the United States and the Soviet Union and to proceed to constructive friendly cooperation. This aim is close to the hearts of the American people and their Government. It found its expression in wartime cooperation, and the United States was deeply disappointed when Soviet postwar actions disrupted the conditions for its continuation. The conclusion of a German treaty in peace and freedom and based on the freely expressed will of the German people would, indeed, allow the U.S.S.R. and the U.S. to come much closer to the attainment of this goal.

With regard to Berlin, the United States is not insisting upon the maintenance of its legal rights because of any desire merely to perpetuate its presence there. It is insisting on, and will defend, its legal rights against attempts at unilateral abrogation because the freedom of the people of West Berlin depends upon the maintenance of those rights. The support and approval of the people of West Berlin for the system under which they live has been made amply clear over the years. Their overwhelming support for their government in free elections is a dramatic example of this. That the

---

[12] Delivered to the Soviet Ministry of Foreign Affairs at Moscow on July 17. Similar notes were delivered on the same day by the French and British Ambassadors.

United States is not wedded to one particular arrangement for Berlin is demonstrated by the all-Berlin solution which was proposed at Geneva in 1959. It has accepted the possibility of practical arrangements intended to improve the present situation in Berlin until such time as an over-all solution of the German problem can be achieved. It is sorry to note that all the proposals it has made to that end have been rejected by the Government of the U.S.S.R. However, the United States also supports the clearly expressed wish of the West Berliners that no change be made in the status of their city which would expose them, at once or gradually over a longer time, to the domination of the regime which presently controls the surrounding areas.

The United States Government continues to believe that there will be no real solution of the German problem, nor any real tranquility in Central Europe, until the German people are reunified in peace and freedom on the basis of the universally recognized principle of self-determination. It is because of this conviction that the United States Government, with its Allies, has repeatedly proposed solutions for the German problem based on these principles—unfortunately without evoking a positive response from the Soviet Government.

Thus, they proposed to the Soviet Government on May 14, 1959 the Western Peace Plan, which was acclaimed throughout the world as a constructive offer. The detailed proposals in the Peace Plan were intended as a practical step-by-step approach to the problem of a Central European settlement based on the principle of self-determination, to which the Soviet Government professes to adhere, but which is conspicuous by its absence in Soviet proposals.

The Soviet *aide memoire* argues that the time has already passed when the situation in Germany could be left unchanged. The United States Government is persuaded that a change for the better is to be desired. But at the same time it is certain that world opinion has noted that In the decade between the end of the Soviet blockade of Berlin and the renewed threat to Berlin in the Soviet note of November 27, 1958 the German problem did not disturb world peace. And Just as the world could not fail to note who was responsible for disturbing the peace on those two occasions, it will surely condemn any attempt by any one of the Four Powers to change the existing situation in West Berlin against the will of the other Three and against the overwhelming desire of the vast majority of the people of Berlin and Germany, who are most directly concerned.

To justify the action it wishes to take, the Government of the U.S.S.R. alleges that without a peace treaty there is danger of conflagration in Europe. The U.S. Government does not consider that this argument has any merit. Minor incidents which occur from time to time in the present situation are settled through exercise of those quadripartite responsibilities which, in themselves, constitute the most effective protection against any local aggravation of the situation growing into a real threat to the peace.

Contrary to the unfounded assertion in the Soviet *aide memoire*, the Western Powers vigorously carried out the programs to eradicate Nazi militarism, to eliminate vestiges of the Third Reich, to prevent the rebirth of aggressive forces, and to chart a course by which Germany could recover its respect and play a constructive role in international affairs. The Federal Republic of Germany is the proof of the successful achievement of these aims by the West.

The Federal Republic's foreign and military policies accept significant restraints. It has undertaken not to manufacture atomic, chemical, and biological weapons, and has accepted international control to insure that this undertaking is honored. All of the Federal Republic's combat forces are completely integrated into NATO, which has only defensive—not aggressive—aims. The Federal Republic does not seek, or intend to develop, an independent nuclear capability or the transfer of nuclear weapons to its national jurisdiction. It looks to its legitimate defense requirements entirely within the NATO framework. In addition, the Federal Government has publicly stated that the Federal Republic does not con template the use of force to achieve reunification or to alter existing boundaries. It has also consistently taken significant steps to integrate itself peacefully and firmly Into the Western European community—steps which would never be taken by a government bent on a militaristic course.

After the end of World War II, the United States and its Western Allies demobilized their military forces in the expectation of a peaceful world order. However, post-war Soviet policies compelled the organization of the military defense of the North Atlantic Treaty area. Without the armed threat to Western Europe, the purely defensive Alliance to which the United States is fully committed and in which the Federal Republic participates might well never have developed. The pursuit by the U.S.S.R. of its unilateral objectives in Eastern Europe convinced the present members of NATO that Soviet power would be extended into any area westward which did not have the ability to defend itself. Should the U.S.S.R. make unilateral moves In its German policy, contrary to binding international agreements, the NATO countries could only interpret such moves as a purposeful threat to their national interests.

The Soviet Government, in its *aide memoire*, is presenting the Western Powers with a demand that they accept Its solution of the German problem. Despite the protestations of the Soviet Government that it does not intend to harm the interests of the United States or other Western Powers in Europe, it remains the firm conviction of the Western Powers that the end result of the Soviet proposals would harm not only their interests, but also those of the German people, and—since they endanger the peace—those of the entire world.

The counterpart of the Soviet position is that unless the Western Powers accept its German 'solution, the Soviet Government will try to obtain what it wants by unilateral action.

The Soviet Government thus threatens to violate its solemn international obligations, to determine unilaterally the fate of millions of Germans without their consent, and to use force against its World War II Allies if they do not voluntarily surrender their rights and vital positions. The Soviet Government must understand that such a course of action is not only unacceptable, but is a more serious menace to world peace, for which it bears full responsibility before all mankind.

At the end of World War II, the victorious Powers entered into a number of agreements to settle the German problem, based on the principle that questions concerning Germany as a whole were a matter for joint action by the victorious Powers. A peace settlement with Germany is foremost among those questions. The Potsdam Agreement of 1945 for instance, refers to "the preparation of a peace settlement for Germany to be accepted by the government of Germany when a government adequate for the purpose is established."

Under international law, the Soviet Government cannot ignore these agreements in order to conclude unilateral arrangements with a part of Germany; nor would such action invalidate the rights of the United States Government and the other governments responsible for the settlement of the German question, since these rights derive absolutely from the unconditional surrender of Nazi Germany, and were not granted by, or negotiated with, the Soviet Union. This has repeatedly been acknowledged by the Soviet Government, as recently *as* at the Vienna meetings and in Chairman Khrushchev's address of June 15, 1961. For the same reasons, the United States Government does not admit that its rights and obligations toward Germany as a whole can be affected by unilateral negotiations of peace settlements with a part of Germany.

The obligation to maintain the unity of Germany was affirmed by the victorious Powers from the beginning. It was acknowledged by the Soviet Union in 1955, at a Conference attended by Chairman Khrushchev, in the Geneva directive of the Four Heads of Government, which says:

"The Heads of Government [of France, the United Kingdom, the Soviet Union, and the United States], recognizing their common responsibility for the settlement of the German question and the re-unification of Germany, have agreed that the settlement of the German question and the re-unification of Germany by means of free elections shall be carried out in conformity with the national interests of the German people. ..."

What the Soviet Union proposes, unless the Three Powers formally abandon their efforts to reunify Germany, is to determine by itself the fate of Germany through an agreement with the authorities of the so-called "German Democratic Republic," which is not freely chosen, but has been created by the Soviet Union as an instrument of Soviet foreign policy.

By its signature of the United Nations Charter and in numerous statements, the Soviet Government is committed to respect for the principle of self-determination. But, in contradiction of this, by denying freedom of choice to seventeen million East Germans it has not permitted freedom of choice to the German people as a whole. And it is now proposing to perpetuate that denial by concluding a final settlement with a regime which is not representative of these people, does not enjoy their confidence, and is, in fact, no more than its own creation and an extension of its own authority. Under these circumstances, the part of Germany subject to that regime cannot be regarded as an independent sovereign state, and a "peace treaty" with the part of Germany's territory termed "German Democratic Republic" by the Soviet Government could have no validity in international law, nor could it affect in any way whatsoever the rights of the Western Powers.

According to the thesis repeatedly expounded by the Soviets, the "separate peace treaty" would, upon its conclusion, terminate the rights of the West in, and with regard to, Berlin. These assertions are untenable and fallacious from a legal point of view, both because such a separate treaty would be legally ineffective, and because neither the Soviet Union nor East Germany can, for the reasons stated above, unilaterally deprive the three Western Powers of their original rights in, and regarding, Berlin. Rights of access to Berlin are inherent in the rights of the Western Powers to be in Berlin. The procedures for the exercise of these rights have been defined in numerous agreements between the Four Governments and were confirmed by the Soviet Government in the Paris Agreement of June 20, 1949 on the termination of the Berlin blockade, and in practice over many years. They cannot be unilaterally abrogated by any act of the Soviet Government. If any one of the Four withdraws from these arrangements, then it is clearly the responsibility of the other Three to make such dispositions with respect to the exercise of their access rights as they deem appropriate.

The Soviet Union further asserts that a "peace treaty," whether signed by all the interested parties or not, would bring about the establishment of West Berlin as a "demilitarized Free City." As proposed, this would bring with it the cessation of the rights of the Western Allies in Berlin, including the right of access.

The United States considers entirely unfounded the Soviet claims that this unilateral act could deprive the other three participants in the joint occupation of Berlin of their basic rights in the City—rights derived from the Nazi surrender, as indicated, and expressed in binding and valid agreements, to which the Soviet Union is a party. The agreements of September 12, 1944 and May 1, 1945 establishing the occupation arrangements for the City were joint undertakings by the occupying powers, all of whom derived rights and obligations from them. The obligation of the Soviet Union to assure the normal functioning of transport and communication between Berlin and the western zones of Germany was reaffirmed in the Four Power Agreement of June 20, 1949. This legal situation was thus jointly created by the Four Powers and cannot be altered except by the common consent of all of them.

The United States wishes particularly to reiterate, in discussing the legal aspects of Berlin's status, that Soviet references to Berlin as being situated on the territory of the so-called "German Democratic Republic" are entirely without foundation. This can be readily and clearly established by reference to the attached copy of the Protocol of September 12, 1944. The Protocol makes clear that Berlin was not a part of, or located on, the territory to be occupied as a zone by any one of the powers under the Agreement. With respect specifically to the area now constituting the so-called "German Democratic Republic" the Protocol clearly stated that a specified area, described by metes and bounds, "will be occupied by armed forces of the U.S.S.R., with the exception of the Berlin area, for which a special system a occupation is provided below." The Protocol subsequently clearly specified that "The Berlin area ... will be jointly occupied by armed forces of the U.S., U.K., and U.S.S.R., assigned by the respective Commanders-in-Chief." The Soviet Government approved the Protocol on February 6, 1945, and since that time there have been no legal alterations in the special status of Berlin.

The Soviet Union claims that the "free city" of West Berlin would be able to maintain freely its communications with the outside world and determine its domestic order by the free expression of the will of its people. Since, however, the "free city" would in fact be isolated within the so-called "German Democratic Republic," which according to the Soviet proposal would control all access to and from the city, it is of significance to examine the stated intentions of the leaders of that regime with respect to West Berlin.

The United States notes in particular the statements made by Mr. Ulbricht on June 15 in which he made clear his regime would seek to close Tempelhof Airport, West Berlin's principal airport and a vital part of its communications with the outside world. In addition, Mr. Ulbricht announced he "considered it a matter of course" that the refugee centers in West Berlin would be closed. These camps are maintained by West Berlin for the constant stream of refugees fleeing from East Germany, and Ulbricht's statement makes clear the degree to which his regime intends to interfere in West Berlin where it suits his purpose. In view of such statements, it is not surprising if neither the West Berliners nor the Western Powers are reassured by professions of peaceful intent. In this connection, it is relevant to ask why the Soviet Union has chosen to raise the question at all if it has not had in mind a fundamental change in West Berlin.

It is evident that the present status of the City, which the Soviet Union chooses to characterize as an "occupation regime" which "has already outlived itself," is actually an arrangement that—under the existing abnormal division of Germany—does not constitute any threat to peace. Attempts by the Soviet Union to destroy that arrangement, in pursuit of its political goals, are certain to jeopardize gravely the very peace in the name of which the Soviet action is taken. With respect to the nature of these goals in Berlin itself, it is significant that the Soviet Union, having previously occupied East Berlin and violated its Four Power status by establishing there an alleged "G.D.R." government, now proposes that its troops will be among those stationed in a "free city" of West Berlin. The Soviet Government would thus seek to extend its postwar empire by the absorption of the Flastern sector of Berlin and to shift the Four Power principle from all of Berlin to the Western part of the city alone.

The immediate cause of this threat to peace arises from the announced intention of the Soviet Government to present the three Western Powers with a *de facto* situation based on the false assertion that they would no longer be entitled to remain in Berlin, or to have free access thereto. Such a move could lead to highly dangerous developments, and would be totally devoid of legal effect. The United States considers the exercise of its rights together with its British and French Allies, in order to maintain the freedom of over two million people in West Berlin, a fundamental political and moral obligation.

The international dispute arising out of Soviet claims would have the gravest effects upon international peace and security and endanger the lives and well-being of millions of people. It would be irresponsible on the part of the nations directly concerned not to use available means to settle such a dispute in a peaceful manner.

As in the past, the United States Government is always prepared to consider in agreement with its Allies a freely negotiated settlement of the unresolved problems of Ger many. Such a settlement must be in conformity with the principle of self-determination and with the interests of all concerned. The United States Government for its part has never contemplated confronting the Soviet Union with a *fait accompli.* It hopes that for its part the Soviet Government will renounce any idea of taking such action, which, as noted, would have unforeseeable consequences. It thinks it necessary to warn the Soviet Government in all seriousness of the grave dangers of such a course, and to express the hope that the Soviet Government will rather aim, as does the United States Government, at the creation of conditions in which a genuine and peaceful settlement of outstanding problems can be pursued.

Peace and freedom are not merely words nor can they be achieved by words or promises alone. They are representative of a state of affairs.

A city does not become free merely by calling it free. For a city or a people to be free requires that they be given the opportunity without economic, political or police pressure to make their own choice and to live their own lives. The people of West Berlin today have that freedom. It is the objective of our policy for them to continue to have it.

Peace does not come automatically from a "peace treaty." There is peace in Germany today even though the situation is "abnormal." A "peace treaty" that adversely affects the lives and rights of millions will not bring peace with it. A "peace treaty" that attempts to affect adversely the solemn commitments of three great powers does not bring peace with it.

There is no reason for a crisis over Berlin. If one develops it is because the Soviet Union is attempting to invade the basic rights of others. All the world will plainly see that the misuse of such words as "peace" and "freedom" cannot conceal a threat to raise tension to the point of danger and suppress the freedom of those who now enjoy it.

Annex III

Three Power Agreement of 1944

Protocol

between the Governments of the United States of America, the United Kingdom, and the Union of Soviet Socialist Republics, on the zones of occupation in Germany and the administration of "Greater Berlin."

The Governments of the United States of America, the United Kingdom of Great Britain and Northern Ireland, and the Union of Soviet Socialist Republics have reached the following agreement with regard to the execution of Article u. of the Instrument of Unconditional Surrender of Germany:

1. Germany, within her frontiers as they were on the 31st December, 1937, will, for the purposes of occupation, be divided into three zones, one of which will be allotted to each of the three Powers, and a special Berlin area, which will be under joint occupation by the three Powers.

2. The boundaries of the three zones and of the Berlin area, and the allocation of the three zones as between the U.S.A., the U.K. and the U.S.S.R. will be *as* follows:

Eastern Zone

The territory of Germany (including the province of East Prussia) situated to the East of a line drawn from the point on Lübeck Bay where the frontiers of Schleswig-Holstein and Mecklenburg meet, along the western frontier of Mecklenburg to the frontier of the province of Hanover, thence, along the eastern frontier of Hanover, to the frontier of Brunswick; thence along the western frontier of the Prussian province of Saxony to the western frontier of Anhalt; thence along the western frontier of Anhalt; thence along the western frontier of the Prussian province of Saxony and the western frontier of Thuringia to where the latter meets the Bavarian frontier; thence eastwards along the northern frontier of Bavaria to the 1937 Czechoslovakian frontier, will be occupied by armed forces of the U.S.S.R., with the exception of the Berlin area, for which a special system of occupation is provided below.

North-Western Zone

The territory of Germany situated to the west of the line defined above, and bounded on the south by a line drawn from the point where the western frontier of Thuringia meets the frontier of Bavaria; thence westwards along the southern frontiers of the Prussian provinces of Hessen-Nassau and Rheinprovinz to where the latter meets the frontier of France will be occupied by armed forces of _____.

South-Western Zone

All the remaining territory of Western Germany situated to the south of the line defined in the description of the North-Western Zone will be occupied by armed forces of _____.

The frontiers of States (Länder) and Provinces within Germany, referred to in the foregoing descriptions of the zones, are those which existed after the coming into effect of the decree of 25th June, 1941 (published in the Reichsgesetzblatt, Part I, No. 72, 3rd July, 1941).

Berlin Area

The Berlin *area* (by which expression *is* understood the territory of "Greater Berlin" as defined by the Law of the 27th April, 1920) will be jointly occupied by armed forces of the U.S.A., U.K., and U.S.S.R., assigned by the respective Commanders-in-Chief. For this purpose the territory of "Greater Berlin" will be divided into the following three parts:

North-Eastern *part of "Greater Berlin"* (districts of Pankow, Prenzlauerberg, Mitte, Weissensee, Friedrichshain, Lichtenberg, Treptow, Köpenick) will be occupied by the forces of the U.S.S.R.

North-Western part *of "Greater Berlin"* (districts of Reinickendorf, Wedding, Tiergarten, Charlottenburg, Spandau, Wilmersdorf) will be occupied by the forces of _____.

Southern part of "Greater Berlin" (districts of Zehlendorf, Steglitz, Schöneberg, Kreuzberg, Tempelhof, Neukölln) will be occupied by the forces of _____.

The boundaries of districts within "Greater Berlin", referred to in the foregoing descriptions, are those which existed after the coming into effect of the decree published on 27th March, 1938 (Amtsblatt der Reichshauptstadt; Berlin No. 13 of 27th March, 1938, page 215).

3. The occupying forces in each of the three zones into which Germany is divided will be under a Commander-in-Chief designated by the Government of the country whose forces occupy that zone.

4. Mach of the three Powers may, at its discretion, include among the forces assigned to occupation duties under the command of its Commander-in-

Chief, auxiliary contingents from the forces of any other Allied Power which has participated in military operations against Germany.

5. An Inter-Allied Governing Authority (*Kommandatura*) consisting of three Commandants, appointed by their respective Commanders-in-Chief, will be established to direct jointly the administration of the "Greater Berlin" Area.

6. This Protocol has been drawn up in triplicate in the English and Russian languages. Both texts are authentic. The Protocol will come into force on the signature by Germany of the Instrument of Unconditional Surrender.

The above text of the Protocol between the Governments of the United States of America, the United Kingdom and the Union of Soviet Socialist Republics, on the zones of occupation in Germany and the administration of "Greater Berlin" has been prepared and unanimously adopted by the European Advisory Commission at a meeting held on 12th September, 1944, with the exception of the allocation of the North-Western and South-Western zones of occupation in Germany and the North-Western and Southern parts of "Greater Berlin", which requires further consideration and joint agreement by the Governments of the U.S.A., U.K. and U.S.S.R.

LANCASTER HOUSE,
London, S.W. 1.
12th September, 1944.

Representative of the Government of the U.S.A.
on the European Advisory Commission:
JOHN G. WINANT

Representative of the Government of the U.K.
on the European Advisory Commission:
WILLIAM STRANG

Representative of the Government of the U.S.S.R.
on the European Advisory Commission:
F. T. GOUSEV

Annex IV

Statement by President Kennedy, July 19, 1961

In consultation and full agreement with its British and French allies, and with the benefit of the views of the Federal Republic of Germany, and after consultation with the other member governments of the North Atlantic Treaty Organization, the United States on Monday delivered through *its* Embassy in Moscow its reply to the *aide memoire* on Germany and Berlin received from the Soviet Government on June 4. Our reply speaks for itself and advances what I believe to be an irrefutable legal, moral, and political position. In this statement I should like to convey to the American people and the people of the world the basic issues which underlie the somewhat more formal language of diplomacy.

The Soviet *aide memoire* is a document which speaks of peace but threatens to disturb it. It speaks of ending the abnormal situation in Germany but insists on making permanent its abnormal division. It refers to the Four Power alliance of World War II but seeks the unilateral abrogation of the rights of the other three powers. It calls for new international agreements while preparing to violate existing ones. It offers certain assurances while making it plain that its previous assurances are not to be relied upon. It professes concern for the rights of the citizens of West Berlin while seeking to expose them to the immediate or eventual domination of a regime which permits no self-determination. Three simple facts are clear:

1. Today there is peace in Berlin, in Germany, and in Europe. If that peace is destroyed by the unilateral actions of the Soviet Union, its leaders will bear a heavy responsibility before world opinion and history.

2. Today the people of West Berlin are free. In that sense it is already a "free city"—free to determine its own leaders and free to enjoy the fundamental human rights reaffirmed in the United Nations Charter.

3. Today the continued presence in West Berlin of the United States, the United Kingdom, and France is by clear legal right, arising from war, acknowledged in many agreements signed by the Soviet Union, and strongly supported by the overwhelming majority of the people of that city. Their freedom is dependent upon our exercise of these rights—an exercise which is thus a political and moral obligation as well as a legal right. Inasmuch as these rights, including the right of access to Berlin, are not held from the Soviet Government, they cannot be ended by any unilateral action of the Soviet Union. They cannot be affected by a so-called "peace treaty," covering only a part of Germany, with a regime of the Soviet Union's own creation—a regime which is not freely representative of all or any part of

Germany and does not enjoy the confidence of the 17 million East Germans. The steady stream of German refugees from East to West is eloquent testimony to that fact.

The United States has been prepared since the close of the war, and is prepared today, to achieve, in agreement with its World War II allies, a freely negotiated peace treaty covering all of Germany and based on the freely expressed will of all of the German people. We have never suggested that, in violation of international law and earlier Four Power agreements, we might legally negotiate a settlement with only a part of Germany, or without the participation of the other principal World War II allies. We know of no sound reason why the Soviet Government should now believe that the rights of the Western Powers, derived from Nazi Germany's surrender, could be invalidated by such an action on the part of the Soviet Union.

The United States has consistently sought the goal of a just and comprehensive peace treaty for all of Germany since first suggesting in 1946 that a special commission be appointed for this purpose. We still recognize the desirability of change—but it should be a change in the direction of greater, not less, freedom of choice for the people of Germany and Berlin. The Western peace plan and the all-Berlin solution proposed by the Western allies at Geneva in 1959[13] a were constructive, practical offers to obtain this kind of fair settlement in central Europe. Our objective is not to perpetuate our presence in either Germany or Berlin—our objective is the perpetuation of the peace and freedom of their citizens.

But the Soviet Union has blocked all progress toward the conclusion of a just treaty based on the self-determination of the German people and has instead repeatedly heightened world tensions over this issue. The Soviet blockade of Berlin in 1948, the Soviet note of November 27th, 1958,[14] and this most recent Soviet *aide memoire* of June 4, 1961, have greatly disturbed the tranquility of this area.

The real intent of the June 4 *aide memoire* is that East Berlin, a part of a city under Four Power status, would be formally absorbed into the so-called "German Democratic Republic" while West Berlin, even though called a "free city," would lose the protection presently provided by the Western

---

[13] For texts of Western proposals at the Conference of Foreign Ministers at Geneva in 1959, see *Department of State Bulletin* of June 1, 1959, p. 775; June 8, 1959, p. 819; June 15, 1959, p. 859; June 29, 1959, p. 943; Aug. 3, 1959, p. 147; *Aug.* 10, 1959, p.191; and Aug_ 24, 1959, p. 265.

[14] For text of Soviet note of Nov. 27, 1958, and U.S. reply of Dec. 31, 1958, see ibid. Jan. 19, 1959, P. 79.

Powers and become subject to the will of a totalitarian regime. Its leader, Herr Ulbricht, has made clear his intention, once this so-called "peace treaty" is signed, to curb West Berlin's communications with the free world and to suffocate the freedom it now enjoys.

The area thus newly subjected to Soviet threats of heightened tension poses no danger whatsoever to the peace of the world or to the security of any nation. The world knows that there is no reason for a crisis over Berlin today and that, if one develops, it will be caused by the Soviet Government's attempt to invade the rights of others and manufacture tensions. It is, moreover, misusing the words "freedom" and "peace." For, as our reply states, "freedom" and "peace" are not merely words—nor can they be achieved by words or promises alone. They are representative of a state of affairs.

A city does not become free merely by calling it a "free city." For a city or a people to be free requires that they be given the opportunity, without economic, political, or police pressure, to make their own choice and to live their own lives. The people of West Berlin today have that freedom. It is the objective of our policy that they shall continue to have it.

Peace does not come automatically from a "peace treaty." There is peace in Germany today even though the situation is "abnormal." A "peace treaty" that adversely affects the lives and rights of millions will not bring peace with it. A "peace treaty" that attempts to affect adversely the solemn commitments of three great powers will not bring peace with it. We again urge the Soviet Government to reconsider its course, to return to the path of constructive cooperation it so frequently states it desires, and to work with its World War II allies in concluding a just and enduring settlement of issues remaining from that conflict.

Annex V

The Berlin Crisis—Report to the Nation by President Kennedy, July 25, 1961[15]

Seven weeks ago tonight I returned from Europe to report on my meeting with Premier Khrushchev and the others. His grim warnings about the future of the world, his *aide memoire* on Berlin, his subsequent speeches and threats which he and his agents have launched, and the increase in the Soviet military budget that he has announced have all prompted a series of decisions by the administration and a series of consultations with the members of the NATO organization. In Berlin, as you recall, he intends to bring to an end, through a stroke of the pen, first, our legal rights to be in West Berlin and, secondly, our ability to make good on our commitment to the 2 million free people of that city. That we cannot permit.

We are clear about what must be done—and *we* intend to do it. I want to talk frankly with you tonight about the first steps that we shall take. These actions will require sacrifice on the part of many of our citizens. More will be required in the future. They will require, from all of us, courage and perseverance in the years to come. But if we and our allies act out of strength and unity of purpose—with calm determination and steady nerves, using restraint in our words as well as our weapons—I am hopeful that both peace and freedom will be sustained.

The immediate threat to free men is in West Berlin. But that isolated outpost is not an isolated problem. The threat is worldwide. Our effort must be equally wide and strong and not be obsessed by any single manufactured crisis. We face a challenge in Berlin, but there is also a challenge in southeast Asia, where the borders are less guarded, the enemy harder to find, and the danger of communism less apparent to those who have so little. We face a challenge in our own hemisphere and indeed wherever else the freedom of human beings is at stake.

Let me remind you that the fortunes of war and diplomacy left the free people of West Berlin in 1445 110 miles behind the Iron Curtain. This map makes very clear the problem that we face. The white is West Germany, the East is the area controlled by the Soviet Union; and as you can see from the chart, West Berlin is 110 miles within the area which the Soviets now dominate—which is immediately controlled by the so-called East German regime. We are there as a result of our victory over Nazi Germany, and our

---

[15] Delivered from the White Rouse by television and radio.

basic rights to be there deriving from that victory include both our presence in West Berlin and the enjoyment of access across East Germany.

These rights have been repeatedly confirmed and recognized in special agreements with the Soviet Union. Berlin is not a part of East Germany, but a separate territory under the control of the allied powers. Thus our rights there are clear and deep-rooted. But in addition to those rights is our commitment to sustain—and defend, if need be—the opportunity for more than 2 million people to determine their own future and choose their own way of life.

Determination to Maintain Rights in Berlin

Thus our presence in West Berlin, and our access thereto, cannot be ended by any act of the Soviet Government. The NATO shield was long ago extended to cover West Berlin, and we have given our word that an attack in that city will be regarded as an attack upon us all. For West Berlin, lying exposed 110 miles inside East Germany, surrounded by Soviet troops and close to Soviet supply lines, has many roles. It is more than a showcase of liberty, a symbol, an island of freedom in a Communist sea. It is even more than a link with the free world, a beacon of hope behind the Iron Curtain, an escape hatch for refugees.

West Berlin is all of that. But above all it has now become, as never before, the great testing place of Western courage and will, a focal point where our solemn commitments, stretching back over the years since 1945, and Soviet ambitions now meet in basic confrontation. It would be a mistake for others to look upon Berlin, because of its location, as a tempting target. The United States is there, the United Kingdom and France are there, the pledge of NATO is there, and the people of Berlin are there. It is as secure, in that sense, as the rest of us, for we cannot separate its safety from our own. I hear it said that West Berlin is militarily untenable. And so was Bastogne. And so, in fact, was Stalingrad. Any dangerous spot is tenable if men—brave men—will make it so.

We do not want to fight, but we have fought before. And others in earlier times have made the same dangerous mistake of assuming that the West was too selfish and too soft and too divided to resist invasions of freedom in other lands. Those who threaten to unleash the forces of war on a dispute over West Berlin should recall the words of the ancient philosopher: "A man who causes fear cannot be free from fear."

We cannot and will not permit the Communists to drive us out of Berlin, either gradually or by force. For the fulfillment of our pledge to that city is essential to the morale and security of Western Germany, to the unity of Western Europe, and to the faith of the entire free world. Soviet strategy has long been aimed not merely at Berlin but at dividing and neutralizing all of Europe, forcing us back to our own shores. We must meet our oft-stated pledge to the free peoples of West Berlin—and maintain our rights and their safety, even in the face of force—in order to maintain the confidence of other free peoples in our word and our resolve. The strength of the alliance on which our security depends is dependent in turn on our willingness to meet our commitments to them.

Preparations to Defend the Peace

So long as the Communists insist that they are preparing to end by themselves unilaterally our rights in West Berlin and our commitments to its people, we must be prepared to defend those rights and those commitments. We will at all times be ready to talk, if talk will help. But we must also be ready to resist with force, if force Is used upon us. Either alone would fail. Together, they can serve the cause of freedom and peace. The new preparations that we shall make to defend the peace are part of the long-term buildup in our strength which has been under way since January. They are based on our needs to meet a worldwide threat, on a basis which stretches far beyond the present Berlin crisis. Our primary purpose is neither propaganda nor provocation—but preparation.

A first need is to hasten progress toward the military goals which the North Atlantic allies have set for themselves. In Europe today nothing less will suffice. We will put even greater resources into fulfilling those goals, and we look to our allies to do the same. The supplementary defense buildups that I asked from the Congress in March and May have already started moving us toward these and our other defense goals. They included an increase In the size of the Marine Corps, improved readiness of our reserves, expansion of our air- and sealift, and stepped-up procurement of needed weapons, ammunition, and other items. To insure a continuing invulnerable capacity to deter or destroy any aggressor, they provided for the strengthening of our missile power and for putting 50 percent of our B-52 and B-47 bombers on a ground alert which would send them on their way with 15 minutes' warning.

These measures must be speeded up, and still others must now be taken. We must have sea- and airlift capable of moving our forces quickly and in large numbers to any part of the world.

But even more importantly, we need the capability of placing in any critical area at the appropriate time a force which, combined with those of our allies, is large enough to make clear our determination and our ability to defend our rights at all costs and to meet all levels of aggressor pressure with whatever levels of force are required. We intend to have a wider choice than humiliation or all-out nuclear action.

While it is unwise at this time either to call up or send abroad excessive numbers of these troops before they are needed, let me make it clear that I intend to take, as time goes on, whatever steps are necessary to make certain that such forces can be deployed at the appropriate time without lessening our ability to meet our commitments elsewhere.

Thus, in the days and months ahead, I shall not hesitate to ask the Congress for additional measures or exercise any of the Executive powers that I possess to meet this threat to peace. Everything essential to the security of freedom must be done; and if that should require more men, or more taxes, or more controls, or other new powers, I shall not hesitate to ask them. The measures proposed today will be constantly studied, and altered as necessary. But while we will not let panic shape our policy, neither will we permit timidity to direct our program.

Accordingly I am now taking the following steps:

(1) I am tomorrow requesting of the Congress for the current fiscal year an additional $3,247,000,000 of appropriations for the Armed Forces.

(2) To fill out our present Army divisions and to make more men available for prompt deployment, I am requesting an increase in the Army's total authorized strength from 875,000 to approximately 1 million men.

(3) I am requesting an increase of 29,000 and 63,000 men, respectively, in the active-duty strength of the Navy and the Air Force.

(4) To fulfill these manpower needs, I am ordering that our draft calls be doubled and tripled in the coming months; I am asking the Congress for authority to order to active duty certain ready reserve units and individual reservists and to extend tours of duty; and, under that authority, I am planning to order to active duty a number of air transport squadrons and Air National Guard tactical air squadrons to give us the airlift capacity and protection that we need. Other reserve forces will be called up when needed.

(5) Many ships and planes once headed for retirement are to be retained or reactivated, increasing our airpower tactically and our sealift, airlift, and antisubmarine warfare capability. In addition, our strategic airpower will be increased by delaying the deactivation of B-47 bombers.

(6) Finally, some $1.8 billion—about half of the total sum—is needed for the procurement of non-nuclear weapons, ammunition, and equipment.

The details on all these requests will be presented to the Congress tomorrow. Subsequent steps will be taken to suit subsequent needs.

Comparable efforts for the common defense are being discussed with our NATO allies. For their commitment and interest are as precise as our own.

And let me add that I am well aware of the fact that many American families will bear the burden of these requests. Studies or careers will be interrupted; husbands and sons will be called away; incomes in some cases will be reduced. But these are burdens which must be borne if freedom is to be defended. Americans have willingly borne them before, and they will not flinch from the task now.

A New Start on Civil Defense

We have another sober responsibility. To recognize the possibilities of nuclear war in the missile *age* without our citizens' knowing what they should do and where they should go if bombs begin to fall would be a failure of responsibility. In May *I* pledged a new start on civil defense. Last week I assigned, on the recommendation of the Civil Defense Director, basic responsibility for this program to the Secretary of Defense, to make certain It is administered and coordinated with our continental defense efforts at the highest civilian level. Tomorrow I am requesting of the Congress new funds for the following immediate objectives: to identify and mark space in existing structures—public and private—that could be used for fallout shelters in ease of attack; to stock those shelters with food, water, first-aid kits, and other minimum essentials for survival; to increase their capacityto improve our air-raid warning and fallout detection systems, including a new household warning system which is now under development; and to take other measures that will be effective at an early date to save millions of lives if needed.

In the event of an attack, the lives of those families which are not hit in a nuclear blast and fire can still be saved—if they can be warned to take shelter and *if* that shelter is available. We owe that kind of insurance to our families—and to our country. In contrast to our friends in Europe, the need for this kind of protection is new to our shores. But the time to start is now. In the coming months I hope to let every citizen know what steps he can take without delay to protect his family in case of attack. I know that you will want to do no less.

Meeting the Costs

The addition of $207 million in civil defense appropriations brings our total new defense budget requests to $3.454 billion and a total of $47.5 billion for the year. This is an increase in the defense budget of $6 billion since January and has resulted in official estimates of a budget deficit of over

$5 billion. The Secretary of the Treasury and other economic advisers assure me, however, that our economy has the capacity to bear this new request.

We are recovering strongly from this year's recession. The increase in this last quarter of our year of our total national output was greater than that for any postwar period of initial recovery. And yet wholesale prices are actually lower than they were during the recession, and consumer prices are only one-fourth of 1 percent higher than they were last October. In fact this last quarter was the first in 8 years in which our production has increased without an increase in the overall-price index. And for the first time since the fall of 1959 our gold position has improved and the dollar is more respected abroad. These gains, it should be stressed, are being accomplished with budget deficits far smaller than those of the 1958 recession.

This improved business outlook means improved revenues; and *I* intend to submit to the Congress in January a budget for the next fiscal year which will be strictly in balance. Nevertheless, should an increase in taxes be needed—because of events in the next few months—to achieve that balance, or because of subsequent defense rises, those increased taxes will be requested in January.

Meanwhile to help make certain that the current deficit is held to a safe level, we must keep down all expenditures not thoroughly justified in budget requests. The luxury of our current post-office deficit must be ended. Costs in military procurement will be closely scrutinized—and in this effort I welcome the cooperation of the Congress. The tax loopholes I have specified—on expense accounts, overseas income, dividends, interest, cooperatives, and others—must be closed.

I realize that no public revenue measure is welcomed by everyone. But I am certain that every American wants to pay his fair share and not leave the burden of defending freedom entirely to those who bear arms. For we have mortgaged our very future on this defense, and we cannot fail to meet our responsibility.

Source of Tension Is Moscow, Not Berlin

But I must emphasize again that the choice is not merely between resistance and retreat, between atomic holocaust and surrender. Our peacetime military posture is traditionally defensive; but our diplomatic posture need not be. Our response to the Berlin crisis will not be merely military or negative. It will be more than merely standing firm. For we do not intend to leave it to others to choose and monopolize the forum and the framework of discussion. We do not intend to abandon our duty to mankind to seek a peaceful solution.

As signers of the U.N. Charter we shall always be prepared to discuss international problems with any and all nations that are willing to talk—and listen—with reason. If they have proposals, not demands, we shall hear them. If they seek genuine understanding, not concessions of our rights, we shall meet with them. We have previously indicated our readiness to remove any actual irritants in West Berlin, but the freedom of that city is not negotiable. We cannot negotiate with those who say, "What's mine is mine and what's yours is negotiable." But we are willing to consider any arrangement or treaty in Germany consistent with the maintenance of peace and freedom and with the legitimate security interests of all nations.

We recognize the Soviet Union's historical concerns about their security in central and eastern Europe after a series of ravaging invasions, and we believe arrangements can be worked out which will help to meet those concerns and make it possible for both security and freedom to exist in this troubled area.

For it is not the freedom of West Berlin which is "abnormal" in Germany today but the situation in that entire divided country. If anyone doubts the legality of our rights in Berlin, we are ready to have it submitted to international adjudication. If anyone doubts the extent to which our presence is desired by the people of West Berlin, compared to East German feelings about their regime, we are ready to have that question submitted to a free vote in Berlin and, if possible, among all the German people. And let us hear at that time from the 2½ million refugees who have fled the Communist regime in East Germany—voting for Western-type freedom with their feet.

The world is not deceived by the Communist attempt to label Berlin as a hotbed of war. There is peace in Berlin today. The source of world trouble and tension is Moscow, not Berlin. And if war begins, it will have begun in Moscow and not Berlin.

For the choice of peace or war is largely theirs, not ours. It is the Soviets who have stirred up this crisis. It is they who are trying to force a change. It is they who have opposed free elections. It is they who have rejected an all-German peace treaty and the rulings of international law. And as Americans know from our history on our own old frontier, gun battles are caused by outlaws and not by officers of the peace.

In short, while we are ready to defend our interests, we shall also be ready to search for peace—in quiet exploratory talks, in formal or informal meetings. We do not want military considerations to dominate the thinking of either East or West. And Mr. Khrushchev may find that his invitation to other nations to join in a meaningless treaty may lead to *their* inviting *him to* join in the community of peaceful men, in abandoning the use of force, and in respecting the sanctity of agreements.

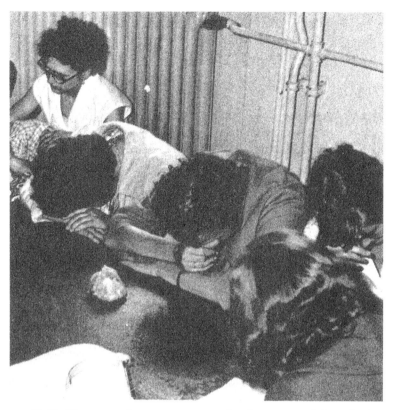

August 1961, Women refugees, overcome by the strain of their flight from East Germany, after having arrived safely with their children at a refugee camp in West Berlin

A Challenge to All Free Nations

While all of these efforts go on, we must not be diverted from our total responsibilities, from other dangers, from other tasks. If new threats in Berlin or elsewhere should cause us to weaken our program of assistance to the developing nations who are also under heavy pressure from the same source, or to halt our efforts for realistic disarmament, or to disrupt or slow down our economy, or to neglect the education of our children, then those threats will surely be the most successful and least costly maneuver in Communist history. For we can afford all these efforts, and more—but we cannot afford *not* to meet this challenge.

177

And the challenge is not to us alone. It *is* a challenge to every nation which asserts its sovereignty under a system of liberty. It is a challenge to all who want a world of free choice. It is a special challenge to the Atlantic Community, the heartland of human freedom. We in the West must move together in building military strength. We must consult one another more closely than ever before. We must together design our proposals for peace and labor together as they are pressed at the conference table. And together we must share the burdens and the risks of this effort.

The Atlantic Community, as we know it, has been built In response to challenge: the challenge of European chaos in 1947, of the Berlin blockade in 1948, the challenge of Communist aggression in Korea in 1950. Now, standing strong and prosperous after an unprecedented decade of progress, the Atlantic Community will not forget either its history or the principles which gave it meaning. The solemn vow each of us gave to West Berlin in time of peace will not be broken in time of danger. If we do not meet our commitments to Berlin, where will we later stand? If we are not true to our word there, all that we have achieved in collective security, which relies on these words, will mean nothing. And if there is one path above all others to war, it is the path of weakness and disunity. Today the endangered frontier of freedom runs through divided Berlin. We want it to remain a frontier of peace. This is the hope of every citizen of the Atlantic Community, every citizen of Eastern Europe, and, I am confident, every citizen of the Soviet Union. For I cannot believe that the Russian people, who bravely suffered enormous losses in the Second World War, would now wish to see the peace upset once more in Germany. The Soviet Government alone can convert Berlin's frontier of peace into a pretext for war.

The steps I have indicated tonight are aimed at avoiding that war. To sum it all up: We seek peace, but we shall not surrender. That is the central meaning of this crisis—and the meaning of your Government's policy. With your help, and the help of other free men, this crisis can be surmounted. Freedom can prevail, and peace can endure.

The Need for Courage and Perseverance

I would like to close with a personal word. When I ran for the Presidency of the United States, I knew that this country faced serious challenges, but I could not realize—nor could any man realize who does not bear the burdens of this office—how heavy and constant would be those burdens.

Three times in my lifetime our country and Europe have been involved in major wars. In each case serious misjudgments were made on both sides of the intentions of others, which brought about great devastation. Now, in the thermonuclear age, any misjudgment on either side about the intentions of the other could rain more devastation in several hours than has been wrought in all the wars of human history.

Therefore I, as President and Commander in Chief, and all of us as Americans are moving through serious days. I shall bear this responsibility under our Constitution for the next 31/) years, but I am sure that we all, regardless of our occupations, will do our very best for our country and for our cause. For all of us want to **see** our children grow up in *a* country at peace and in a world where freedom endures.

I know that sometimes we get impatient; we wish for some immediate action that would end our perils. But I must tell you that there is no quick and easy solution. The Communists control over a billion people, and they recognize that if we should falter their success would be imminent.

We must look to long days ahead which, if we are courageous and persevering, can bring us what we all desire. In these days and weeks I ask for your help and your advice. I ask for your suggestions, when you think we could do better.

All of us, I know, love our country, and we shall all do our best to serve it.

In meeting my responsibilities in these coming months as President, I need your good will and your support— and above all, your prayers.

Annex VI

Excerpts From Statements by Walter Ulbricht[16]

"We consider it a matter of course that the so-called refugee camps in West Berlin must be closed down. ..."

"... those who obtain permission from the GDR (German Democratic Republic) authorities, i.e., from the Ministry of the Interior, may leave the GDR, and those who fail to obtain this permission must not leave. ..."

"A further point is that West Berlin today is situated on GDR territory, that under constitutional law it forms part of GDR territory. ..."

"As regards the state frontier—our frontier runs along the Elbe and so on, and the territory of West Berlin forms part of the territory of the GDR. ..."

In answer to questions about control of air traffic to and from West Berlin:

"Think of the West Berliners. ... Today they are constantly disturbed by the noise of aircraft and they are exposed to the danger—as happened in Munich—of the aircraft crashing into buildings."

(Question: "Am I right in inferring from your words that in the event of such an agreement Tempelhof Airport would be closed down?")

"... Perhaps the airport will close itself down. ..."

"... I should like to tell the questioner that I am sure he is familiar with the international regulations regarding travel, which respect the sovereignty of the individual states. The same arrangements applying to other states must also apply to the GDR. Whether it be by water, land, or in the air, they will be entering the GDR, they will be subject to our control, for these are our communications. We have said so a hundred times. There is no doubt at all. ..."

---

[16] Mr. Ulbricht, No. 1 East German Communist, made these statements in answer to questions at a press conference on June 25, 1961.

Annex VII

Statement by Secretary of State Dean Rusk, August 13, 1961

The authorities in East Berlin and East Germany have taken severe measures to deny to their own people access to West Berlin. These measures have doubtless been prompted by the increased flow of refugees in recent weeks. The refugees are not responding to persuasion or propaganda from the West but to the failures of communism in East Germany. These failures have created great pressures upon communist leaders who, in turn, are trying to solve their own problems by the dangerous course of threats against the freedom and safety of West Berlin.

The resulting tension has itself stimulated flights from the East.

Having denied the collective right of self-determination to the peoples of East Germany, communist authorities are now denying the right of individuals to elect a world of free choice rather than a world of coercion. The pretense that communism desires only peaceful competition is exposed; the refugees, more than half of whom are less than 25 years of age, have "voted with their feet" on whether communism is the wave of the future.

Available information indicates that measures taken thus far are aimed at residents of East Berlin and East Germany and not at the allied position in West Berlin or access thereto. However, limitation on travel within Berlin is a violation of the four-power status of Berlin and a flagrant violation of the right of free circulation throughout the city. Restrictions on travel between East Germany and Berlin are in direct contravention of the Four Power agreement reached at Paris on June 20, 1949. These violations of existing agreements will be the subject of vigorous protest through appropriate channels.

Annex VIII

Text of Protest Letter From the Three Western Commandants to the Soviet Commandant, August 15, 1961

During the night of August 12-13 the East German authorities put into effect illegal measures designed to turn the boundaries between the West sectors of Berlin and the Soviet sector into an arbitrary barrier to movement of German citizens resident in East Berlin and East Germany.

Not since the imposition of the Berlin blockade has there been such a flagrant violation of the Four-Power agreements concerning Berlin. The agreement of June 20, 1949, in which the U.S.S.R. pledged itself to facilitate freedom of movement within Berlin and between Berlin and the rest of Germany, has also been violated.

In disregard of these agreements and of the wishes of the population of this city, for the welfare of which the Four Powers are jointly responsible, freedom of circulation throughout Berlin has been severely curtailed. Traffic between the East sector and the Western sectors of Berlin has been disrupted by the cutting of S-Bahn and U-Bahn service, the tearing up of streets, the erection of road blocks, and the stringing of barbed wire. In carrying out these illegal actions, military and paramilitary units, which were formed in violation of Four-Power agreements and whose very presence in East Berlin is illegal, turned the Soviet sector of Berlin into an armed camp.

Moreover, the East German authorities have now prohibited the many inhabitants of East Berlin and East Germany who were employed in West Berlin from continuing to pursue their occupations in West Berlin. They have thus denied to the working population under their control the elementary right of free choice of place of employment.

It is obvious that the East German authorities have taken these repressive measures because the people under their control, deeply perturbed by the threats on Berlin recently launched by Communist leaders, were fleeing in large numbers to the West.

We must protest against the illegal measures introduced on August 13 and hold you responsible for the carrying out of the relevant agreements.

Annex IX

U.S. Note of August 17, 1961, to Soviet Government, Protesting Closure of Soviet Sector Border in Berlin

The Embassy of the United States presents its compliments to the Minister of Foreign Affairs and upon instructions of its Government has the honor to direct the most serious attention of the Government of the U.S.S.R. to the following.

On August 13, East German authorities put into effect several measures regulating movement at the boundary of the western sectors and the Soviet sector of the City of Berlin. These measures have the effect of limiting, to a degree approaching complete prohibition, passage from the Soviet sector to the western sectors of the city. These measures were accompanied by the closing of the Sector boundary by a sizeable deployment of police forces and by military detachments brought into Berlin for this purpose.

All this is a flagrant, and particularly serious, violation of the quadripartite status of Berlin. Freedom of movement with respect to Berlin was reaffirmed by the quadripartite agreement of New York of May 4, 1949, and by the decision taken at Paris on June 20, 1949, by the Council of the Ministers of Foreign Affairs of the Four Powers. The United States Government has never accepted that limitations can be imposed on freedom of movement within Berlin. The boundary between the Soviet sector and the western sectors of Berlin is not a state frontier. The United States Government considers that the measures which the East German authorities have taken are illegal. It reiterates that it does not accept the pretension that the Soviet sector of Berlin forms a part of the so-called "German Democratic Republic" and that Berlin is situated on its territory. Such a pretension is in itself a violation of the solemnly pledged word of the U.S.S.R. in the agreement on the zones of occupation in Germany and the administration of Greater Berlin. Moreover, the United States Government cannot admit the right of the East German authorities to authorize their armed forces to enter the Soviet sector of Berlin.

By the very admission of the East German authorities, the measures which have just been taken are motivated by the fact that an ever increasing number of inhabitants of East Germany wish to leave this territory. The reasons for this exodus are known. They are simply the internal difficulties in East Germany.

To judge by the terms of a declaration of the Warsaw Pact powers published on August 13, the measures in question are supposed to have been recommended to the East German authorities by those powers. The United States Government notes that the powers which associated themselves with the U.S.S.R. by signing the Warsaw Pact are thus intervening in a domain in which they have no competence.

It is to be noted that this declaration states that the measures taken by the East German authorities are "in the interests of the German peoples themselves." It is difficult to see any basis for this statement, or to understand why it should be for the members of the Warsaw Pact to decide what are the interests of the German people. It is evident that no Germans, particularly those whose freedom of movement is being forcibly restrained, think this is so. This would become abundantly clear if all Germans were allowed a free choice, and the principle of self-determination were also applied in the Soviet sector of Berlin and in East Germany.

The United States Government solemnly protests against the measures referred to above, for which it holds the Soviet Government responsible. The United States Government expects the Soviet Government to put an end to these illegal measures. This unilateral infringement of the quadripartite status of Berlin can only increase existing tension and dangers.

Annex X

Soviet Violations of International Treaties and Agreements Relating to Germany Prior to August 1961

In war never tie your hands with considerations of formality. It is ridiculous not to know the history of war, not to know that a treaty is the means of gaining strength ... the history of war shows as clearly as clear can be that the signing of a treaty after defeat is a means of gaining strength. ... Yes, of course, we are violating the [Brest-Litovsk] treaty; we have violated it thirty or forty times.
—Lenin, Selected Works, vol. VII, pp. 301, 309.

A diplomat's words must have no relation to action—otherwise what kind of diplomacy is it? Words are one thing, actions another. Good words are a mask for the concealment of bad deeds. Sincere diplomacy is no more possible than dry water or iron wood.
—Stalin, Works, vol. II, p. 277.

The Soviet Union has systematically and flagrantly violated the wartime and postwar agreements concluded by the Allies to govern the administration of the occupation and rehabilitation of Germany. In addition to violating those parts of the agreements which were designed to insure the peaceful, democratic, and balanced economic development of all Germany, the U.S.S.R. has persistently sought to terminate unilaterally the rights of the Western Allies which resulted from the victory over Nazi Germany and which were formalized in the agreements concluded with the Soviet Government.

1. Democracy

The Potsdam Protocol of August 1, 1945, and subsequent decisions by the Allied Control Commission guaranteed certain fundamental personal and political freedoms to the German people.

(a) "The judicial system will be reorganized in accordance with the principles of democracy, of justice under law, and of equal rights for all citizens without distinction of race, nationality or religion." (Potsdam Protocol, II, 8)

(b) "Subject to the necessity for maintaining military security, freedom of speech, press and religion shall be permitted, and religious institutions shall be respected. Subject likewise to the maintenance of military security, the formation of free trade unions shall be permitted." (Potsdam Protocol, II, 10)

These basic human freedoms have been consistently and flagrantly violated by the Soviet Union. The legal system was put on a political basis and thousands of people in the Soviet zone were arrested and deported to the U.S.S.R. or sent to concentration camps.

There is no freedom of speech or of the press in the Soviet zone, and freedom of religion has been greatly limited, as in the U.S.S.R. Education has been subordinated to communist aims and principles. Soviet military forces cooperated with the East German regime in putting down the uprisings and strikes which occurred in June 1953.

The increasing flow of refugees escaping from the eastern zone testifies to the continuing denial of basic human freedoms to the people of East Germany.

(c) "So far as is practicable, there shall be uniformity of treatment of the German population throughout Germany." (Potsdam Protocol, II, 2)

The Soviet-dominated East German authorities in June 1952 began an extensive program aimed at the complete Isolation of the East German population from contact with the West and particularly with the population of West Germany. Soviet actions included complete closure of the interzonal frontier with the exception of crossing points for carefully channeled and controlled traffic to and from West Berlin, and prohibition of all visits of West Germans to the Soviet zone except by rarely issued special permits. The U.S.S.R. created a 5-kilometer blocked zone along the frontier from which a substantial portion of the population, including entire villages, was forcibly evacuated.

(d) Free exchange of printed matter and films was authorized in all occupation zones of Germany and Berlin. (Control Council Directive No. 55, June 25, 1947)

Soviet authorities have repeatedly barred from the Soviet zone or Soviet sector of Berlin such materials originating in other zones.

(e) "Local self-government shall be restored through out Germany on democratic principles. ..." (Potsdam Protocol, II, 9, i)

(1) "All democratic political parties with rights of assembly and of public discussion shall be allowed and encouraged throughout Germany." (Potsdam Protocol, II, 9, ii)

(g) "The purposes of the occupation of Germany ... are to prepare for the eventual reconstruction of German political life on a democratic basis and for eventual peaceful cooperation in international life by Germany."

In April 1946 the Soviet authorities forced the merger of the Socialist Party of Germany with the Communist Party of Germany, forming the SED or Socialist Unity Party, with the aim of "capturing" the Socialist voters of Berlin and the east zone. In June 1947 the Soviets "vetoed" the election of Ernst Reuter as Governing Mayor of Berlin and installed their representatives in the police who, operating under Soviet orders, openly defied the legally-elected Berlin government. On June 23, 1948, the Soviets ordered the SET) to carry out riots around the City Hall of Berlin and brought the demonstrators to the scene in Russian Army trucks.

In East Germany the so-called German Democratic Republic was established in October 1949 by Soviet order, without prior discussion or free elections. The regime's first elections were held in 1950 under the "bloc-party" system and the National Front, a communist cover organization. In 1952 the U.S.S.R. refused to grant entry into East Berlin and East Germany of the U.N. Commission to investigate whether there were conditions conducive to free elections.

2. *Economic Questions*

The Potsdam Protocol of August 1, 1945, provided for the treatment of Germany as a single economic unit, envisaged the equitable distribution of essential commodities between the various zones, and limited excessive reparations.

(a) "During the period of occupation Germany shall be treated as a single economic unit." (Potsdam Protocol, II, 14)

(b) "To this end common policies shall be established in regard to ... import and export programs for Germany as a whole ... reparation and removal of industrial war potential, transportation and communications." (Potsdam Protocol, II, 14)

(c) "Allied controls shall be imposed upon the German economy but only to the extent necessary ... to ensure in the manner determined by the Control Commission equitable distribution of essential commodities between the several zones so as to produce a balanced economy throughout Germany and reduce the need for imports." (Potsdam Protocol, II, 15)

On April 5, 1946, in the Allied Control Council's Economic Directorate, the Soviet Union stated that each zone should be responsible for its own trade. The U.S.S.R. thereafter consistently refused to make a common import-export plan workable by submitting a plan for its own zone, even though the Control Council, on September 20, 1945, had approved the establishment of a common program.

(d) "Payment of Reparations should leave enough resources to enable the German people to subsist without external assistance." (Potsdam Protocol, II, 19)

(e) "... industrial capital equipment ... should be removed from the Western Zones of Germany in exchange for an equivalent value of food, coal, potash, zinc, timber, clay products, petroleum products, and such other commodities as may be agreed upon." (Potsdam Protocol, III, 4, a)

The U.S.S.R. exploited and drained German resources in a manner not authorized by the Potsdam Protocol, took large amounts of reparations from current production, and absorbed a substantial part of German industry in the Soviet zone into Soviet state-owned concerns. Although the United States had made 11,100 tons of reparations equipment available to the U.S.S.R. by August 1, 1946, the Soviet Union did not live up to its agreement to ship goods in return to the western zones of Germany.

The result of the Soviet violations of the agreement on reparations and the U.S.S.R.'s refusal to treat Germany as an economic unit was that the United States and the United Kingdom were obliged to give financial support to their zones in Germany to maintain a minimum economy. In effect, the United States, in shipping reparations to the Soviet Union while supporting its own zone to make up deficiencies caused by Soviet violations of the Potsdam Protocol, was permitting the U.S.S.R. to collect reparations from the United States itself, rather than from Germany.

(f) German external assets in Finland, Eastern Austria, Hungary, Bulgaria and Rumania were to be vested in the German External Property Commission. (Control Council Law No. 5, October 30, 1945)

The U.S.S.R. directly appropriated German external assets in these countries without investing and *assignment* by the German External Property Commission.

(g) In conformity with paragraph 14 of the Potsdam Protocol, quadripartite legislation was enacted to provide tax uniformity and stabilization of wages in all zones. (Control Council Laws Nos. 12, February 11, 1946, and 61, December 19, 1947; Control Council Directive No. 14, October 12, 1945)

Soviet authorities permitted the Land governments of Brandenburg and Saxony-Anhalt to grant partial tax exemptions to large groups of wage and salary earners in violation of this legislation. This move was intended to stop the exodus of skilled workers to the western zones, to encourage qualified workers to take jobs in Soviet-owned factories, and to make propaganda for improving the living standards of Soviet Zone workers.

3. *Demilitarization*

On repeated occasions during and after the war, the U.S.S.R. agreed that demilitarization of Germany should be one of the cardinal aims of the occupation.

(a) "The purposes of the occupation of Germany ... are the complete disarmament and demilitarization of Germany. ..." (Potsdam Protocol, II, 3)

(b) "All armed forces of Germany or under German control ... shall be completely disarmed. ... Detachments of civil police to be armed with small arms only, for the maintenance of order and for guard duties, will be designated by the Allied Representatives." (Declaration Regarding Defeat of Germany, June 5, 1945, Art. 2)

(c) "All forms of military training, military propaganda and military activities of whatever nature, on the part of the German people, are prohibited, as well as the formation of any organization initiated to further any aspect of military training and the formation of war veterans' organizations or other groups which might develop military characteristics or which are designed to carry on the German military tradition, whether such organizations or groups purport to be political, educational, religious, social, athletic or recreational or of any other nature." (Four Power Agreement on Additional Requirements to be Imposed on Germany, Sept. 20, 1945, Section I, Paragraph 2)

In 1948 Soviet authorities began building up a sizable "police force" in the Soviet Zone. On May 23, 1950, the United States protested to the U.S.S.R. against the remilitarization of the Soviet zone, calling attention to the fact that some 40,000 to 50,000 men in so-called "Police Alert Units" were receiving basic infantry, artillery and armored training and were equipped with Soviet military weapons.

By the end of 1953 the Soviet zone had a "police force" of 100,000 men, supplemented by an additional 140,200 military personnel, including three mechanized divisions and an air force. By June 1959 East German military and paramilitary forces totaled more than 700,000 men. Although the U.S.S.R. now admits the continuation of the four-power occupation status of Berlin (the Soviets had denied this in 1948, 1952, and 1958 but subsequently reversed their position), it has allowed the presence of East German paramilitary units and armament factories in East Berlin in violation of the Four Power Agreement. Military parades have taken place annually on May Day in East Berlin.

4. *Allied Occupation of Germany*

In violation of wartime and postwar agreements, the Soviet Union has sought to destroy the organs established for the occupation of Germany and to deny to the Western Allies their rights stemming from the military conquest of Germany.

(a) "… supreme authority in Germany will be exercised, on instructions from their Governments, by the Soviet, British, United States, and French Commanders-in-Chief, each in his own zone of occupation, and also jointly in matters affecting Germany as a whole. The four Commanders-in-Chief will together constitute the Control Council." (Four Power Statement on Control Machinery in Germany, June 5, 1945, Paragraph 1)

On March 20, 1948, the Soviet commander unilaterally adjourned a meeting of the Council and abruptly walked out, thereby precipitating a rupture of the operations.

(b) "The administration of the 'Greater Berlin' area will be directed by an Inter-Allied Governing Authority, which will operate under the general direction of the Control Council and will consist of four Commandants, each of whom will serve in rotation as Chief Commandant." (Four Power Statement on Control Machinery in Germany, June 5, 1945, Paragraph 7)

On June 16, 1948, the Soviet representative walked out of a meeting of the Inter-Allied Governing Authority *(Kommandatura)*. On July 1, 1948, Soviet authorities announced that they would no longer participate in any meetings. These acts finally destroyed the quadripartite control machinery of Berlin.

(c) [Occupation of Berlin will be carried out] … in accordance with arrangements between the respective commanders, including in these arrangements simultaneous movement of the national garrisons into Greater Berlin and provision of free access by air, road, and rail from Frankfurt and Bremen to Berlin for United States forces." (Letter of the President of the United States to Soviet Premier Stalin of June 14, 1945, to which Stalin replied on June 18, 1945: "On our part all necessary measures will be taken in Germany and Austria in accordance with the above stated plan.")

The Soviets imposed rail and road restrictions on Allied traffic to Berlin from the western zones on April 1, 1948. The Allies inaugurated a "little airlift" which was expanded to a full airlift on June 26, 1948, 2 days after the Soviets imposed a total blockade. On July 1, 1948, the Soviet Chief of Staff of the U.S.S.R. delegation to the Inter-Allied Governing Authority told his British, French, and American counterparts that four-power administration of Berlin no longer existed.

(d) "... the occupation authorities, each in his own zone, will have an obligation to take the measures necessary to ensure the normal functioning and utilization of rail, water, and road transport for such movement of persons and goods and such communications by post, telephone, and telegraph." (Council of Foreign Ministers Communiqué, Paris, June 20, 1949, Paragraph 5)

On September 20, 1955, the U.S.S.R. transferred to the East German Government control over road, railroad and air traffic in and out of Berlin in violation of the 1949 agreement. In December 1955 the Soviets threatened to interrupt the Berlin barge service and higher tolls were levied on barges bound for Berlin in May 1958. Since January 13, 1950, the Soviet authorities have intermittently interfered with traffic between Berlin and Western Germany.

5. *Prisoners of War*

(a) "German prisoners of war located in the territory of the Allied Powers and in all other territories will be returned to Germany on December 31, 1947." (Report of the Council of Foreign Ministers, April 23, 1947)

The Soviet Union reaffirmed this obligation in submitting its plan for repatriation on June 30, 1947. On January 3, 1949, the United States protested to the Soviet Union for its failure to furnish information on repatriation of war prisoners, noting that only 447,367 prisoners were known to have been repatriated out of the 890,532 war prisoners which Soviet Foreign Minister Molotov announced on March 12, 1947, were still in Soviet custody.

(b) "... repatriation of war prisoners will be completed during 1949." (Soviet note of January 24, 1949)

On May 5, 1952, the Soviet news agency Tass announced that the last group of German POW's numbering 17,538 had been repatriated. It added that there were 9,717 prisoners still being held, because they had been convicted of grave crimes, and 3,815 in addition still being investigated. At this time it was estimated that the Soviet Government held more than 100,000 German prisoners, most of whom had been convicted on various pretexts to hard labor and were therefore no longer considered war prisoners. During the period from May 1950 to August 1955, some 11,000 German prisoners were released by the U.S.S.R. and following a special plea by the West German Government during the negotiations leading to the exchange of diplomatic representatives in September 1955, the Soviets released 11,000 additional prisoners. In addition, the Soviet Government has refused to repatriate more than 100,000 German civilians deported during and after the war from eastern Germany and eastern Europe. The Ad Hoc Commission on repatriation of war prisoners reported in September 1957 that the Soviet Government had not even replied to a request to discuss further the prisoner of war issue.

6. *Eastern, Frontiers*

Both the Yalta Agreement and the Potsdam Protocol stipulated that final delimitation of the German-Polish frontier should await a peace settlement with Germany.

(a) "... the final delimitation of the Western frontier of Poland should thereafter await the Peace Conference." (Yalta Agreement, VII)

(b) "The three Heads of Government reaffirm their opinion that the final delimitation of the western frontier of Poland should await the peace settlement" (Potsdam Protocol, VIII B)

Immediately after this pledge was made, the U.S.S.R. in effect recognized the Oder-Western Neisse line as the German-Polish frontier, allowing the Soviet-controlled Lublin Polish Government to occupy the land and evacuate the Germans who had been living there. On July 6, 1950, the Soviet controlled governments of Poland and eastern Germany signed an agreement recognizing the Oder-Western Neisse line, in violation of the Yalta and Potsdam Agreements.

Annex XI

Selected Bibliography

OFFICIAL PUBLICATIONS

(Publications for which a price is indicated may be purchased from the Superintendent of Documents, Government Printing Office, Washington 25, D.C. Those listed as "free" may be obtained from the Office of Public Services, Department of State, Washington 25, D.C., or, in the case of publications other than those issued by the Department of State, from the source indicated in the listing. Publications listed as "out of print" may be consulted in a number of public and university libraries throughout the United States.)

DEPARTMENT OF STATE PUBLICATIONS

Department of State Bulletin. Official statements and documents concerning Germany and Berlin, including exchanges of communications, are published in the weekly *Bulletin.* The *Bulletin* is indexed in the *Readers' Guide to Periodical Literature* and is available in many public, school, and university libraries. 52 issues, domestic, $8.50; foreign, $12.25.

Foreign Relations of the United States: The Conferences at Malta and Yalta, *1945.* Pub. 6199. $5.50.

Foreign Relations of the United States: The Conference of Berlin (The Potsdam Conference), 1945, 2 vols. Pubs. 7015, 7163. Vol. I, $6.00; vol. II, $6.50.

Occupation of Germany: Policy and *Progress.* Pub. 2783. Out of print.

Germany, 1947-1949: The Story in Documents. Pub. 3556. Out of print.

The Berlin Crisis: A Report on the Moscow Discussions, 1948. Pub. 3298. Out of Print.

The United States and Germany, *1945-1955.* Pub. 5827. 250.

American Foreign Policy, 1950-1955, Basic Documents, 2 vols. Pub. 6446. $5.25 each vol.

American Foreign Policy, Current Documents, vols. for 1956 and 1957. Pubs. 6811 and 7101. $4.75 and $5.25.

Foreign Ministers Meeting, Berlin Discussions, January 25-February 18, 1954. Pub. 5399. 704t.

London and Paris Agreements, September-October 1954. Pub. 5659. Out of print.

The Geneva Conference of Heads of Government, July 18-2,8,1955. Pub. 6046. 350.

The Geneva Meeting of Foreign Ministers, October 27 November 16,1955. Pub. 6156. $1.

The Soviet Note on Berlin: An Analysis. Pub. 6757. 250. *Foreign Ministers Meeting, May-August 1959, Geneva.* Pub. 6882. $1.75.

Background of Heads of Government Conference, 1960: Principal Documents, 1955-1959, With Narrative Summary. Pub. 6972. $1.25.

RECENT PAMPHLETS

Berlin—City Between Two Worlds. Pub. 7089. 20t. *President Eisenhower's Report to the Nation, May 25, 1960—Secretary Herter's* Report *to the Senate Foreign Relations Committee, May 27, 1960.* Pub. 7010. 150.

President Kennedy's Report to the People on *His Trip to* Europe, *May 30-June 6, 1961.* Pub. 7213. 150.

The Berlin Crisis: Report to *the Nation by President Kennedy, July 25, 1961.* Pub. 7243. 150

PUBLICATIONS OF THE OFFICE OF THE CHIEF OF MILITARY HISTORY, DEPARTMENT OF THE ARMY

Forrest C. Pogue, *The Supreme Command* [European Theater of Operations], *United States Army in World War II* (Washington, 1954). $6.50.

PUBLICATIONS OF THE OFFICE OF THE U.S. HMII COMMISSIONER FOR GERMANY

Report on *Germany* (quarterly, 1949-1952). Out of print.

Documents on German Unity, 4 vols. (Frankfurt, 1951-1953). Out of print.

Elmer Plischke. *Berlin: Development of its Government and Administration.* 1952. Out of print.

CONGRESSIONAL PUBLICATIONS

A Decade of American Foreign Policy, Basic Documents, 1941-49. Senate Document No. 123, 81st Cong., 1st sess. Out of print.

Documents on *Germany, 1944-1959, Background Documents* on *Germany, 1944-1959, and a Chronology of Political Developments Affecting Berlin, 1945-1956.*

86th Cong., 1st sess., committee print for Senate Committee on Foreign Relations. Free, from Senate Committee on Foreign Relations, Washington, D.C.

UNOFFICIAL PUBLICATIONS

(NOTE: The Department of State can assume no responsibility for the accuracy of information contained in unofficial publications.)

James F. Byrnes. *Speaking Frankly* (New York, 1947)

Winston S. Churchill. *Triumph and Tragedy* (Boston, 1953)

Lucius D. Clay. *Decision in Germany* (New York, 1950)

John Foster Dulles. *War or Peace* (New York, 1950)

Dwight D. Eisenhower. *Crusade in* Europe (Garden City, 1948)

O. M. von der Gablentz, editor. *Documents on the Status of Berlin, 1944-1959, abridged translation of* Dokumente *zur Berlin-Frage, 1944-1959* (Berlin, 1959)

Philip E. Mosely. "Dismemberment of Germany" and "The Occupation of Germany", reprinted in *The Kremlin and World Politics* (New York, 1960)

B. Ruhm von Oppen. *Documents on* Germany *under Occupation, 1945-1954* (New York, 1955)

Edward R. Stettlnius, Jr. *Roosevelt and the Russians: The Yalta Conference* (New York, 1949)

Harry S. Truman. Memoirs, 2 volumes (Garden City, 1955-56)

Five Successive Secretaries of State on Berlin

"The United States and its allies have assumed certain basic obligations to protect the freedom of the people of West Berlin. Western forces are in the city by right and remain there to protect those freedoms. The people of West Berlin welcome and support those forces, whose presence gives tangible expression to our obligation. It is obvious that the United States could not accept the validity of any claim to extinguish its position in Berlin by unilateral action."

— SECRETARY OF STATE DEAN RUSK
(Statement at news conference, June 22, 1961)

"One fact must be faced squarely. Fear and appeasement will not in the long run reduce the danger of war. Only courage and a firm stand on our rights and principles can do this. Once the Communist rulers soberly realize the depth of our solemn Berlin commitment, we believe they will refrain from putting to trial by force the present right and obligation of the Western Powers to preserve the freedom of the people of West, Berlin."

— SECRETARY OF STATE CHRISTIAN A. HERTER
(Radio-television address to the Nation, May 7, 1959)

"We possess rights in relation to Berlin which derive from the wartime agreements. We do not believe that the Soviet Union can evade those obligations by setting up a puppet regime in East Germany and East Berlin and claim that it now has authority. We plan to hold the Soviet Union to its very formal and clear obligations with respect to Berlin and access to Berlin. ..."

—SECRETARY OF STATE JOHN FOSTER DULLES
(Statement at news conference, December 20, 1955)

"We have given notice, in plain and unmistakable language, that we are in Berlin *as* a matter of right and of duty, and we shall remain in Berlin until we are satisfied that the freedom of this city is secure. We have also indicated in unmistakable terms that we shall regard any attack on Berlin from whatever quarter as an attack against our forces and ourselves."

— SECRETARY OF STATE DEAN G. ACHESON
(Address at laying of cornerstone of American Memorial Library, Berlin, June 29, 1952)

"We are in Berlin as a result of agreements between the Governments on the areas of occupation in Germany, and we intend to stay."

— SECRETARY OF STATE GEORGE C. MARSHALL
(Press statement, June 30, 1948)

Berlin Brigade
Special Services Division Presents

Compiler's Preface to

Berlin Brigade Special Services Division Presents

This booklet was published in two editions, but with the same text in each. One in 1964 and another in 1966. The text is heavily based on the text of the previous *Special Services Berlin Tour* of 1958. Deletions from the 1958 text are shown as ~~strikethroughs~~, and additions are shown in a sans serif font. Text that is the same in both editions is in this font.

The 1958 edition had a different set of photographs. Those can be seen in *Berlin in Early Cold-War Army Booklets*.

Some differences between the 1958 and the 1960s tour booklets are minor. The 1958 booklet, for examples, describes the **Titania Palast** as "~~a modernistic theater~~," while the 1960s booklet drops the description. The description of the Tiergarten likewise changes ever so slightly: "With the help of ~~E.R.P. funds~~ the European Recovery Plan ~~unemployed~~ out-of-work Berliners were employed in remodeling the park."

Though it has been 20 years since the end of WWII, the 1960s tour books still remark that: "There are blocks of ruins as far as one can see." On the other hand, some structures, such as the Marienkirche, though "rather badly damaged during the war ... have since been restored." The 1958 tour book says that the Kurfuerstendamm "was heavily damaged by street fighting and from aerial bombs, but gradually it is coming back." The 1960s tour book makes no mention of damage to the Ku-Damm.

Various unit identifications have changed in the course of time. ~~Berlin Command~~ (~~BC~~) has been replaced by Berlin Brigade, and ~~Tempelhof Central Airport~~ by Tempelhof Air Base.

The major differences are found in the new reality of the Berlin Wall. The tour of the Soviet Sector of Berlin (East Berlin) is now "for US Armed Forces uniformed personnel **only.** Personnel must be in possession of their ID card." No such requirement, or even division of the tour into "East" and "West" is contained in the 1958 tour booklet.

The 1960s tour takes a different route than the 1958 tour. Instead of proceeding to Treptower Park like the 1958 tour did, the 1960s tour leaves Tempelhof Central Airport "Via Mehringplatz [where] we enter Friedrichstrasse and stop at Checkpoint Charlie, US Army Checkpoint at the border-crossing between the American and the Soviet Sector of Berlin." This reflects the new constraints on where Americans can and cannot cross the sector border with East Berlin. There is no mention of *Friedrichstrasse* or *Checkpoint Charlie* in the 1958 tour booklet.

The rhetoric of the Cold War has been turned up a notch. In the 1958 tour booklet, "Many people were killed or wounded" in the uprising on 17 June 1953. The 1960s booklet adds: "And even today, some of them are still in jail." As the tour passes down Bernauer Strasse, the booklet points out that: "We see several markers which were put on the sidewalks by West Berliners where refugees died in their efforts to make their way to freedom."

The "Introduction" to the **Entertainment Guide** is exactly the same in both the 1958 and in the 1960s editions. There are differences in the various lists of entertainment and shopping venues. For example, the 1960s edition lists 11 Theaters, while the 1958 edition only lists 9.

The booklet has been reformatted from its original size (4¾ X 6⅝) to fit the format of this book (6X9). Additional compiler comments within the text will be enclosed in [square brackets]. No other editing has been done to the text. Only blatant typographical errors have been corrected. The **emphasis** is that of the original.

The quality of the photographs is limited by the quality of the available originals.

Table of Contents

Foreword

This booklet is designed to give you a general background of Berlin with a discussion of the points of interest which this guided tour covers. It is hoped, at the same time, that it will be of use in making your visit to Berlin interesting and worthwhile.

~~The Special Services Division, Berlin Command, conducts a bus tour of Berlin each Wednesday, Saturday and Sunday, starting from the US Army Shopping Center at 1300 hrs. and lasting approximately four hours. These tours include the Soviet Sector. Reservations must be made 24 hours in advance by calling 74 43 153. A small service charge is assessed each person. The tour may also be joined in front of the Harnack House, or at the Tempelhof Officers' Open Mess "Columbia House" Tempelhof Air Base.~~

Special Services Division, Berlin Brigade, conducts tours of both East and West Berlin every Wednesday, Saturday and Sunday, during the summer months, however, the West Berlin tours will operate daily, starting from the US Army Shopping Center located across the street from the US Headquarters. The tours depart the Shopping Center at 1300 hours and make stops at the Harnack House at 1310 hours and the Columbia House at 1330 hours. The tour entering the Soviet Sector of Berlin (East Berlin) is for US Armed Forces uniformed personnel **only.** Personnel must be in possession of their ID card. The West Berlin tour is for military and civilian personnel and their dependents. Both tours last approximately 3½ hours, and the cost is 75¢ per person. Reservations are required at least 24 hours in advance. Reservations may be made by calling Berlin military 6523. If calling from a civilian phone, dial 819-6523.

Sightseeing in Berlin today is a unique experience. One cannot help being conscious of the profound changes since the nineteen-thirties and the difference between the two parts of Berlin as a result of the political circumstances of the present time. This comparison explains why this tour is not only a "sightseeing tour" in the usual sense but also an excellent means of information regarding life behind the "Iron Curtain".

With the building of the wall dividing East and West Berlin on 13 August 1961, the Iron Curtain was lowered in the heart of this city to end Berlin's mission as the living 'bridge between the people in both parts of Germany. In the days just prior to the building of the wall, the highest number of refugees from East Berlin and the Soviet Zone were arriving in the Western sectors of the divided city. They came by the thousands each day before the door of freedom was finally shut and the escape routes severed. However, a small trickle of refugees still make their way into the West by swimming the canals, climbing or crashing the walls, always risking discovery by communist border guards and shots from communist sub-machine guns.

East and West Berliners may not see each other any longer, but they will not give up hope that one day freedom will be given back to those millions of people who live under communist pressure behind the Iron Curtain.

Brief History of Berlin

Berlin is first mentioned in history in the early part of the 13th century. It was located on the banks of the river Spree, opposite Koelln. Both villages were well known markets for fish, grain, and wood on the commercial highway from Leipzig to Stettin at the Baltic Sea.

The names of both villages are of Wendish origin, but stories about them have not really been confirmed. Berlin is supposed to mean "sandy field", which indeed is true of the area around Berlin. Koelln is said to stand for "built on wooden planks above the water". Some people also connect the name Berlin with Albrecht the Bear, founder of the Margraviate of Brandenburg who held the title Margrave from 1150 to 1170, but it is almost certain that Berlin was not founded during his time.

The oldest parts of Berlin-Koelln were situated on the Museum Island and south of it. When Emperor Sigismund appointed the Burgrave of Nuremberg, Frederick von Hohenzollern, viceroy of the Mark Brandenburg in 1415, the nobles of the Mark became rebellious, and the struggle was not ended until his son Frederick "with the Iron Tooth" conquered Berlin-Koelln with 600 horsemen and built a strong citadel on the island of Koelln. This castle was rebuilt and extended during the centuries, and became the Schloss or Royal Palace of the Hohenzollern Emperors up to the time of Kaiser Wilhelm II.

In the beginning of the 13th century the double town was united under the name of Berlin. Rapid development began when King Frederick I made the town the royal residence and the capital of the kingdom of Prussia in 1701. Each succeeding Hohenzoller added to Berlin's beauty and importance and neighboring villages and towns grew likewise, so that boundary lines became almost indistinguishable. All attempts at unification, however, failed until 1911 when the formation of Greater Berlin began. The process came to an end in 1920 with the integration of the village Steglitz, which at that time was the largest one in Prussia with a population of 115,000 people.

The late date of the creation of Greater Berlin is why every district or "Bezirk" even today still has its "Buergermeister" and its town hall functioning under the Governing Mayor or "Regierender Buergermeister" of Berlin. Likewise there are about twenty streets with the name "Berliner Strasse", and several main streets change their name whenever entering another district.

Before the war Berlin was Germany's political and commercial center of 4,5 million people living in an area of 340 square miles. This made Berlin the third largest city in the world in area and fourth largest in population.

The Soviet Army captured Berlin on 2 May 1945 after encircling the city and taking most districts in house-to-house fighting. According to agreements with the Western Allies Berlin was divided into four sectors.

The American Army took over the US Sector of Berlin during the first week of July 1945. The Stars and Stripes was flown in Berlin, for the first time, on 4 July 1945.

The war left Berlin with nearly 2 billion cubic feet of rubble. The population decreased by almost 1,5 million people. Since the beginning of the blockade in June 1948, Berlin has been split into two parts; the west sectors and the Soviet sector. Every city wide organization was divided; there are now two currencies, two police forces, two city councils, and two municipal transport companies.

The 11 month long operation" Airlift" was carried out, during which time the Western Allies, with the aid and cooperation of the West Germans and West Berliners, airlifted into Berlin all of the goods that were necessary to keep the city alive. The Soviets finally lifted the blockade on 12 May 1949.

On 17 June 1953, East Berliners and East Germans revolted against the communist regime; the revolt was, however, crushed by Russian tanks. This date, 17 June, was declared a national holiday in the free part of Germany, the so-called "Day of German Unity". In the following years political pressure in eastern Germany grew constantly, and the number of refugees increased to 1,000 and more a day.

The event on 13 August 1961 brought this flow of refugees to a stop, when the sector borders between the western and the eastern half of the city were sealed off and the 34 mile long barbed wire barriers and concrete wall were built by the communists.

East Tour

We start at the "Harnack House", the American Officers'-Civilians' Open Mess of Berlin **Brigade** ~~is located at 16 Ihnestr. Dahlem~~.

Originally the guest house of the famous Kaiser-Wilhelm-Institute, Harnack House was designed to house distinguished foreign scientists who came from all parts of the world to do research work here. It was named after the first president of the society, Adolf von Harnack. During a later period it was headed by Albert Einstein.

When the first American Army personnel entered Berlin in July 1945 they found Harnack House practically undamaged, so with a clatter of field ranges and supply trucks, mess sergeants took over. A large amount of the original furniture still remains and is being used in the club. Besides housing the Officers'-Civilians' Open Mess of Berlin Brigade, Harnack House has a restaurant, two floors of rooms for visitors, a beauty parlor and barber shop, and a newsstand.

The buildings surrounding Harnack House, for the most part, belonged to and made up the Kaiser-Wilhelm-Institute ~~of Dahlem~~; those not too badly damaged were taken over by the **Free University of Berlin** ~~and are crowded with eager young students from the West and East Sectors of the city~~.

~~The Administration Building and some of the main lecture halls including the Auditorium Maximum or Henry Ford Building of the **Free U** are right beside Harnack House and the streets surrounding the spacious lawns of the club are always gay with young students coming and going either on foot or on bicycle.~~

The Free University was founded in 1948 by a number of students which fled East Berlin's Humboldt University. Under the motto *"Veritas, Justitia, Libertas"*, 2,140 students began their first semester in December 1948. Since then the number of students has grown to over 15,500. The Auditorium Maximum was donated by the Henry Ford Foundation, and is located right beside the Harnack House.

Ihnestrasse is a most attractive street in the spring when the beautiful old chestnut trees are in bloom. Residential streets in the new districts of Berlin are all planted with trees, a specific variety to each street and in many cases, following the idea of the famous Unter den Linden, the street is named after the trees that shade it. There is an Unter den Eichen (Under the Oaks) and a Kastanienstrasse (Chestnut-Street), and so on.

The US Sector of Berlin consists of six districts or "Bezirken": Zehlendorf, Schoeneberg, Kreuzberg, Tempelhof, Neukoelln and Steglitz. Of these, Zehlendorf and Steglitz are the newest- and most attractive. They are modern, mainly residential with clean streets and innumerable parks containing small bodies of water. Most of the houses have balconies gay in summer with flowers and foliage and they are usually surrounded by gardens enclosed by grill work fences.

After leaving Harnack House we drive through ~~attractive~~ winding residential streets, all tree bordered, and turn right into Koenigin-Luise-Strasse which ~~runs into~~ becomes Grunewaldstrasse. On the left we pass the modern catholic church of Dahlem, bombed and now rebuilt. Farther down on the same side are two other buildings of the Free University, one of them a newly built Medical School. On the right is the rear entrance to the **Botanical Gardens** with the main entrance located on Unter den Eichen. Because of the large and extensive selection of plants the Botanical Gardens are considered to be one of the finest in Europe.

From Grunewaldstrasse we enter Schloss Strasse in the Steglitz district. On our left we see the town hall of Steglitz, **Rathaus Steglitz,** built of red brick like so many local government buildings of Berlin.

Schloss Strasse is a good street not only for shopping but also for seeing the Berliner. It is always crowded with people. The traffic is heavy and the shops offer a very fine choice. At night it is bright with neon signs advertising movies, restaurants, and shops.

On the left is the new Wertheim Department Store, the first rebuilt department store after the war, continuing the tradition of the old "Wertheim" now located in the Soviet Sector and totally bombed.

One block down on the same side we see ~~a modernistic theater called~~ the **Titania Palast.** It was from 1945-1948 a recreational center of the US Army and then handed back to German ownership. It has since been renovated and acoustic conditions improved, and is now used for movie and stage productions including light plays, concerts, variety and radio shows, lectures, and as an assembly hall. It has a seating capacity of 1,800 and has seen successions of famous artists, musicians, and Hollywood stars since 1945.

~~Again there is a town hall,~~ **Rathaus Friedenau,** ~~and the street changes its name. It is now Rheinstrasse; later it becomes Hauptstrasse, but it is still crowded with traffic and the shops look prosperous.~~

After Innsbrucker Platz by turning left we come to John-F.-Kennedy-Platz to see the **Rathaus Schoeneberg.** [Photograph on the facing page.] Before the war this was a Rathaus like so many others, but after the Berlin Blockade caused a separation in the city's administrative set-up, it was chosen as the seat of the West Berlin government. Here are located the offices of the governing mayor of West Berlin as well as those of local administration of the Schoeneberg district.

The tower of the building was especially reconstructed to hold the ten-ton **Freedom Bell,** a gift from the United States to the people of Berlin. The bell's deep throated tones can be heard each day at noon. This great bell, one of the largest in the world, was designed by Walter Dorwin Teague, one of America's leading industrial designers, and was brought to Berlin on United Nations Day, 24 October 1950. Inscribed on its rim is the following message paraphrased from the address of Abraham Lincoln at Gettysburg: "That this world, under God, shall have a new birth of freedom".

An elevator has been installed in the tower and visitors may go up to see the bell and at the same time, get a fine view of the city. ~~Coming to Grunewaldstrasse we turn right and pass on our left the~~ **Allied Control Authority Building.**

~~Situated in Kleistpark, the~~ **ACA Building** ~~was, until the beginning of the blockade, the Headquarters for the highest quadripartite governing body~~

~~in Germany. The four flags, Soviet, French, British and American still are flown on tall flagstaffs in front of it. This imposing structure once housed the Prussian State Court, the second highest court in Germany, where those who took part in the plot against Hitler's life on July 20, 1944 were tried and sentenced.~~

Crossing Hauptstrasse we go up ~~Monumenten Strasse~~ Kolonnenstrasse over the S-Bahn tracks, and as we approach Tempelhof we ~~see rising above the roof tops the attractive monument on~~ pass on our left Viktoria Park with the **Kreuzberg Hill**, ~~surrounded by a well laid out park. This hill, which certainly is not impressive in height, used to be~~ which was the highest elevation of the city before postwar rubble mountains were created.

On the hill stands the attractive Kreuzberg monument, built in the Gothic style in 1821, dedicated to the Prussian War of Liberation. ~~It was designed by Schinkel, one of Germany's most famous artists.~~ It is claimed that on a fine day all of Berlin, with the river Spree winding around it, can be seen from the summit of the hill.

And now we see the building of **Tempelhof Central Airport** looming up ahead of us. ~~One of the finest airports in the world,~~ Tempelhof obtained its name from the village originally created by the Templar Knights in the year 1319 and named Tempelhof.

The air field emerged from World War II a shambles, and tons of debris had to be cleared away in time to receive President Truman and Prime Minister Churchill when they arrived for the Potsdam Conference in 1945.

Prior to its utilization as an airport~~, which began~~ in 1919, the field had served as an exercise and drill ground for the Berlin Garrison. Dating back to the time of Frederick William I (1721) the field was the scene of parades by the Royal Guard Corps in the spring and fall of each year.

Construction of the modern airport buildings was begun in 1937 and had not been completed at the end of the war. The arc-shaped hangars are of steel construction, uniquely built to permit aircraft parking under a roof supported by large cantilever beams. The upright beams were set in reinforced concrete foundations and anchored to the terminal building by specially designed steel erection equipment.

Although destined never to realize its purpose, the entire roof of the hangar construction, nearly one mile in length, was laid in tiers to form a semi-circular stadium, designed to seat thousands of spectators for air and ground demonstrations.

The landing field is a well-drained, sodded area of 312 acres, bordered on one side by a concrete block apron approximately 950 feet wide and 3,500 feet long. Length of the runway is 5,300 feet; width 140 feet.

In addition to the landing field and the hangars, one of the more interesting areas of the base is "Eagle Square". This ornate quadrangle forms the main entrance to the base, ~~recently handed back to German ownership~~. Since the occupation of Germany began, the area had been known as "Eagle Square" because of the large eagle which surmounted the center wall. Once a typical Nazi eagle, it was Americanized by a coat of white paint ~~over its head and an American coat of arms over the old Swastika~~. However, this statue was removed in mid-1961. Facing "Eagle Square" is the **Platz der Luftbruecke** named by the city of Berlin to commemorate the airlift, and the impressive **Airlift Monument.**

The Soviet army took possession of the airport in May 1945, and although the buildings were little damaged by bombing, extensive burning by the Russians and pilfering by the general public presented a tremendous job of reconstruction to the first American troops to arrive in Berlin on 2 July 1945.

From 1945 until September 1947, Tempelhof was operated as an installation of the European Air Transport Service; on 20 September 1947, control of the base was transferred to the United States Air Force in Europe.

As Russian restrictions on land travel became more complicated in the spring of 1948, West Berlin began to depend more and more on the United States Air Force for transportation and for providing necessary supplies. On 1 April, USAFE C-47's and C-54's began a' 24-hour schedule between Rhein Main Air Base and Tempelhof, but on 6 April 1948, the travel restrictions were temporarily relaxed and land travel resumed. However, the

211

period of relaxed restrictions was brief and on 20 June 1948, it was necessary to recommence supplying the city by air. "Operation Vittles", later known as the Combined Airlift Task Force, came into existence on 26 June 1948, and the Berlin Airlift began.

Flying 109,228,502 miles or an equivalent of 227.8 trips to the moon, the Berlin Airlift transported 2,324,257 tons of cargo to the blockaded city of Berlin. In addition to Tempelhof, the center of control in Berlin, Gatow Airport in the British Sector and Tegel Airport in the French Sector were utilized as landing fields to receive the tremendous amounts of coal, flour, and miscellaneous items required to supply the more than two million inhabitants of West Berlin.

The blockade of Berlin officially ended on 12 May 1949, and in August the Airlift began a phase-out period which lasted until 30 September 1949, when the operation was finally stopped.

At the beginning of 1951, one half of the airport was de-requisitioned by the Air Force and handed back to German trusteeship. ~~Three commercial air-lines are using this civilian portion of the airport now: Pan American World Airways, British European Airways, and Air France.~~ Two main commercial airlines are using this civilian portion of the airport now: Pan American World Airways and British European Airways. Air France operates out of Tegel Airport.

[The 1958 tour continues to Treptower Park at this point, while the 1964 tour takes another route.]

212

Continuing down Mehringdamm the next point of interest is Hallesches Tor, a former city gate to Berlin, and the American Memorial Library, a memorial to the airlift, donated from a special fund for the benefit of German cultural institutions set up by John McCloy, former US High Commissioner in Germany. With 300,000 volumes and over 40,000 card holders it is the largest public library in Germany, and has the largest library circulation.

Via Mehringplatz we enter Friedrichstrasse and stop at Checkpoint Charlie, US Army Checkpoint at the border-crossing between the American and the Soviet Sector of Berlin. Of the seven border crossing points between East and West Berlin, Checkpoint Charlie is the only border crossing point for foreigners.

~~Crossing over the former **Schloss Bruecke** (Castle Bridge) renamed Marx Engels-Bruecke, we leave the island and start down the famous ...~~ Entering the Soviet Sector the tour leads us to the famous **Unter den Linden,** Berlin's most famous boulevard, 900 yards in length from the Brandenburg Gate to Marx-Engels-Bruecke, laid out by Frederick William, the Great Elector, in the middle of the 17th century. It was so named because of the double avenue of lime or linden trees planted along it.

On either side of **Unter den Linden** can be seen the ruins of what were once the finest palaces, embassies, museums, libraries and great hotels in Germany. The drive down what was formerly one of Europe's most beautiful streets will show you clearly the destructiveness of total war. Nearly all public 'buildings and most of the commercial centers are now heaps of rubble or broken fragments of walls. ~~Unter den Linden is part of the Soviet Sector of Berlin.~~

~~On the left is a grey building containing~~ The first building on our right is the head office of the Freie Deutsche Gewerkschaitsbund (FDGB), the East Zone's trade union.~~, later on the right is the center of the Freie Deutsche Jugend (FDJ), the communist youth organization.~~

~~Facing the Opera on the other side of Bebelplatz is~~ We then pass the destroyed palace of Emperor William I. On the left, opposite the palace, is the National Library, which once housed one of the world's largest collections of books. The collection, begun in 1659 by the Great Elector, was built up to 150,000 volumes by Frederick the Great; before War II it had grown to two million books.

~~Just behind the opera house and facing the square was all that remained of Berlin's Catholic Cathedral, St. Hedwig's. Its facade was a perfect miniature reproduction of the great Pantheon at Rome. Built during~~

~~the reign of Frederick the Great, it was completely destroyed during bombing~~
~~in 1943. It is now under repair.~~

Next on our right we see Bebelplatz, formerly Opernplatz, with Berlin's Catholic Cathedral, St. Hedwig's. Its facade was a perfect miniature reproduction of the great Pantheon at Rome. Built during the reign of Frederick the Great, it was completely destroyed during bombing in 1943 and has recently been restored.

Also on Bebelplatz just beyond the cathedral, is the red-bannered and slogan-decorated SED Headquarters, operating in a completely renovated building formerly housing main offices of the Dresdener Bank. The SED Party is sponsored by the Soviet Union and is the leading political organization of the Soviet Sector and Zone of Germany. This building, aside from the far more historical ones surrounding it, has been completely remodeled and repainted. It shows no evidence of bomb damage.

Facing Bebelplatz from the other side is the rebuilt State Opera House, built under Frederick the Great in 1743. This opera house has proved to be an ill-fated building. having been burnt to the ground twice in its history and finally, in 1943, bombed to a shambles by Allied Air Forces.

Next to the State Opera House once stood the Kronprinzenpalais, the residence of the sons and daughters of the German rulers. Frederick the Great was the first Crown Prince to live in this small palace on Unter den Linden. Then came Frederick William III (1797-1840). In 1797 Emperor William I was born here, and from 1858-1888 it served as the winter residence of Crown Prince Frederick III. In 1900 it was opened to the public as a state museum.

Across the avenue on the left is the University of Berlin. founded in 1810 by Wilhelm von Humboldt, philosopher and statesman. Prior to 1939 over twenty thousand students were enrolled in this university. After the occupation and the dividing of Berlin, many of the postwar students left the Soviet Sector to study at West Berlin's Free University.

Also on the left is the **Zeughaus** or Arsenal. It was built at the end of the 17th century in an ornate French baroque style and for over 200 years was used as a museum for weapons of war and a hall of fame for the Prussian army. The building at present houses a "History Museum" controlled by the East Government. Next to the arsenal stands the former Royal Guard House which after 1919 contained the **Tomb of the German Unknown Soldier,** World War I. Behind it is the **House of Soviet Culture** in the building that was formerly the Academy of Voice Culture, renowned for the excellent acoustics of its concert hall.

216

The **House of Soviet Culture, or House of German-Soviet Friendship,** containing lecture halls, library, art galleries and the **Maxim Gorki Theater,** was opened in March 1947 to inform the Germans of Soviet culture.

Crossing over the former **Schloss Bruecke** (Castle Bridge), renamed Marx-Engels-Bruecke, we enter the **Museum Island,** a perfect island in the Spree River, connected by several bridges. It was formerly the heart of the **Old City** and was named after the five Berlin art museums located on the island. The massive shell of the **Schloss,** the Royal Palace of the Prussian Rulers, dominated the scene when the occupation troops first marched into Berlin in 1945. Later on, the Soviets dynamited it and pulled it down to make way for their **Red Square,** now named Marx-Engels-Platz. The original building on this site was a stronghold built in 1441-1451 by Frederick II, Elector of Brandenburg. Frederick the Great was born in the castle and Kaiser Wilhelm II occupied it until his exile to Holland.

On the north side of the island is the **Lustgarten,** originally part of the palace garden and converted into a drill ground by Frederick William I, and now included in the **Red Square.**

The Dom or Cathedral, was Berlin's main protestant church. It was built in 1904 as the house of worship for the Royal family. Buried beneath the massive structure are the remains of many of the kings and emperors of the House of Hohenzollern.

Although the cathedral was not too severely damaged during the war, services have been held in the basement only on a small scale since the winter of 1945.

North of the Dom, clustered around the far side of the former Lustgarten, are the ruins of Berlin's most famous museums, which gave this island the name Museum Island. These museums included the National Gallery - paintings of the 19th century; the Old Museum — Greek and Roman art; the New Museum - Egyptian collection; the Pergamon Museum — Greek, old German and Western Asiatic art and the Emperor Frederick Museum — devoted to Persian and Ismaelic art. All five museums were extensively damaged; however, most of the collections had been previously removed.

Leaving Museum Island behind we enter Liebknechtstrasse and ahead of us is the Marienkirche, one of the oldest churches in Berlin. It was built in the 14th century, and rebuilt in 1892-1894. Its singularly plain Gothic spire, 295 feet high, was added to the old church in 1790.

In the hall below the church tower of the Marienkirche is the famous and weird mural painting done about 1470 called "The Dance of Death". Rather badly damaged during the war, the roof and spire have since been restored, and the church is now in use both for Lutheran services and concerts of sacred music.

Turning into Spandauer Strasse we see the City Hall of Greater Berlin, now used only by the communist administration of the East Sector. This huge structure was built in 1861-1869 near an older city hall and was considered one of the show places of prewar Berlin. The massive 210 foot tower is still standing.

Via ~~Leninallee~~ Rathausstrasse we approach **Alexanderplatz,** located near the geographical center of Greater Berlin. It once was the busiest traffic intersection in Berlin with five main streets converging and was surrounded by many big office buildings and department stores. In the background on the left used to be the huge **Police Headquarters** built in 1885-1890. It was also used by the Gestapo and had prison cells in the basement and heavy barred windows.

There is also a large department store which is called H.O., one of chain operated stores by the East Zone Government where ~~rationed food and goods could be purchased at inflated prices without coupons. Since May 1958, food ration cards are no longer required. Food is now purchased without coupons for the first time since 1939~~ goods can be purchased at inflated prices.

The tour then enters **Lenin Allee,** showing one of the most heavily bombed areas of Berlin, and then follows Friedenstrasse and Fruchtstrasse, passing the **East station** (former Schlesischer Bahnhof) which has become the main railroad station of the Soviet Sector ~~with trains leaving and arriving [in] from all directions~~. We then drive along the banks of the **River Spree** with a number of storage houses and factories in the area.

After crossing the Spree River at Treptow Bridge we enter the **Treptower Park,** one of the finest parks in Berlin. It was laid out in 1876 on the banks of the widest part of the river Spree. The broad, elm tree bordered avenue leading to the park was marked on all the maps as Treptower Chaussee, but it has been renamed Puschkin Allee by the Soviets.

The center of the magnificent old park has been converted by the Soviets into a Red Army War Memorial which they call **"The Garden of Remembrance".** The memorial was designed by Russian architects and built by German laborers working 18 months in day and night shifts.

The visitors enter on foot through one of the two sandstone gates erected on either side of the park. Visitors are asked not to smoke in the area of this national monument.

A wide path, with trimmed hedges on either side, leads from the gate to a stone statue symbolizing Mother Russia mourning her sons killed in the battle of Berlin.

Turning left, the path widens and continues ~~for at least 80 yards~~ to the top of a flight of wide steps where two huge red flags carved from red granite ~~in modernistic style~~, droop forward like curtains drawn aside. Before each flag a bronze soldier kneels, helmet in hand, head bowed.

Steps descend on the farther side down to an extensive lawn which is divided into five grass plots. ~~Under these nobody is buried, while 200 rest beneath the hill at the end.~~ On the summit of a hill in the distance towers the huge bronze statue of a Red Army soldier on top of the Hall of Fame.

On both sides of the lawn 3,400 Red Army soldiers, killed in the Battle of Berlin, are buried in mass graves. In front of the graves eight white stone blocks with carved reliefs depict the life of the workers of the Soviet Union and the Red Army. Each block bears an inscription by Joseph Stalin. These reliefs are most interesting and worth studying.

Climbing the flight of steps at the far end of the lawn, one enters the perfectly round Hall of Fame on top of the small hill. Here, inside a circular mosaic, rich in color and gold leaf, Russian peasants are pictured in costumes of every part of the Soviet Union, mourning around the grave of the Russian heroes. Overhead, in the center of the dome, burns a star which is a huge replica of the most valuable Soviet World War II decoration, "The Order of Victory". On a pedestal in the center of the small room, under glass, is a parchment book containing the names of the buried soldiers.

The towering bronze figure of the Red Army soldier on top the Hall of Fame is bare-headed and carries on his left arm a small child symbolizing the future of the Soviet Union. In his right hand he holds a long two-edged sword with which he is cutting up a swastika lying at his feet. The statue is 36 feet tall and 40 tons in weight.

Returning from the Russian memorial the tour takes us along the embankment of the Spree river as far as Warschauer Strasse, then to **Frankfurter Tor,** where we turn into **Karl-Marx-Allee,** the former **Stalin-Allee.** Most of the buildings here were completely razed by bombing and street fighting when the Red Army troops entered Berlin. The style of the new buildings erected in 1952-53 is typically Russian. The **Stalin Statue** has been removed.

Karl-Marx-Allee, the former Stalin-Allee

At the end of Karl-Marx-Allee we see once more Alexanderplatz, and following Rathausstrasse the tour takes us back to Unter den Linden.

At the end of Unter den Linden we see on our right the building of the **Freie Deutsche Jugend (FDJ),** the communist youth organization, and on our left the **Soviet Embassy,** an ornate ~~new~~ structure built on the site of the old Russian Embassy at a cost of $ 4,000,000 to house Soviet representatives.

Just beyond the **Soviet Embassy,** at the corner of Wilhelmstrasse, are the ruins of the **Adlon Hotel,** once the most luxurious hotel on the continent, receiving in the grand manner diplomats, foreign correspondents and world travelers. The **Adlon** ~~Hotel~~ was used as the setting of Vicky Baum's well-known novel *Grand Hotel.*

We now turn into **Wilhelmstrasse,** formerly lined with government buildings and considered in prewar days the most aristocratic part of Berlin. Now there is little to see except total destruction. ~~But here again it is the case of being interested in what once existed, in knowing where the historic buildings one has read so much about, once stood.~~

Soviet Embassy on Unter den Linden

The **Reich's Foreign Office** was on the right, at numbers 75-76, but even the house numbers can no longer be found. Again on the right, number 77 was the President's Palace, at one time the official residence of General von Hindenburg, President of Germany under the Weimar Republic. This residence and the other buildings on Wilhelmstrasse were destroyed during the heavy street fighting in the last days of the war. The Red Army fought its way down this street to the **Reichschancellery** on 30 April 1945.

Wilhelmstrasse opens out into Wilhelmplatz, now Ernst-Thaelmann-Platz, and on the right side of the square stood the **Reichschancellery**.

The **Reichschancellery** was Hitler's official residence as well as his office. It was built during 1936-1938, modern in style, but richly decorated in the interior with gold mosaic and inlays of gold leaf, marble, and fine wood. From the first floor balcony facing the Platz Hitler showed himself to his followers massed in the large square below.

Under the gardens of the **Reichschancellery** Hitler's personal air raid shelter was built, 36 feet deep. It was said to have been the most elaborate air raid shelter in Germany—steam-heated and air-conditioned, furnished with every luxury. It is in this underground palace that Hitler and Eva Braun died in a suicide pact.

The chancellery was partially destroyed during one single air raid and further damaged during the last days of fierce fighting in this area. The Red Army looted most of the furnishings and then burned out the ornate interior. Finally, in 1948, the ruins were removed. The Communists claim they intend to make a beautiful people's park where Hitler's famous **Reichschancellery** once stood.

Across from the **Reichschancellery** were the offices of Dr. Joseph Goebbels' **Ministry of Propaganda.** They have now been rebuilt and remodeled into headquarters for the **Nationalrat,** the Soviet-sponsored Upper House for East Berlin and the East Zone of Germany.

At the corner of Wilhelmstrasse and Leipziger Strasse is the building which housed Nazi Germany's **Air Ministry.** It escaped the war with practically no damage and is presently occupied by a number of departments of the East Zone's government.

We then turn into Leipziger Strasse, formerly an important business street, and leave **Potsdamer Platz** on our right.

In prewar days **Potsdamer Platz** was one of the busiest traffic intersections of the city. During the Soviet blockade of Berlin in 1948-1949 it became quite a hot spot, for here the ~~three sectors~~ American and the British and the Soviet sector meet and East faces West. During the period of the blockade, the Soviets put up a barricade to keep the West Berliners from coming over into their territory.

In the fall of 1950 the free press of West Berlin erected on the British side a tall sign, illuminated at night, on which news bulletins were run for the benefit of the Germans on the other side of the Iron Curtain.

This was also the scene of the uprising on 17 June 1953, started on Stalinallee by workers who were in protest against a 10% work-increase without pay demanded by the government. Thousands of others joined them in the march toward the sector border, where they were stopped by Russian tanks. Many people were killed or wounded. And even today, some of them are still in jail.

The square, formerly surrounded by stately and well-known hotels and business houses, is now nothing but a wide open space since most of the ruins were removed. East of the Potsdamer Platz, on the entrance to Leipziger Strasse, once stood the famous **Wertheim Department Store.**

On the other side one can still see the wrecked **Potsdamer Bahnhof,** Berlin's first railroad station, which has been in existence since 1835 and where the first train left for Potsdam. It was a small but artistically attractive building.

Also on this side is the **Haus Vaterland,** a unique prewar restaurant in which ~~you~~ patrons wandered at will from "country to country", ~~eating the national food, drinking the national wines, hearing the national music and~~

223

---

being waited upon by enjoying the food, wines and music of each nation represented and being served by waiters and waitresses dressed in national costumes. Even the scenery of the specific country was reproduced outside the windows and on the walls. The old **Haus Vaterland** attracted practically everyone who came to Berlin. It was severely damaged by bombing and fire.

This section of the city took a heavy pounding; Berlin was the target of 71,095 tons of bombs dropped in 154 raids by the United States 8th and 15th Air Forces and the British Royal Air Force. There were blocks of ruins as far as one could see.

Returning to Checkpoint Charlie, we leave the Soviet Sector and re-enter the American Sector.

Driving along the wall we pass the site of the Anhalter Bahnhof, an important railroad station which was bombed during the war.

The tour then takes us into the Tiergarten area which is now in the British Sector. It was once the private property of the crown and a hunting reservation for royalty where the deer roamed in herds. Frederick the Great had his famous architect Knobelsdorff layout a portion of it in the stiff Versailles style of gardens and later Frederick William continued the beautifying.

The park was opened to the public in the 19th century; restaurants, stables and an open air theater sprang up around it, and it soon became as important to the Berliner as the Bois de Boulogne is to the Parisian.

A good deal of the battle of Berlin was fought in this area. Trenches and fox holes were dug in the gardens and the beautiful old trees were either destroyed during the fighting or cut down by the Berliners to be used for fuel during the frightfully cold winter of 1945-1946. The rose gardens were plowed up and planted as vegetable gardens and acres of the park were planted in potatoes to keep the people of Berlin alive.

With the help of E.R.P. funds the European Recovery Plan unemployed out-of-work Berliners were employed in remodeling the park. An extensive reforestation project was carried out, with German towns from all over the Western Zones sending gifts of trees.

A ride along the Street of the 17th of June, formerly Charlottenburger Chaussee, renamed as a memorial of the uprising in the East Sector, then takes us to the Brandenburger Tor. The gate is in the Soviet Sector and we see it blocked by the wall.

Brandenburger Tor has been the center of every important event in Berlin's history since 1791. German historians have called it "The Guard of Stone at the Threshold of Prussia". It was originally built as a town gate, and served as a sort of line of demarcation between the city and the western outskirts. Despite all changes and the growing of the city it has remained the gateway to Berlin. In appearance it is in many ways imitation, architecturally, of the antique town gate of Athens and Propylaea of the Acropolis of Greece.

For two centuries **Brandenburger Tor** was the triumphant entrance gate for victorious Prussian troops every time they returned from the conquest of other lands. All foreign rulers and dignitaries coming to Berlin entered here; every state procession, funeral, or show of Prussian might; even the athletes coming in for the Olympic Games, all entered the city through this gate. Finally, in May 1945, the Red Army stormed through it to capture the city.

The famous quadriga — the **Victory Car,** a Roman chariot drawn by four galloping horses — on top of the gate hung in shreds when the occupying troops first entered the city. After the battle of Jena in 1806, when Napoleon marched into Berlin, he had the chariot removed, packed and sent to Paris. Berliners used to take pride in the fact that the Parisians never saw

225

it, because when Marshal ~~Blücher~~ Bluecher defeated Napoleon eight years, later he brought it back before the French had time to unpack the original 36 cases in which it had been shipped to France.

During World War II the chariot was almost totally destroyed and in 1946 the Soviets removed what was left of it. ~~Recently the~~ The restoration of the gate was done by East Berlin construction firms, and the chariot was 'recast by a West Berlin art foundry and reinstalled atop the gate. The reconstruction of the gate was the first and only **Mutual** effort made by ~~both the~~ city administrations of both East and West Berlin since the division of Berlin. Thus, all Berliners can be proud to have their **Brandenburger Tor** back anew except that Eastern authorities removed the Iron Cross and the Prussian Eagle from the laurel wreath prior to the installation of the chariot, and apart from the fact that the flag flying on top the chariot has the communist emblem in it.

On the right, as ~~one leaves~~ we leave **Brandenburger Tor** behind and ~~looks~~ look down the wide **Street of the 17th of June,** is the old Koenigsplatz, now renamed Platz der Republik, and the monumental **Reichstag.** During the days of the monarchy and the Weimar Republic, the **Reichstag** was the meeting place of the German parliament. It was built in 1884-1894 in florid Italian Renaissance style, to serve as the Prussian House of Parliament.

Most of the building was destroyed by fire on the night of 28 February 1933. The National Socialists accused the Communist party of having started the fire as a signal of a nationwide revolution, and the world accused the Nazis of having done it themselves as an excuse to seize power by force. Hitler never had the **Reichstag** rebuilt; he moved his own parliament into the **Kroll Opera House.**

Next on the right rises the **Soviet War Memorial,** which is a semicircular sandstone arch with a bronze Red Army soldier on top pointing at defeated Berlin. The Soviets unveiled this memorial in 1945 at ceremonies commemorating the Russian October Revolution. Two Red Army soldiers stand here on guard day and night.

The inscription on the monument reads: "Eternal glory to heroes who fell in the struggle against German fascist invaders for freedom and independence of the Soviet Union." It is said that the Soviets had this memorial ready for the capture of Berlin and that it was brought into the city from Russia in sections. Its construction took six weeks and commenced when all of the city was Soviet-occupied in 1945, before the Western powers took over their control. This is why the monument stands in the British Sector. To avoid incidents, the British put barbed wire around this place and one British soldier is on duty there to guard the two Russian soldiers.

In the center of the Tiergarten is the Grosser Stem, a circular space where the Street of the 17th of June is crossed by roads radiating in all directions. Here the Siegessacule or Victory **Column** rises impressively.

This column, built in 1873, commemorates the victories of the Prussian armies in the Franco-Prussian war of 1870-1871. It formerly stood before the Reichstag in the center of the square now known as the Platz der Republik. Rising to a height of 193 feet, it is topped by a gilded figure of victory called by the Germans the "Goddess of Victory".

The Allied Forces made such a target of this wide and beautiful road called Street of the 17th of June that Hitler had it covered with an extensive and elaborate camouflage net. In ~~many accounts of~~ the last days of Berlin~~, it is claimed that~~ planes carrying messages to Hitler, ~~while he was~~ then living underground in his bunker ~~air raid shelter~~ at the chancellery, actually landed and took off on this street.

North of the Grosser Stern is the Bellevue Castle, originally built in 1785 and almost completely destroyed during World War II. After its reconstruction it was designated as the official residence of the President of the Federal Republic of Germany while he is in Berlin. The attractive park around the castle is open to the public.

Also on the right is the Hansa Area, an exclusive pre-war residential section. After being almost totally destroyed in 1943, nothing but ruins remained for a period of 12 years.

In 1957, the Hansa Area was the scene of the International Building Exhibition, where modern concepts of architecture and town-building were demonstrated in a self-contained settlement. More than 50 architects of international repute built a "town of tomorrow" — a futuramic city — with skyscrapers and one-family houses, a movie theater, two churches, a school, a library and a shopping center.

An American contribution to the International Building Exhibition is the Congress Hall, located north on the outskirts of the Tiergarten next to the Spree River. Funds for this ultra-modern building—unique in Europe—were raised by the Benjamin Franklin Foundation. The hall is used for all public conventions.

Turning left at the Victory Column or Siegessaeule into Hofjaegerallee we pass on the right ~~used to be located~~ the site of two of the largest air raid shelters or Bunkers of Berlin. The larger of the two shelters accommodated over 30,000; the smaller one was reserved for military personnel engaged in the air defense of the city. When the fighting was over the bunkers were turned into hospitals. For the first year after the fall of the city they were also used as shelters for the homeless of the district ~~and later dynamited~~.

Continuing, we enter the area around Luetzow Platz, a badly bombed section which suffered one of the first radar-directed air raids in 1943. This area is now under reconstruction. Among others, the **Hilton Hotel** is one of the new buildings on Budapester Strasse.

At the end of the street we encircle the **Kaiser-Wilhelm-Gedaechtnis-Kirche, or Emperor William Memorial Church.** It was built in 1895, dedicated by Kaiser-Wilhelm II to his grandfather, and is quite a landmark for the present day Berliners. In the prewar days it was the society church of the city and the site of many fashionable weddings.

The church was partially destroyed by aerial bombing and received further destruction when SS troops made a last stand here in the end of April 1945 as the Soviets entered the city. ~~This landmark is now being rebuilt.~~

The main tower of the memorial church was one of the highest points in or near Berlin, 315 feet high. In it hung an electrically operated peal of five bells cast from the metal of captured cannons. ~~The peal was worked by electricity.~~ On the walls of the church there still are very fine mosaic pictures. ~~The organ gallery could accommodate 80 musicians and over 300 singers.~~ The ruin of the tower remains as a war-monument and the new church was built to plans by Prof. Egon Eiermann. At nighttime you will have a wonderful view, when the lamps in the inner part of the church make the glass windows shine brightly in their beautiful colors.

The huge building on your right will be the highest building of Berlin when completed, and it will be 22 stories in height. It will contain theaters, restaurants, a department store and an ice skating rink. The estimated cost is $ 18,000,000.

The **Zoological Gardens** are on the North side of the church with an entrance on Budapester Strasse. This Zoo with its approximately ~~2,200~~ 3,100 animals is one of the finest in Europe. The Aquarium, part of the Zoo, ~~is well worth visiting (if one is interested in fish and sea animals). In the garden popular concerts are given.~~ is, next to the Oceanarium in Florida, the largest in the world with more than 8,000 aquatic animals.

Radiating from the church square several wide shopping streets: Kurfuerstendamm, Tauentzienstrasse, Rankestrasse, Budapester Strasse and Kantstrasse. ~~On Kantstrasse, No. 12, is the theater formerly known as **Theater des Westens** and now used as the **City Opera House**, the only opera house in the Western Sector of Berlin.~~

~~Nobody visits Berlin without coming to shop on **Kurfuerstendamm**. It is the Fifth Avenue of the city, the style center of Germany, most gay with shops, restaurants, outdoor cafes in summer that remind one of Paris, night spots, hotels, and movie theaters. It was heavily damaged by street fighting and from aerial bombs, but gradually it is coming back.~~

Almost nobody visits Berlin without coming to shop on **Kurfuerstendamm.** It is the "Fifth Avenue" of Berlin, the liveliest place in the city, where you find many open air cafes, restaurants of all kinds, big hotels, a great variety of shops, theaters, and approximately 80 nightclubs in the area offering all types of evening entertainment.

On Kurfuerstendamm at the corner of Joachimstaler Strasse is the home of the famous **Kranzler Cafe.** The original site was on Unter den Linden at the corner of Friedrichstrasse in the East Sector, founded in 1825. At the corner of Uhlandstrasse we see on our left the **Maison de France,** the French Information Center in Berlin, with the French Consulate and a restaurant offering French cuisine at reasonable prices.

The tour continues down Kurfuerstendamm to its end. From a railroad bridge, in the distance on the right, we see the **Funkturm,** a ~~450~~ 490-foot radio tower which looks something like the famed Eiffel Tower in Paris. There is a restaurant a third of the way up and an elevator to take you up to the very top of the lofty mast to see a bird's eye view of Berlin.

We then enter the Grunewald district, a beautiful residential area ~~The route back is tree-bordered,~~ skirting the Grunewald (Green Forest), 11,350 acres that were once a royal hunting preserve, consisting mainly of tall, straight pines. There are several natural lakes in this forest, which extends from the elegant Western residential section of the city to the banks of the Havel River, Berlin's great waterway to the sea. On Sundays and holidays large crowds of Berliners pour into the Grunewald to walk, ride, bicycle, swim and sun themselves.

Driving down Clay-Allee (named in honor of General Lucius D. Clay, former U.S. Military Governor of Berlin ~~and commander-in-chief U.S.~~) we re-enter the U.S. Sector and see the American Community housing area with the Outpost Theater, the Berlin American School, the Berlin Brigade Chapel and the U.S. Army Shopping Center on the right. U.S. Headquarters is on the left.

Here, within a quarter mile radius, are all the installations found in a normal American civic center. The Shopping Center, a one story structure, was originally built by Army engineers as an officers' and civilians' mess hall in 1946.

Occupying the two main wings are ~~the quartermaster sales commissary, which sells groceries and meats to family and bachelor messes,~~

the main post exchange, a counterpart of a small-town department store, ~~In this building also are located~~ the main post office, a cafeteria, beauty and barber shops, beverage store, tailor shop, watch and radio repair shop, theater ticket office, telephone- and telegraph services, the American Express, and a newsstand ~~and a central office for the payment of rentals and subsistence accounts of all persons connected with the Army.~~

U.S. Army Shopping Center

At the intersection of Clay-Allee, Saargemuender Strasse and Argentinische Allee is U.S. **Headquarters Berlin,** formerly known as OM GUS (Office of Military Government U.S.) serving as headquarters. for the U.S. Department of State, U.S. Army ~~personnel~~ Berlin and Berlin Brigade.

When American troops entered Berlin in July 1945 they established headquarters here in the shambles that had once been the proud, modern Luftgau buildings, the command post for the aerial defense of the eastern region of Germany. They found these buildings painted a dirty gray-green for camouflage purposes, battered by bombs and artillery, and ~~guttered~~ gutted by fire. All the first floors were ripped out to provide firewood, the doors ~~knocked in~~ and windows broken and everything that could be pulled out had been looted by the Red Army.

A German plane lay in the middle of Saargemuender Strasse, right at the corner of Clay-Allee: it had hit the right wing of the Luftgau building as it came down in flames and that part of the roof was burned away. Beside the main gate, where the official cars are now parked, there were groups of shallow graves with crude wooden stars painted blood red, marking the spot where Red Army soldiers had been hastily buried.

The U.S. Sector of Berlin was formally occupied on 6 July 1945. On 20 July 1945, President Truman left the Tripartite Conference at Potsdam to attend the flag raising ceremonies in the compound. He was accompanied by Generals Eisenhower, Bradley, Patton, Clay and Floyd S. Parks, the Commanding General, Berlin District.

The flag which was raised in the compound that day had been flown over the United States Capitol on 8 December and 11 December 1941, when war had been declared first on Japan, then on Germany and Italy. This same flag had been flown triumphantly over Rome on 4 July 1944 after the surrender of Italy and later it was raised in Tokyo at General MacArthur's command on 8 September 1945.

In the Headquarters Compound are now located ~~U.S. Mission Berlin, USCOB, the United States Consulate, Navy Headquarters and Berlin Command Headquarters.~~ the Office of the United States Commander, Berlin, the U.S. Mission of Berlin and Berlin Brigade Headquarters.

Across from the headquarters compound, at Clay-Allee and Saargemuender Strasse is ~~Club 48~~ **Club 50**, the non-commissioned officers' club, built by the Army. On Argentinische Allee are more apartments built by the Army to house military and civilian personnel working for the government.

Behind the Shopping Center is the ~~Command~~ Brigade athletic center with gym, tennis courts, bowling alleys and athletic fields.

West Tour

[The descriptions of the places visited on the "West Tour" are in many instances identical to the ones used on the "East Tour," which have already been marked to show how they compare to the 1958 tour. Paragraphs that are identical with those in the "East Tour" are marked at the end by the tag ¶=¶.]

We start at the "Harnack House", the American Officers'-Civilians' Open Mess of Berlin Brigade. ¶=¶

Originally the guest house of the famous Kaiser-Wilhelm-Institute, Harnack House was designed to house distinguished foreign scientists who came from all parts of the world to do research work here. It was named after the first president of the society, Adolf von Harnack. During a later period it was headed by Albert Einstein. ¶=¶

When the first American Army personnel entered Berlin in July 1945 they found Harnack House practically undamaged, so with a clatter of field ranges and supply trucks, mess sergeants took over. A large amount of the original furniture still remains and is being used in the club. Besides housing the Officers'-Civilians Open Mess of Berlin Brigade, Harnack House has a restaurant, two floors of rooms for visitors, a beauty parlor, barber shop, and a newsstand. ¶=¶

The buildings surrounding Harnack House, for the most part, belonged to and made up the Kaiser-Wilhelm-Institute; those not too badly damaged were taken over by the **Free University of Berlin.** ¶=¶

The Free University was founded in 1948 by a number of students which fled East Berlin's Humboldt University. Under the motto *"Veritas, Justitia, Libertas"*, 2,140 students began their first semester in December 1948. Since then the number of students has grown to over 15,500. The Auditorium Maximum was donated by the Henry Ford Foundation, and is located right beside the Harnack House. ¶=¶

Ihnestrasse is a most attractive street in the spring when the beautiful old chestnut trees are in bloom. Residential streets in the new districts of Berlin are all planted with trees, a specific variety to each street and in many cases, following the idea of the famous Unter den Linden, the street is named after the trees that shade it. There is an Unter den Eichen (Under the Oaks) and a Kastanienstrasse (Chestnut Street), and so on. ¶=¶

The U.S. Sector of Berlin consists of six districts or "Bezirken": Zehlendorf, Schoeneberg, Kreuzberg, Tempelhof, Neukoelln and Steglitz. Of these Zehlendorf and Steglitz are the newest and most attractive. They are modern, mainly residential with clean streets and innumerable parks containing small bodies of water. Most of the houses have balconies gay in summer with flowers and foliage and they are usually surrounded by gardens enclosed by grill work fences. ¶=¶

After leaving **Harnack House** we drive through winding residential streets, all tree bordered, and turn right into Koenigin-Luise-Strasse which becomes Grunewaldstrasse. On the left we pass the modern catholic church of Dahlem, bombed and now rebuilt. Further down on the same side are two other buildings of the Free University, one of them a newly-built Medical School. On the right is the rear entrance to the **Botanical Gardens** with the main entrance located on Unter den Eichen. Because of the large and extensive selection of plants the Botanical Gardens are considered to be one of the finest in Europe. ¶=¶

From Grunewaldstrasse we enter Schloss Strasse in the Steglitz district. On our left we see the townhall of Steglitz, **Rathaus Steglitz,** built of red brick like so many local government buildings of Berlin. ¶=¶

Schloss Strasse is a good street not only for shopping but also for seeing the Berliner. It is always crowded with people. The traffic is heavy and the shops offer a very fine choice. At night it is bright with neon signs advertising movies, restaurants, and shops. ¶=¶

On the left is the new Wertheim Department Store, the first department store rebuilt after the war, continuing the tradition of the old "Wertheim" now located in the Soviet Sector and totally bombed. ¶=¶

One block down on the same side we see the **Titania Palast.** It was from 1945-1948 a recreational center of the US Army and then handed back to German ownership. It has since been renovated and acoustic conditions improved, and is now used for movie and stage productions including light plays, concerts, variety and radio shows, lectures, and as an assembly hall. It has a seating capacity of 1,800 and has seen successions of famous artists, musicians and Hollywood stars since 1945. ¶=¶

After Innsbrucker Platz by turning left we come to John-F.-Kennedy-Platz to see the **Rathaus Schoeneberg.** Before the war this was a Rathaus like so many others, but after the Berlin Blockade caused a separation in the city's administrative set-up, it was chosen as the seat of the West Berlin government. Here are located the offices of the governing mayor of West Berlin as well those of local administration of the Schoeneberger district. ¶=¶

The tower of the building was especially reconstructed to hold the ten-ton **Freedom Bell,** a gift from the United States to the people of Berlin. The bell's deep throated tones can be heard each day at noon. This great bell, one of the largest in the world, was designed by Walter Dorwin Teague, one of America's leading industrial designers, and was brought to Berlin on United Nations Day, 24 October 1950. Inscribed on its rim is the following message paraphrased from the address of Abraham Lincoln at Gettysburg: "That this world, under God, shall have a new birth of freedom". ¶=¶

An elevator has been installed in the tower and visitors may go up to see the bell and at the same time get a fine view of the city. ¶=¶

Crossing Hauptstrasse we go up Kolonnenstrasse over the S-Bahn tracks, and as we approach Tempelhof we pass on our left Viktoria Park with **Kreuzberg Hill,** which once was the highest elevation of the city before postwar rubble mountains were created. ¶=¶

On the hill stands the attractive Kreuzberg monument, built in the Gothic style in 1821, dedicated to the Prussian War of Liberation. It was designed by Schinkel, one of Germany's most famous artists. It is claimed that on a fine day all of Berlin, with the river Spree winding around it, can be seen from the summit of the hill. ¶=¶

And now we see the buildings of **Tempelhof Central Airport** looming up ahead of us. Tempelhof obtained its name from the village originally created by the Templar Knights in the year 1319 and named Tempelhof. ¶=¶

The air field emerged from World War II a shambles, and tons of debris had to be cleared away in time to receive President Truman and Prime Minister Churchill when they arrived for the Potsdam Conference in July 1945. ¶=¶

Prior to its utilization as an airport in 1919, the field had served as an exercise and drill ground, for the Berlin Garrison. Dating back to the time of Frederick William I (1721), the field was the scene of parades by the Royal Guard Corps in the spring and fall of each year. ¶=¶

Construction of the modern airport buildings was begun in 1937 and had not been completed at the end of the war. The arc-shaped hangars are of steel construction, uniquely built to permit aircraft parking under a roof supported by large cantilever beams. The upright beams were set in reinforced concrete foundations and anchored to the terminal building by specially designed steel erection equipment. ¶=¶

Although destined never to realize its purpose, the entire roof of the hangar construction, nearly one mile in length was laid in tiers to from a semi-circular stadium, designed to seat thousands of spectators for air and ground demonstrations. ¶=¶

The landing field is a well-drained, sodded area of 312 acres, bordered on one side by a concrete block apron approximately 950 feet wide and 3,500 feet long. Length of the runway is 5,300 feet, width 140 feet. ¶=¶

In addition to the landing field and the hangars, one of the more interesting areas of the base is "Eagle Square." This ornate quadrangle forms the main entrance to the base, recently handed back to German ownership. Since the occupation of Germany began, the area had been known as "Eagle Square" because of the large eagle which surmounted the center wall. Once a typical Nazi eagle, it was Americanized by a coat of white paint over its head and an American coat of arms over the old swastika. However, this statue was removed in mid-1961. Facing "Eagle Square" is the **Platz der Luftbruecke.** named by the city of Berlin to commemorate the airlift, and the impressive **Airlift Monument.** ¶=¶

The Soviet army took possession of the airport in May 1945, and although the buildings were little damaged by bombing, extensive burning by the Russian and pilfering by the general public presented a tremendous job of reconstruction to the first American troops to arrive in Berlin on 2 July 1945. ¶=¶

From 1945 until September 1947, Tempelhof was operated as an installation of the European Air Transport Service; on 20 September 1947, control of the base was transferred to the United States Air Force in Europe. ¶=¶

As Russian restrictions on land travel became more complicated in the spring of 1948, West Berlin began to depend more and more on the United States Air *Force* for transportation and for providing necessary supplies. On 1 April USAFE C-47's and C-54's began a 24-hour schedule between Rhein Main Base and Tempelhof, but on 6 April 1948, the travel restrictions were temporarily relaxed and land travel resumed. However, the period of relaxed restrictions was brief and on 20 June 1948 it was necessary to recommence supplying the city by air. "Operation Vittles", later known as the Combined Airlift Task Force, came into existence on 26 June 1948, and the Berlin Airlift began. ¶=¶

Flying 109,228,502 miles or an equivalent of 227.8 trips to the moon, the Berlin Airlift transported 2,324,257 tons of cargo to the blockaded city of Berlin. In addition to Tempelhof, the center of control in Berlin, Gatow Airport in the British Sector and Tegel Airport in the French Sector were utilized as landing fields to receive the tremendous amounts of coal, flour, and miscellaneous items required to supply the more than two million inhabitants of West Berlin. ¶=¶

The blockade of Berlin officially ended on 12 May 1949, and in August the Airlift began a phase-out period which lasted until 30 September 1949, when the operation was finally stopped. ¶=¶

At the beginning of 1951, one half of the airport was de-requisitioned by the Air Force and handed back to German trusteeship. Two main commercial airlines are using this civilian portion of the airport now: Pan American World Airways and British European Airways. Air France operates out of Tegel Airport. ¶=¶

Continuing down Mehringdamm the next point of interest is **Hallesches Tor,** a former city gate to Berlin, and the **American Memorial Library,** a memorial to the airlift, donated from a special fund for the benefit of German cultural institutions set up by John McCloy, former US High Commissioner in Germany. With 300,000 volumes and over 40,000 card holders it is the largest public library in Germany, and has largest library circulation. ¶=¶

[At this point, the "West Tour" takes a different path than the "East Tour."]

The tour then takes us along the Landwehrkanal, through Alexandrinenstrasse to Stallschreiberstrasse, showing us some of the most heavily destroyed areas in Berlin, presently under reconstruction. On Stallschreiberstrasse we start our trip along the Wall, with Checkpoint Charlie as our first stop. Checkpoint Charlie is the US Army Checkpoint at the border crossing between the American and the Soviet Sector of Berlin. Of the seven border crossing points presently in operation, Checkpoint Charlie is the only crossing point for foreigners.

Continuing our tour along the Wall we cross Wilhelmstrasse, formerly the "Street of Ministries", lined with government buildings and considered in prewar days as the most aristocratic part of Berlin. Now there is little to see except total destruction. But here again it is the case of being interested in what once existed, in knowing where the historic buildings one has read so much about, once stood.

Wilhemstrasse formerly housed the Reich's Foreign Office, the President's Palace, the Reichschancellory, the Ministry of Propaganda, and at the corner of Leipziger Strasse, Nazi Germany's Air Ministry, which escaped the war with practically no damage and is at present occupied by a number of departments of the East Zone's Government. Next

239

to the former Air Ministry we see a burnt out red brick building, formerly the headquarters of the Gestapo.

On our left we pass the site of the Anhalter Bahnhof, in prewar days one of the biggest railroad stations in Berlin, bombed during the war and no longer in use. Next to the Anhalter Bahnhof is a World War II air raid shelter.

Turning right we follow Landwehrkanal and cross Potsdamer Strasse, leaving Potsdamer Platz on our right. In prewar days Potsdamer Platz was one of the busiest traffic intersections of the city. During the Soviet blockade of Berlin in 1948-1949 it became quite a hot spot, for here the American and the British and the Soviet sector meet and East faces West. During the period of the blockade, the Soviets put up a barricade to keep the West Berliners from coming over into their territory. In the fall of 1950 the free press of the West erected on the British side a tall sign, illuminated at night, on which news bulletins were run for the benefit of the Germans on the other side of the Iron Curtain. ¶=¶

This was also the scene of the uprising on 17 June 1953, started on Stalinallee by workers who were in protest against a 10% work-increase without pay demanded by the government. Thousands of others joined them in the march toward the sector border, where they were stopped by Russian tanks. Many people were killed or wounded. And even today, some of them are still in Jail. ¶=¶

The square, formerly surrounded by stately and well-known hotels and business, is now nothing but a wide open space since most of the ruins were removed. East of the Potsdamer Platz, on the entrance to Leipziger Strasse, once also stood the famous **Wertheim Department** Store. ¶=¶

On the other side one can still see the wrecked **Potsdamer Bahnhof,** Berlin's first railroad station, which has been in existence since 1835 and where the first train left for Potsdam. It was a small but artistically attractive building. ¶=¶

Also on this side is the **Haus Vaterland,** a unique prewar restaurant in which patrons wandered at will from "country to country", enjoying the national food, wines and music of each nation represented and served by waiters and waitresses dressed in national costumes. Even the scenery of the specific country was reproduced outside the windows and on the walls. The old **Haus Vaterland** attracted practically everyone who came to Berlin. It was severely damaged by bombing and fire. ¶=¶

This section of the city took a heavy pounding; Berlin was the target of 71,095 tons of bombs dropped in 154 raids by the United States 8th and 15th

Air Forces and the British Royal Air Force. There are blocks of ruins as far as one can see. ¶=¶

At the corner of Potsdamer Strasse and Reichpietsch Ufer we see the ruins of a building, bombed before it ever was finished, planned to be the "Haus des Fremdenverkehrs" (House of Tourism). Beyond, on our right, we see the new **Philharmonie,** the new home of the Berlin Philharmonic Orchestra, on Kemperplatz. The section between Potsdamer Strasse on the east, the "Zoologischer Garten" (Zoo) on the west, the Landwehrkanal on the south, and the Tiergarten on the north was prewar Berlin's diplomatic quarter. With the exception of the slightly damaged Italian and Japanese embassies, the entire area lies· in ruins.

We enter Stauffenbergstrasse, formerly Bendlerstrasse, named after Colonel Count von Stauffenberg, the leading officer in the unsuccessful bomb plot against Hitler which took place on 20 July 1944. Number 10-11 Stauffenbergstrasse was the **Oberkommando** des Heeres (Army High Command). Four army officers, including Stauffenberg, were shot in the courtyard of this building, and as we drive past the main gate we see a statue dedicated to the victims of this anti-Nazi revolt.

The tour then takes us into the **Tiergarten,** Berlin's "Central Park", which is in the British Sector. It was once the private property of the crown and a hunting reservation for royalty where the deer roamed in herds. Frederick the Great had his famous architect Knobelsdorff layout a portion of it in the stiff Versailles style of gardens and later Frederick William II continued the beautifying. ¶=¶

The park was opened to the public in the 19th century; restaurants, stables, and an open air theater sprang up around it, and it soon became as important to the Berliner as the Bois de Boulogne is to the Parisian. A good deal of the battle of Berlin was fought in this area. Trenches and fox holes were dug in the gardens and the beautiful old trees were either destroyed during the fighting or cut down by the Berliners to be used for fuel during the frightfully cold winter of 1945-1946. The rose gardens were plowed up and planted in potatoes to keep the people of Berlin alive. ¶=¶

With the help of European Recovery Plan funds, out-of-work Berliners were employed in remodeling the park. An extensive reforestation project was carried out, with German towns from all over the Western Zones sending gifts of trees. ¶=¶

We leave **Luetzowplatz** on our left, a badly bombed section which suffered one of the first radar-directed air raids in 1943. This area is now under reconstruction and when completed will be Berlin's new business and government quarter. [Not precisely identical. The difference is marked.]

Turning right the tour leads us through Hofjaegerallee to the **Victory Column or Siegessaeule.** On our left was the site of two of the largest air raid shelters or **Bunkers** of Berlin. The larger of the two shelters accommodated over 30,000; the smaller one was reserved for military personnel engaged in the air defense of the city. When the fighting was over the bunkers were turned into hospitals. For the first year after the fall of the city they were also used as shelters for the homeless of the district.

The **Siegessaeule or Victory Column** rises impressively in the center of the Tiergarten, the so-called **Grosser Stem.** This column, built in 1873, commemorates the victories of the Prussian armies in the Franco-Prussian war of 1870-1871. It formerly stood before the Reichstag in the center of the square now known as the "Platz der Republik". Rising to a height of 193 feet, it is topped by a gilded figure of victory called by the Germans the "Goddess of Victory".

Running down the center of the **Tiergarten** is the **Street of the 17th of June,** formerly Charlottenburger Chaussee, renamed as a memorial to the uprising in the East Sector in 1953.

The Allied Air Forces made such a target of this wide and beautiful road that Hitler had it covered with an extensive camouflage net. In the last days of Berlin planes carrying messages to Hitler, then living underground in his air raid shelter at the chancellery, actually landed and took off on this street.

On our left we pass the **Soviet War Memorial,** which is a semicircular sandstone arch with a bronze Red Army soldier on top ' pointing at defeated Berlin. The Soviets unveiled this memorial in 1945 at ceremonies commemorating the Russian October Revolution. Two Red Army soldiers stand here on guard day and night. The inscription on the monument reads: "Eternal glory to heroes who fell in the struggle against German fascist invaders for freedom and independence of the Soviet Union". It is said that the Soviets had this memorial ready for the capture of Berlin and that it was brought into the city from Russia in sections. Its construction took six weeks and commenced when: all of the city was Soviet-occupied in 1945 before the Western powers took over their control. This is why the monument stands in the British Sector. To avoid incidents, the British put barbed wire around this place and one British soldier is on duty there to guard the two Russian soldiers.

At the end of the Street of the 17th of June we reach the **Brandenburger Tor or Brandenburg Gate,** since 1791 the center of every important event in Berlin's history. German historians have called it "The Guard of Stone at the Threshold of Prussia". It was built originally as a town gate and served as a sort of line of demarcation between the city and the western outskirts. Despite all changes and the growing of the city it has remained the gateway to Berlin. In appearance it is in many ways an imitation, architecturally, of the antique town gate of Athens and the Propylaea of the Acropolis of Greece.

For two centuries Brandenburger Tor was the triumphant entrance gate for victorious Prussian troops every time they returned from the conquest of other lands. All foreign rulers and dignitaries coming to Berlin entered here, every state procession, funeral, or show of Prussian might, even the athletes coming in for the Olympic Games, entered the city through this gate. Finally, in May 1945, the Red Army stormed through it to capture the city. ¶=¶

The famous quadriga — the Victory **Car,** a Roman chariot drawn by four galloping horses - on top of the gate, hung in shreds when the occupying troops first entered the city. After the battle of Jena in 1806, when Napoleon marched into Berlin he had the chariot removed, packed and shipped to Paris. Berliners used to take pride in the fact that the Parisians never saw it because when Marshal Bluecher defeated Napoleon eight years later he brought it back before the French had time to unpack the original 36 cases in which it had been shipped to France. ¶=¶

During World War II the chariot was almost totally destroyed and in 1946 the Soviets removed what was left of it. The restoration of the gate was· completed by East Berlin construction firms; the chariot was recast by a West Berlin art foundry and reinstalled atop the gate. ¶=¶

The reconstruction of the gate was the first and only **Mutual** effort made by city administration of both West and East Berlin since the division of the city. Thus all Berliners can be proud to have their **Brandenburger Tor** back anew except that Eastern authorities removed the Iron Cross and Prussian Eagle from the laurel wreath prior to the installation of the chariot and apart from the fact that the flag flying atop the gate has the communist emblem in it. ¶=¶

~~On the right, as the tour starts down the wide **Charlottenburger Chaussee** which runs right down the center of the **Tiergarten,** is **Koenigs Platz** with the ruins of the monumental **Reichstag.**~~ We now turn left and pass Platz der Republik, formerly Koenigsplatz, and the monumental Reichstag. During the days of the monarchy and the Weimar Republic, the Reichstag was the meeting place of the German parliament. It was built in

1884-1894 in florid Italian Renaissance style to serve as the Prussian House of Parliament.

Most of the building was destroyed by fire on the night of 28 February 1933. The National Socialists accused the Communist party of having started the fire as a signal of a nationwide revolution, and the world accused the Nazis of having done it themselves as an excuse to seize power by force. Hitler never had the Reichstag rebuilt; he moved his own parliament into the Kroll Opera House.

Facing the Platz der Republik on our left is the Congress Hall, a contribution of the Benjamin Franklin Foundation to the "Interbau Berlin"', the International Building Exhibition in 1957. The architect was H. A. Stubbins. Each of the two concrete arches spanning the huge concrete base are 367 feet long with a maximum height of 60 feet. Each of these arches weighs 600 tons. They seem to hover in the air held by some mysterious force. The Congress Hall has a large auditorium capable of seating 1,200-1,400 persons, seven smaller halls for conferences, offices and refreshment rooms, as well as an exhibition hall, lounges, and post office. It is presently used for all public conventions.

We then cross the River Spree, which forms the Humboldt Harbor on our right. On the other side of Humboldt Harbor we see the sector border fenced off with barbed wire. Also on the other side of the harbor is the compound of the Charitee, one of Berlin's oldest and biggest hospitals. The tour then enters the French Sector, and we continue driving along the wall.

Muellerstrasse, the main street of the Wedding district, is blocked off by the wall, and as we turn into **Liesenstrasse** we see all houses on our right bricked off from the Western side. The drive takes us along a walled-off cemetery into Gartenstrasse, where we have a fenced-in railroad station on our right, and into **Bernauer Strasse.**

Bernauer Strasser where apartment houses located in East Berlin, facing the West, are the actual border, was one of the most famous escape routes for refugees before 13 August 1961. To prevent mass escapes from these apartment houses the communists bricked in all the doors and windows and placed barbed wire on the roof tops. Despite these measures, in the days following 13 August 1961, several East Berliners leaped from first, second, third, fourth floors and the roofs in hopes of landing in the West Berlin fire department nets, which were spread for them on the pavement, while "VoPos" tried to hold them back or shot at them. Unfortunately, some did not succeed, and as we drive along Bernauer Strasse, we see several markers which were put on the sidewalks by West Berliners where refugees died in their efforts to make their way to freedom.

To prevent people from looking across the borderline the communists put up view screens on the side streets, and the end of Bernauer Strasse is one huge barricade.

The **Versoehnungskirche or Church of Reconciliation** at the beginning of Bernauer Strasse cannot fulfill its mission any longer. On 13 August 1961 the entrance was blocked for those members of

the congregation who happened to live on the Western side, and no services have been held in this church since.

You might see groups of West Berliners assembling on the sidewalks here to wave and send greetings and signs of friendliness across the barriers, hoping that freedom, justice and the dignity of man will one day be restored to their friends and relatives on the Eastern side.

Returning from **Bernauer Strasse** we pass the **Berlin Court of Justice** and reenter the **Tiergarten area.**

We cross the **Spree River** on Luther Bruecke and then see the **Bellevue Castle** on our right. The castle, originally built in 1785, was almost completely destroyed during World War II. After its reconstruction it was designated as the official residence of the President of the Federal Republic of Germany while he is in Berlin. The attractive park around the castle is open to the public.

Turning right from the **Victory Column** we enter the **Hansa Area,** an exclusive prewar residential section. After being almost totally destroyed in 1943, nothing but ruins remained for a period of 12 years. ¶=¶

In 1957, the **Hansa Area** was the scene of the **International Building Exhibition,** where modern concepts of architecture and Town building were demonstrated in a self-contained settlement. More than 50 architects of international repute built a "Town of tomorrow" - a futuramic city - with 1,200 housing units ranging from one-family houses to 16 storied skyscrapers, two churches, a school, a library, and a shopping center. ¶=¶

Here, on the east side of the North Hansa district, the new Academy of Art was erected to plans by the Berlin architect Duettman, with funds from the Henry R. Reichold Foundation. The tour then leads us back on the Street of the 17th of June, and through the **Charlottenburg Gate** we enter the district of Charlottenburg.

On our left we see the campus of Berlin's **Technical University,** the oldest university of Berlin, which was originally the Royal Academy of Architecture founded by Frederick William III in 1799. The university now has approximately 9,300 students who study the humanities as well as engineering, mining, shipbuilding and all other technical subjects.

Ahead of us now is **Ernst-Reuter Platz,** named after the former Lord Mayor of Berlin. This area also suffered total destruction during World War II, and now houses offices of big industrial concerns, such as IBM, Telefunken, Osram and Saba.

Otto-Suhr-Allee then leads us to the **Charlottenburg Castle** and on our way we see the **Charlottenburg City** Hall on our right.

The **Charlottenburg Castle** is a long, low, graceful French-type palace, originally designed as the country residence of Sophia Charlotte, wife of Frederick I. The main part was built in 1695 by A. Nehring, the south wing and dome were added in 1701-1707 by the Swedish architect Eosander von Goethe and the east wing or Neues Schloss (New Castle) was finally added by von Knobelsdorff in 1740 at the request of Frederick the Great. In 1788 the former Schlosstheater (Castle Theater) was built at the end of the west wing by Langhans. The central part of the castle was damaged in 1943 but is now completely restored.

The Equestrian statue of the **Great Elector of Brandenburg** by Andreas Schlueter in the main courtyard of the Castle is the most famous example of German baroque sculpture. It was created in 1698-1703 and originally stood on the Castle Bridge near the main Berlin castle.

The palace gardens on the banks of the Spree, now a public park, were laid out in 1694 by the famous French landscape gardener Le Notre shortly after he created the gardens of Versailles ~~and they are still as lovely as ever~~. In the garden also stands the mausoleum of Queen Luise of Prussia with the famous marble sculpture by Christian Rauch.

The castle now houses parts of the National Gallery as well as the museum for early history.

The tour then leads us on to Bismarckstrasse, where we pass the new West Berlin **Opera House** on our left, designed by Prof. Bornemann and opened on the occasion of the Berlin Festival Weeks in October 1961. The opera house was built on the site of the bombed-out **Deutsches Opernhaus.** It has a seating capacity of 1,899 and it is renowned for its outstanding acoustics.

On our right we then see the **Schiller Theater,** one of the largest theaters in Berlin, also a post-war construction, with a seating capacity of 1,071.

The tour then leads us via **Ernst-Reuter-Platz** into Hardenbergstrasse and the **Zoo Area.**

On our left we see again the campus of the **Technical University.** Then follows the **Academy of fine Arts,** and next to it is the **College of Music,** which has one of the most diversified curricula

247

of any music school in Germany. Belonging to the Academy of Music is West Berlin's **Concert Hall.**

Hardenbergstrasse is also the city's financial district, with the **Stock Exchange,** reopened in 1952, the **Chamber of Industry and Commerce,** and the main office of the **Berliner Bank** on the other side of Hardenbergstrasse. Next on our right is the **Amerika House,** the U.S. Information Center in Berlin, with a library, exhibitions, a workshop, and a film section.

We then pass under the bridge of the **Zoological Garden Station,** the only terminal in West Berlin for rail traffic with West Germany. The entrance to Berlin's **Zoological Gardens** is opposite the railway terminal.

This **Zoo,** with its approximately 3,100 animals, is one of the finest in Europe. Popular concerts are given in the garden. Part of the **Zoo** is the **Aquarium,** which is, next to the Oceanarium in Florida, the largest in the world with more than 8,000 aquatic animals. ¶=¶

The Zoo area is one of the most prominent features of the "Berlin of Tomorrow" where reconstruction was recently completed. On our left we see a 16-story office building, housing the Women's Clothing Industry Center (DOB Center). Next to it is a twin cinema with two auditoriums to seat 1,200 and 550 persons, and beyond this a long six-story building extending to Budapester Strasse. Restaurants are located between the shops and commercial buildings. Standing a little back is a smaller nine-story building with two fresh-air stories, and a four story garage.

On our right we then pass the **Kaiser-Wilhelm-Gedaechtnis-Kirche,** or **Emperor William Memorial Church.** It was built in 1895, dedicated by Kaiser Wilhelm II to his grandfather, and is quite a landmark for the present day Berliners. In the prewar days it was the society church of the city and the site of many fashionable weddings. ¶=¶

The church was partially destroyed by aerial bombing and received further destruction when SS troops made a last stand here in the end of April 1945 as the Soviets entered the city. ¶=¶

The main tower of the memorial church was one of the highest points in or near Berlin, 315 feet high. In it hung an electrically operated peal of five bells cast from the metal of captured cannons. On the walls of the church there still are very fine mosaic pictures. The ruin of the tower remains as a war monument and a new church was rebuilt to plans by Prof. Egon Eiermann. At nighttime you will have a wonderful view, when the lamps in

248

the inner part of the church make the glass windows shine brightly in their beautiful colors. ¶=¶

The huge building on your right will be the highest building of Berlin when completed, and it will be 22 stories in height. It will contain theaters, restaurants, a department store and an ice skating rink. The estimated cost is $18,000,000. ¶=¶

Radiating from the church square are several wide shopping streets: Kurfuerstendamm, Tauentzienstrasse, Rankestrasse, Kantstrasse and Budapester Strasse ~~On Kantstrasse, No. 12, is the theater formerly known as Theater des Westens and now used as the City Opera House, the only opera house in the Western Sector of Berlin.~~ with the **Hilton Hotel,** which was opened in 1958. We then enter **Kurfuerstendamm,** West Berlin's Broadway, the liveliest place in the city, where you find many open air cafes, restaurants of all kinds, big hotels, a great variety of shops, theaters, and approximately 80 nightclubs on and off Kurfuerstendamm offering all types of evening entertainment.

On Kurfuerstendamm at the corner of Joachimstaler Strasse is the home of the famous **Kranzler Cafe.** The original site was on Unter den Linden at the corner of Friedrichstrasse in the East Sector, founded in 1825. ¶=¶

Also on our right is the **Hotel Kempinski.** At Kurfuerstendamm and the corner of Uhlandstrasse we see on our left the **Maison de France,** housing the French Consulate, the French Information Center and a restaurant offering French cuisine at reasonable prices.

Kurfuerstendamm, as the center of West Berlin's life, is a postwar supplement for the **Unter den Linden,** once the most beautiful street of the city, which is now part of the Soviet Sector.

~~Nobody visits Berlin without coming to shop on **Kurfuerstendamm.** It is the Fifth Avenue of the city, the style center of Germany, most gay with shops, restaurants, outdoor cafes in summer that remind one of Paris, night spots, hotels, and movie theaters. It was heavily damaged by street fighting and from aerial bombs, but gradually it is coming back.~~

"Ku-Damm", as it is called by the Berliners, was laid out by Kurfuerst (Elector) Joachim II as part of a series of roads connecting the center of Berlin with the Grunewald Hunting Lodge. In the late 19th century Bismarck began the remodeling of the street, thinking of making it the Champs Elysees of Berlin. In World War II the Ku-Damm was heavily damaged by street fighting and from aerial bombs.

From a railroad bridge at the end of the Kurfuerstendamm we can see in the distance on our right the **Funkturm,** a ~~450~~ 490-foot radio tower which looks something like the famed Eiffel Tower in Paris. There is a restaurant a third of the way up ahd an elevator to take you up to the very top of the lofty mast to see a bird's eye view of Berlin.

Around the Funkturm are other points of interest which the tour does not pass, but which you may visit on your own. The radio tower is surrounded by the **Ausstellungshallen** for exhibition and fairs.

The new buildings of the fair grounds are quite modern, and they were only partly destroyed during the war. These halls are used very much like the Madison Square Garden of New York City. ~~Dog Shows, Flower Shows, Industrial Shows, and every imaginable kind of show is staged here.~~ "GRUENE WOCHE" (AGRICULTURAL WEEK), dog shows, flower shows, industrial shows, and various other kinds of public displays are staged here.

Facing one of the halls is the Broadcasting Building, "Haus des Rundfunks", which once contained **Radio Berlin.** The Soviets took over control after the war, and according to the Potsdam agreement were allowed to stay. It was then the communist radio station for the Soviet Sector and Zone. However, in 1952 the communists ~~are no longer~~ ceased broadcasting from this building and moved all their equipment and staff over into the Soviet Sector. There was only a handful of Red Army soldiers on guard until July 1956, when the Soviets decided to hand the building over to the West Berlin authorities. Since April 1958 SFB (Sender Freies Berlin) has used this building as its broadcasting station.

Also in this area is the restored **Deutschlandhalle,** reopened in 1957, with a seating capacity of 14,000; Berlin's biggest indoor hall of sports.

~~Not far from the Funkturm is the huge Reichskanzlerplatz with the NAAFI, the recreation and shopping center of British troops, with a Family Shop and the "Jerboa Theater".~~ The **NAAFI,** recreation and shopping center of British troops in Berlin, with a family shop and the "Jerboa Theater" is located on Theodor-Heuss-Platz, formerly Reichskanzler-platz.

From there, Reichsstrasse leads into Olympische Strasse where the world-famous **Olympic Stadium** is located.

The stadium and surrounding structures were built for the 1936 Olympic Games. The seating capacity of the main stadium is approximately 100,000. It was not badly damaged by bombing and it is still most impressive. Beside the main stadium there is a polo field, tennis courts, race track, and an extensive swimming pool. There is also an open-air theater, to accommodate 25,000 spectators, which was modeled after the Hollywood Bowl.

South of the stadium, the visitors will find one of Germany's most extravagant post-war buildings—the **Corbusier Haus**—a single building with 527 apartments on 17 floors. The route back is tree-bordered, skirting the Grunewald (Green Forest), 11,350 acres that were once a royal hunting preserve, consisting mainly of tall, straight pines. There are several natural lakes in this forest, which extends from the elegant Western residential section of the city to the banks of the Havel River, Berlin's great waterway to the sea. On Sundays and holidays large crowds of Berliners pour into the Grunewald to walk, ride, bicycle, swim and sun themselves. [Almost identical]

Driving down Clay-Allee (named in honor of General Lucius D. Clay, former U.S. Military Governor of Berlin) we re-enter the U.S. Sector and see the **American Community** housing area with the *Outpost Theater*, the **Berlin American School**, the **Berlin Brigade Chapel** and the **U.S. Army Shopping Center** on the right. U.S. Headquarters is on the left. Here, within a quarter mile radius, are all the installations found in a normal American civic center. The Shopping Center, a one story structure, was originally built by Army engineers as an officer's and civilians' mess hall in 1946. Occupying the two main wings are the main post exchange, a counterpart of a small-town department store, the main post office, a cafeteria, beauty and barber shops, beverage store, tailor shop, watch and radio repair shop, theater ticket office, telephone- and telegraph services, the American Express and a newsstand. ¶=¶

At the intersection of Clay-Allee, Saargemuender Strasse and Argentinische Allee is U.S. Headquarters Berlin, formerly known as OMGUS (Office of Military Government, U.S.) serving as headquarters for the U.S. Department of State, U.S. Army Berlin and Berlin Brigade. ¶=¶

When American troops entered Berlin in July 1945 they established headquarters here in the shambles that had once been the proud, modern Luftgau buildings, the command post for the aerial defense of the eastern region of Germany. They found these buildings painted a dirty gray-green for camouflage purposes, battered by bombs and artillery, and gutted by fire. All the first floors were ripped out to provide firewood, the doors and windows broken and everything that could be pulled out had been looted by the Red Army. ¶=¶

A German plane lay in the middle of Saargemuender Strasse, right at the corner of Clay-Allee: it had hit the right wing of the Luftgau Buildings as it came down in flames and that part of the roof was burned away. Beside the main gate, where the official cars are now parked, there were groups of shallow graves with crude wooden stars painted blood red, marking the spot where Red Army soldiers had been hastily buried. ¶=¶

The U.S. Sector of Berlin was formally occupied on 6 July 1945. On 20 July 1945, President Truman left the Tripartite Conference at Potsdam to attend the flag raising ceremonies in the compound. He was accompanied by Generals Eisenhower, Bradley, Patton, Clay and General Floyd S. Parks, the Commanding General, Berlin District. ¶=¶

The flag which was raised in the compound that day had been flown over the United States Capitol on 8 December and 11 December 1941, when war had been declared first on Japan, then on Germany and Italy. This same flag had been flown triumphantly over Rome on 4 July 1944 after the surrender of Italy and later it was raised in Tokyo at General MacArthur's command on 8 September 1945. ¶=¶

In the Headquarters compound are now located the Office of the United States Commander, Berlin, the U.S. Mission Berlin and Berlin Brigade Headquarters. ¶=¶

Across from Headquarters Compound, at Clay-Allee and Saargemuender Strasse is **Club 50,** the non-commissioned officers' club, built by the Army. On Argentinische Allee are more apartments built by the Army to house civilian and military personnel working for the government. ¶=¶

Behind the Shopping Center is the Brigade athletic center with gym, tennis courts, bowling alleys and athletic field. ¶=¶

Entertainment Guide

In compiling the entertainment guide, every effort has been made to direct the visitor to the best and most interesting places in Berlin. It is realized that a guide book of this nature must necessarily serve a variety of tastes and personalities ranging from the Sunday afternoon art gallery crowd to the Saturday night boxing enthusiasts. Although some of the rarer types of amusement have been avoided, it is felt that the following description will be helpful to the majority of entertainment seekers.

Scarcely more than a list has been made of most of the theaters, concert halls, and places where sporting events are held; the attractions change often and it is necessary to consult local periodicals and information booths to determine the current programs.

Restaurants and night clubs have been given brief descriptions in order that you may be able to anticipate the type of food, services, and entertainment featured at each of the establishments. Only the most unusual and traditionally superior places have been included. The waiters generally speak English.

Museums have been included in this section rather than under sightseeing because it is felt that the vastness of Berlin is prohibitive to spending much time in such places during ordinary sightseeing tours. Before the war Berlin was one of the major museum cities of the world and although many of her treasures were lost or destroyed, her collections are being rapidly restored.

Movie schedules and other activities of particular interest to the American community are shown in the *Berlin Observer*, published each Friday by Berlin Brigade, and a complete program of Berlin entertainment is announced weekly by the Official Travel Office in the form of a pamphlet. These pamphlets are available at travel offices, information centers, newsstands, hotels, and the Special Services Tours Office.

Theaters

All the following are public Berlin theaters and the performances are generally in German. Tickets for nearly all theater performances may be obtained at the Shopping Center, Ticket Counter, telephone ~~74-43-880~~ 819-6591.

DEUTSCHE OPER BERLIN
34/37 Bismarckstrasse   Tel. 34-4449

~~STAEDISCHE OPER~~
Theaters Des Westens
12 Kantstrasse, (near the "Zoo" Station)   Tel. ~~32-36-56~~ 32-1020

SCHILLER THEATER
110 Bismarckstrasse   Tel. 32-5061

SCHLOSS PARK THEATER
48 Schlosstrasse   Tel. 72-1213

THEATER AM KURFUERSTENDAMM
207 Kurfuerstendamm   Tel. ~~91-37-42~~ 91-2489

RENAISSANCE THEATER
6 Hardenbergstrasse   Tel. 32-4202

KOMOEDIE
206 Kurfuerstendamm   Tel. 91-38 93

TRIBUENE
18/20 Otto-Suhr-Allee ~~on Ernst-Reuter-Platz~~   Tel. 34-2600

HEBBEL THEATER
29 Stresemannstrasse   Tel. ~~66-22-12~~ 18-2212

BERLINER THEATER
50/52 Nuernberger Strasse   Tel. 24-2444

DIE VAGANTEN
Theater an der Spree, Congress Hall   Tel. 32-4529
Kellertheater, 12 Kantstrasse   Tel. 32-4529

~~**TITANIA-PALAST**~~
~~5 Schloss-Strasse~~   ~~Tel. 72-36-72~~

Museums

DAHLEM MUSEUM
23 Arnimallee   Tel. 76-0011
Opening times: Tues, Thurs, Fri and Sat: 0900-1700 hrs; Sun: 1000-1700 hrs; Wed: 0900-1800 hrs (Wed free entrance).
This museum which houses the largest collection of West Berlin's art treasures has secured the city's place of eminence in the world of art. It continues the traditions of the former Kaiser-Friedrich-Museum and the National Gallery (both in the Soviet Sector).

SCULPTURE COLLECTION
In the right wing. Here you can see the approximately 3,300 year old limestone bust of the Egyptian Queen Nofretete. The bust was discovered upon excavations by the German Oriental Society in Tell-el-Amarna in 1912.

ART GALLERY
~~Telephone 76-32-85. Open from 1000-1700 Tuesday, Thursday, Friday and Sunday, and from 1000-2000 Wednesday and Saturday. Admission 50 pfennings. Many famous 13th-to 16th-century Dutch and Italian paintings formerly owned by the German State Museum, destroyed during the war.~~
Also in the right wing, exhibits a great number of 13th to 19th century Italian paintings, 600 paintings of Dutch masters from the 13th to 18th century, a Rembrandt collection—with 26 paintings the largest single group of Rembrandt oils in the world, included are the "Man with the golden Helmet", "Samson and Delilah" and "The Moneychanger", also here 17 of Rubens' works, a collection of masterpieces by the French Impressionists, and an excellent selection of early and medieval German art works.

~~THE ETHNOLOGICAL MUSEUM~~ MUSEUM OF ETHNOLOGY
~~Telephone 76-32-85. Same hours as the art gallery. Admission 50 pfennigs.~~
In the left wing, contains exhibits depicting the manners and customs of the various races or people in the world.

~~SCHLOSS~~ CHARLOTTENBURG CASTLE
Luisenplatz   Tel. ~~92-02-11~~ 34-0586
~~Open daily from 1000—1800. Admission 50 pfennig. Quite a landmark, with its low wrought-iron gates and its two square posts surmounted by the slim fighting gladiators. A long, low, graceful French type palace, the main part was built in 1695 by Schlueter and the side wings and dome added in~~

~~1701 07 by Swedish architect Eosander von Goethe. The left wing contained a nice little private theater. It was designed as the country residence of Sophia Charlotte, wife of Frederick I. They lived in the central part which is now completely burnt out.~~

~~The rococo decorations of the rooms in the right wing of the palace that is now open to the public are interesting. A great deal of the art and furnishings had been carefully and safely stored away and gradually, as the rooms are restored, things are being brought back to their original settings. Unfortunately, the Golden Gallery was completely destroyed. Only the Porcelain Chamber, which was filled with Chinese porcelain presented to Queen Sophia Charlotte by British merchants in 1684, has survived and the porcelain collection will again be open to the public.~~

~~The palace gardens on the banks of the Spree, now a public park, were laid out in 1694 by the famous French landscape-gardener, Le Notre, shortly after he did those at Versailles and they are still as lovely as ever. The mausoleum of Queen Luise is in the garden.~~

HISTORICAL ROOMS
Open daily from 1000-1800 hrs, entrance fee DM 1,-

NATIONAL GALLERY
Opening times: see Dahlem Museum
200 paintings 19th and 20th century, amongst others Caspar David Friedrich, Courbet, Feuerbach, Menzel, Renoir, Monet, Manet, Corinth, Liebermann, Munch, Kokoschka and Kirchner.

MUSEUM OF ANTIQUE ART
In the Stueler Pavillon opposite Charlottenburg Castle a special museum exhibiting Greek vases, small bronze items and antique jewels.
Opening times here: Tues, Thurs, Fri, Sat & Sun 1000-1700 hrs, Wed 1400-2100 hrs.

TWENTIETH CENTURY GALLERY
2 Jebenstrasse (opposite "Zoo" Station), Tel. 32-5181/597
Opening times: Tues thru Sat 0900-1700 hrs, Sun 1000-1500 hrs.
Paintings and sculptures by Munch, Picasso, Braque, Chagall, Klee, etc.

ART LIBRARY
2 Jebenstrasse Tel. 32-5181 ~~extension 684~~ 706
Contains an extensive art literature collection, formerly owned by the German State Museum.
Opening times: Mon, Wed, Fri 1300-2100 hrs, Tues & Thurs 0900-1700 hrs, Sat 0900-1300 hrs, admission free.

GEORG KOLBE MUSEUM
25 Sensburger Allee Tel. 94-2144
~~Open Wednesday and Sunday from 1000-1700 (during the winter months 1000-1500). Admission 75 pfennings.~~
Opening times: Wed & Sun 1000-1500 hrs.
A large collection of Georg Kolbe's sculptures.

GIPSFORMEREI DES EHEMALIGEN STAATLICHEN MUSEEN
17-18 Sophie-Charlotte-Strasse Tel. 34-2367
Opening times: Mon thru Fri 0900-1600 hrs, Sat 0900-1200 hrs, free admission. Exhibition and sale of reproductions of sculptures from the former German State Museum.

~~JAGDSCHLOSS~~ GRUNEWALD HUNTING LODGE
Am Grunewaldsee Tel. 84-7897
~~Open daily except Monday from 1000-1800 from April to September, from 1000-1600 from November until February. Admission 30 pfennigs. Built in 1542 in the Renaissance style for Joachim II. Has a good collection of 17th Century Dutch paintings.~~ Opening times: Tues thru Sun 1000-1800 hrs. Collection of German and Dutch paintings 15th to 19th century.

~~SCHLOSS PFAUENINSEL~~ PEACOCK ISLAND CASTLE
Wannsee, Peacock Island   Tel. 80-6033
Open daily ~~1000-1800~~ 1000-1700 hrs, closed on Mondays. ~~Admission 50 pfennings.~~
Located on an island in Wannsee. Built originally as a country palace for Frederick William II in the 18th century, English architecture and landscaping.

HUMBOLDT ~~SCHLOSS~~ CASTLE
Tegel, ~~Gabrielenstrasse~~ Tel. ~~45 90 56~~ 43-9056
Open Wed, Sat & Sun only, ~~admission 50 pfennigs.~~1400-1800 hrs.
Built as a hunting lodge for the ~~Grossen Kurfursten~~ Great Elector, it was transferred to the von Humboldt family in 1765. Most of the exhibits are furnishings and relics from Wilhelm and Alexander von Humboldt. It was rebuilt in 1822-24 by the famous Berlin architect Schinkel.

AERONAUTICAL MUSEUM
45-49 Schuette-Lanz-Strasse, Lichterfelde Ost (Lilienthal Memorial)
Tel. 73-5905
Development of aeronautical history in pictures, documents, models and original pieces. Open daily except Mon, from 1000-1800 hrs.

Sports

BOATING

Wannsee ~~Rest and Recreation Center~~ U.S. Army Harbor, 17/19 Am Sandwerder, Wannsee (normally closed from 1 December until Spring)

Reservation for boats: Call ~~74 43 405~~ 74-6555 (Harbor Master).

BOWLING

~~BC~~ Berlin Brigade Sports Center behind Shopping Center, Tempelhof Air base, McNair Barracks, Andrews Barracks.

BASEBALL, BASKETBALL and FOOTBALL

In season at the ~~BC~~ Berlin Brigade Sports Center and at Tempelhof Central Airport.

BICYCLE RACES

Periodically at Sportspalast and Deutschlandhalle.

BOXING MATCHES

Berliners are enthusiastic ~~followers of~~ boxing fans and there are frequent bouts at the Waldbuehne ~~(part of the Olympic Stadium)~~, Sportpalast, Deutschlandhalle and Olympic Stadium.

GOLF

Special Services operates an 18-hole course on 22 Golfweg, Wannsee Call ~~74 43 406~~ 74-6533 for reservations.

GERMAN FOOTBALL (Soccer)

German and international games are played at the local stadiums and occasionally at the Olympic Stadium ~~throughout the season~~.

MOTORCYCLE and AUTOMOBILE RACES

Held on ~~special track (~~the Avus~~) near the Funkturm Exhibition Halls~~, one of the fastest racing tracks in Europe.

SULKY RACES

~~German~~ Horse races are held periodically on the track at Mariendorf.

SWIMMING

An indoor swimming pool is located at Andrews Barracks. Military medical authorities do not permit American military and civilian personnel to swim in the lakes and public swimming pools in Berlin.

TENNIS

~~In addition to the tennis courts at Tempelhof Air Base, Berlin Command has courts and instructors at the Sport Center behind the Shopping Center, four courts at the Harnack House, and indoor courts at 26 Saargemuender Strasse. To reserve courts call 74 44 385 or 74 42 833.~~

Following a list of Berlin Brigade courts:

Indoor courts at 26 Saargemuender Strasse,	Tel. 74-6833.
Outdoor courts at 45 Huettenweg,	Tel. 74-6168.
Courts at Tempelhof Central Airport:	
Outdoor courts at the base,	Tel. 74-5242

Restaurants

~~To mention but a few where some of the world's best cooking may be had~~ ~~and whose restaurants and chefs are internationally famous.~~ [The restaurant recommendations were considerably changed. *Restaurants that were included in the 1958 tour guide are marked with an *asterisk.]

Following is a list of a few restaurants which offer you some of Berlin's best cuisine:

ABEN
103 Kurfuerstendamm, Tel. 88-73036. Original Berlin dishes as well as international food.

*BOERSENSTUBEN
12 Hardenbergstrasse, Tel. 32-7310. A sea food specialty house. Open daily except Sundays and Holidays for lunch and dinner.

*FUNKTURM RESTAURANT
11 Messedamm, Tel. 92-0406. On the first platform of the radio tower. Not only excellent food but also exciting view of the city.

HILTON RESTAURANTS
2-18 Budapester Strasse, Tel. 13-0381.
ROTISSERIE with grill specialties.
COFFEE HOUSE for quick menus.
SMOERGASBORD, the only restaurant that specializes in Swedish food.

*KEMPINSKI
27 Kurfuerstendamm, corner Fasanenstrasse, Tel. 91-0691.
Excellent meals and wines served from noon until midnight.

*KOTTLER
30 Motzstrasse, Tel. 24-3893. A fine restaurant near the downtown area. The theme of the place is Southern Germany and there is a zither player. Open from 1200 hrs daily.

*MAISON DE FRANCE
211 Kurfuerstendamm, Tel. 91-8147. ~~A French dining, dancing and imbibing~~ ~~spot in the grand manner.~~ Excellent French cuisine at reasonable prices, orchestra.

RITZ
26 Rankestrasse, Tel. 24-7250. European, Indian and Asiatic specialties.

SCHLICHTER
11 Martin-Luther-Strasse, Tel. 24-6134. A first class wine restaurant.

BLOCKHAUS NIKOLSKOE
Nikolskoer Weg (off Koenigstrasse),Wannsee, Tel. 80-7914.
An idyllic restaurant overlooking the Havel River and Peacock Island, offering excellent food.

Nightclubs

~~Night Tour of Berlin — This tour is conducted privately. "Peter's Party" meets at 8:00 p.m. at the Main Transient Billets, 19 Ihnestrasse, and ends at approximately 2:00 a.m. On request guests will also be met at any other hotel. The Cost is DM40.00. This covers transportation, entrances fees, cover charges and allows for the first round of drinks in each of the five different establishments visited. For reservations call Peter, Tel. 89 40 32. If contacts are made before 6:00, arrangements can be made to go on the same evening.~~ [The nightclub recommendations were considerably changed. *Nightclubs that were included in the 1958 tour guide are marked with an *asterisk.]

Berlin offers a great variety of evening entertainment.

Here is a list of a few places which might be of interest to you:

*CIRO
31 Rankestrasse, Tel. 24-4319. A gay and friendly bar-restaurant. ~~Open all night from 9 p.m.~~

EDEN SALOON
Kurfuerstendamm corner Wilmersdorfer Strasse and 21 Damaschkestrasse, Tel. 88-79416. A very original, bohemian type place for young people.

HILTON—EL PANORAMA
2-18 Budapester Strasse, Tel. 13-0381. Open daily starting 1200 hrs, afternoon teas daily except Mondays. Two bands and a floorshow entertain at night. From here you have one of the finest views over Berlin at night.

OLD FASHIONED BAR
167 Kurfuerstendamm, Tel. 91-4482. Table reservations are required. One of the most fashionable nightspots in Berlin.

*RESI
32-38 Hasenheide, ~~corner Graefestrasse, Neukoelln,~~ Tel. 66-6500. ~~Dancing, colorful and exciting, 12 piece orchestra and the world's most impressive water ballet.~~ Berlin's biggest dancing place. The main attraction is the world-famous water show, to be seen every night at 2230 and 0030 hrs.

Shopping Guide of Berlin

The extreme destruction of Berlin's inner city during the war and the subsequent geographical division by the occupying powers has resulted in a great deal of shifting in the city's business districts.

Although Kurfuerstendamm, in the British Sector now, was ~~before the war and remains today~~ always among the most exclusive shopping ~~street (frequently referred to by Americans and Germans alike as Berlin's Fifth Avenue)~~ areas, most of the business activity formerly located on Leipziger, Friedrich and Unter den Linden Streets (now in the Soviet Sector) has been reestablished in the western sectors. Commonly called "the new city", the largest street of the postwar shopping district begins as Potsdamer Strasse at Potsdamer Platz, a juncture for the American, British and Soviet Sectors, running southwest, changes to Hauptstrasse, Rheinstrasse, Schlosstrasse, Unter den Eichen, Berliner Strasse and Potsdamer Chaussee, before it runs its course. The best shopping district is along the parts of the street that are called Rhein- and Schlosstrasse. The northern end of the street (Potsdamer Strasse) also has several good shops, mostly for cameras, porcelain and books.

Two other recently developed business streets, Tempelhofer Damm directly in front of Tempelhof ~~Central Airport~~ Air Base and Karl-Marx-Strasse to the rear of the base, both running north and south, offer hundreds of shops carrying every type of item imaginable for ordinary daily needs. Most of the firms in these districts carry only staple products and do not compare with the specialty shops of Kurfuerstendamm or Schlosstrasse.

Kurfuerstendamm is a glittering maze of movie theaters, sidewalk restaurants, and beautiful shop windows. Jewelry, furs, fashions, furniture, art, automobiles, antiques—window after window and block after block—make Kurfuerstendamm a paradise for window shoppers and serious purchasers alike. Nearly all the firms are well established and reliable and their products genuine. This is the mecca for Berlin's fashion conscious citizens and the potpourri of her international guests. Kurfuerstendamm is mobbed with trades people and shoppers by day and radiant with neon at night. Even if you don't buy a pin, you're sure to enjoy an expedition to this street.

In an effort to simplify shopping for the Berlin visitor we have compiled the following list of a few of the better and most conveniently located shops in the city. The list has been restricted to certain types of shops (auction houses, porcelain, cameras, antiques, jewelry, and souvenirs) because it seems logical that these items are likely to be of greater interest to individuals making brief visits to the city. It is to be understood that this is merely an introductory and very incomplete list of Berlin shops and is only intended as a sample of the almost limitless discoveries you will probably make for yourself.

Antiques

Berlin has a fabulous street of antique shops—Keithstrasse. If you are going from Tempelhof Airport, you can use the local bus Nr. A 19 to Kleiststrasse. Just before you get to Wittenbergplatz U-Bahn station you are in an antique shop Utopia. On both sides of the street you'll find a total of fourteen (at the last count) shops, jammed with everything from mortars and pestles to elephant tusks. Try to go when you have a little time on your hands and make the rounds before you buy. ~~Next door may be a better bargain~~. In the surrounding area—on Eisenacher Strasse (twelve shops), Motzstrasse, Fasanenstrasse and Winterfeldtstrasse there are more stores which are worthwhile visiting. [None of the shops from the 1958 edition of the guide were included in the 1964 edition.]

FLORA EISENBLAETTER
Berlin W 30, 15 Winterfeldtstrasse (near Sportpalast)   Tel. 24-1581

KLEWER
Berlin W 30, 12a Viktoria-Luise-Platz   Tel. 13-2969

KUNSTKABINETT CHRISTOPHE
Charlottenburg 2, 40 Bleibtreustrasse   Tel. 91-9918

A. LINEWITSCH
Berlin W 30, 111 Eisenacher Strasse   Tel. 26-1352

WILHELM WEICK
Berlin W 30, 10 Eisenacher Strasse   Tel. 24-7500

Cameras

TALBOT
45 Kurfuerstendamm   Tel. 91-4191

BRIESBMEISTER
110 Potsdamer Strasse   Tel. 13-1377
and 91 Mehringdamm

WEGERT
26a & 188 Kurfuerstendamm   Tel. 13-0301
and 12 Budapester Strasse
and 29 Ihnestrasse ~~at Garystrasse~~ (close to the Harnack House)Tel. 76-0101
~~Onkel Toms Hütte~~   ~~Tel 84 25 41~~
and 4 stores in other districts.

Jewelry & Watches

In the Kurfuerstendamm and Schlosstrasse areas are many old and well-known jewelers, but quite a large number of Berlin's experts were forced to set up shop after the war in out-of-the-way streets or in private residential buildings. It is the same in Berlin as in any other city—an unsuspecting layman can be easily cheated by a dishonest jeweler. To be safe, have your repairs done and make your purchases only at legitimate establishments and avoid the sidewalk characters with the alleged big bargains. The jewelers listed below have large selections of the better makes of watches and jewelry and also have excellent repair departments:

HUELSE
228 Kurfuerstendamm   Tel. 91-3342

MARTIN KUEHNOEHL
32 Schlosstrasse   Tel. 72-2379

MARTHA NAGEL
34 Schlos Strasse   Tel. 72-2760

GERTRUD SCHLOEMP
237 Kurfuerstendamm   Tel. 91 -4764

HEINZ WIPPERFELD
30 Budapester Strasse   Tel. 13-1369
and 193 Kurfuer,stendamm   Tel. 91-1150

~~Leather Goods~~

~~Berlin has some of the largest selections of fine leather goods to be found anywhere. In almost every block of the major business districts will be found at least one shop groaning with beautiful luggage, hand bags, brief cases, and every conceivable item which could be manufactured from leather. There are many hand-tooled pieces to be found and a wide variety of bar gadgets, games, card cases, picture frames and the like for gifts and souvenirs. The ones listed below are worth a visit.~~

~~GOLD-PFEIL~~
~~16 Tauentzienstrasse~~   ~~Tel. 24 11 92~~
~~109 Schloss-Strasse~~   ~~Tel. 72 46 03~~

~~Rudolf & Rudolph~~
~~126 Scholss-Strasse~~   ~~Tel. 72 59 20~~

Porcelain

If you're a fancier of old Meissen or fine porcelain in general, you should be able to spend many happy hours consorting with the keepers of Berlin's spectacular arrays of dishes, vases, figurines, etc. We believe it is safe to state that no other place in Germany can offer such extensive collections of fine pieces. There are hundreds of porcelain dealers in Berlin, but the following are mentioned as a few that have become standard haunts of the American community. Porcelain is another item that warrants a bit of looking around before you buy. [Only the KPM was on the 1958 list. All the others are new to the 1960s list.]

~~KPM~~ STAATLICHE PORZELLAN-MANUFAKTUR
48 Budapester Strasse   Tel. 13-3050
and 1 Wegelystrasse (Tiergarten)   Tel. 39-9201

ROSENTHAL
226 Kurfuerstendamm   Tel. 91-1753
and 2 Budapester Strasse (Hilton Hotel)   Tel. 13-2693

KADEWE Department Store
21-24 Tauentzienstrasse   Tel. 24-9171

ERICH BAUCH
2 Tempelhofer Damm   Tel. 66-6011
(Platz der Luftbruecke)

Specialty Shops (Porcelain, crystal, silver, gifts)

~~There are also several firms in Berlin that have specialty shops which sell several different types of modern porcelain, silverware, ceramics, gifts and souvenirs.~~ Listed below are several shop which specialize in novelty items of all types:

[The shops on the 1958 are marked with an *asterisk.]

C. DIETRICH
221 Bundesallee   Tel. 24-4377
Ivory-, amber goods.

GAWANKE
101 Schlosstrasse   Tel. 72-6035
Gifts and souvenirs, glassware, silver, antiques.

GROSCHUPP
30 Schlosstrasse   Tel. 72-3279
Gifts, carvings, silver, jewelry.

RETA KUNSTSALON
204 Kurfuerstendamm   Tel. 91-4597
Antique jewelry, garnet-jewelry, Meissener porcelain, antiques.

*STADERMANN
165 Kurfuerstendamm   Tel. 91-9579
Modern Rosenthal and Hutschenreuther porcelain, plated silver articles.

*STASSEN
235 Kurfuerstendamm   Tel. 91-4521
Gifts and souvenirs, plated silver, leather, glassware, perfume.

International Hotels in Berlin
[The hotels on the 1958 list are marked with an *asterisk.]

*AM ZOO
25 Kurfuerstendamm   Tel. 91-0491

*ASTORIA
2 Fasanenstrasse   Tel. 32-6767

*BERLIN
63-69 Kurfuerstenstrasse   Tel. 13-0291

*BERLIN HILTON
2-18 Budapester Strasse   Tel. 13-0381

*BRISTOL HOTEL KEMPINSKI
27 Kurfuerstendamm   Tel. 91-0891

*CONTINENTAL
53 Kurfuerstendamm   Tel. 91-4323

FLUGHAFEN
Tempelhof Central Airport   Tel. 66-4430

GEHRHUS
Grunewald, 4 Brahmsstrasse   Tel. 89-3232

LICHTBURG
10 Paderborner Strasse   Tel. 97-7606

PARKHOTEL ZELLERMAYER
15 Meinekestrasse   Tel. 91-0551

*ROXY
34 Kurfuerstendamm   Tel. 91-0321

SAVIGNY
21 Brandenburgische Strasse   Tel. 91-0301

*SAVOY
9-10 Fasanenstrasse   Tel. 32-5055

*STEINPLATZ
197 Uhlandstrasse   Tel. 32-3951

*STEPHANIE
38-39 Bleibtreustrasse   Tel. 91-3993

THOBER
99 Kurfuerstendamm   Tel. 88-77586

*TUSCULUM
68 Kurfuerstendamm Tel. 32-5096

*WINDSOR
8-9 Knesebeckstrasse Tel. 32-4237

References:

1. *Berlin*, a HICOG Berlin Element publication.

2. *Tempelhof-Berlin: An Illustrated Guide*, an Air Force publication.

3. Adams, Vivian [SIC] W., *Tour of Berlin*.

F.

I. Berlin 1961

Appendices

Document 1

+ dringendes fs. nr. 4288   * 110861 *   * 1535 *
an   fa. flora fuer mehring
von fa. senkmueller / 11.8.61
meldung nr.   • - 90 712
betr.:   schliessung der sektorengrenzen
pol/nb sbz/ostberlin 13910/16754/nor. uqu. norman
takt.zeit : 12.-18.8.1961   fest.zeit : 10.8.1961 – gespraechserkundung.

norman rief am 10.8.61 gegen 11.45 uhr quelle telefonisch an und teilte mit,
er habe soeben aus ostberliner sed-quelle erfahren, dass massnahmen
vorbereitet werden, die sektorengrenzen zwischen dem 12. und 18.8.1961 zu
schliessen, um den nicht mehr kontrollierbaren fluechtlingsstrom zu
unterbinden.

nor.uqu. war nicht bereit, den namen ihres informanten zu nennen.

 sol.: •-90 712 pol/nb sbz/ostberlin 13910/16754 nor. uqu. norman 12.-
18.8.1961 10.8.1961 10.8.61 11.45 12. und 18.8.1961 nor.uqu.

                        *****

URGENT Cable No. 4288   11 August 1961 15:35 hours
TO: fa. Flora for Mehring
FROM: fa. Senkmeuller / 11 August 1961
Report No. 90712
SUBJECT: Closing of the Sector Border
pol/nb sbz/ostberlin 13910/16754/nor. uqu. Norman
Tact.Time: 12.-18.8.1961 DOI: 10.8.1961 – Report of Conversation.

Norman called on 10 August 1961 at about 11:45 and reported that he had
just learned from East Berlin SED source that measures were being prepared
to close the sector border between 12 and 18 August 1961 in order to halt the
uncontrollable flow of refugees.

Nor.uqu was not prepared to give the name of his informant

sol.: •-90 712 pol/nb   sbz/ostberlin   13910/16754 nor.uqu. norman 12.-
18.8.1961 10.8.1961 10.8.61 11.45 12. und 18.8.1961 nor.uqu.

Document 2

Aus Bonn:

1. In der Sitzung des Bundeskabinetts am 17.8.1961 berichtete ein Bundesminister aus „einwandfreier Quelle", mindestens die Berliner Stadtkommandanten der USA und Großbritanniens hätten bereits vor dem 13.8.1961, spätestens am 12.8.1961 mittags, Kenntnis von den beabsichtigten Sperrmaßnahmen Pankows gehabt.

Das Bundeskabinett beschloß daraufhin strengste Geheimhaltung dieses Tatbestandes. KRONE informierte nur einzelne Mitglieder der CDU-Fraktion.

2. In seiner Unterredung mit dem Bundeskanzler ließ SMIRNOW gewisse Andeutungen über eine vorherige sowjetische/amerikanische „Verständigung" bezüglich Absperrmaßnahmen fallen.

3. In der Washingtoner Arbeitsgruppe kam es nach dem 13.8.1961 zu ernsten Meinungsverschiedenheiten über das Verhalten des Westens nach dem Rechtsbruch Pankows.

GREWE soll am Abend des 17.8. vertraulich von „unglaublichen anglo-amerikanischen Extratouren" gesprochen haben.

From Bonn:

1. During the session of the Federal Chancellor's Cabinet on 17 Augusts 1961 a Federal minister reported from a "indisputable source" that at least the American and British Commandants of Berlin had been informed before 13 August 1961, by at least mid-day on 12 August 1961, of East Germany's planned [border] closing measures.

The Federal Cabinet decided to maintain the strictest secrecy about the facts of the case. [Heinrich] KRONE only informed a few members of the CDU Faction.

2. In a discussion with the Federal Chancellor, [Soviet Ambassador] SMIRNOW let certain hints fall about a prior Soviet/American "understanding" about the closing.

3. There were serious differences of opinion in the Washington Working Group after 13 August 1961 about the West's attitude to the East German breach of the law.

On the evening of 17 August, [Ambassador to the United States Dr. Wilhelm] GREWE was allegedly reported to have spoken confidentially of "unbelievable Anglo-American bloody-mindedness."

Document 3

Central Intelligence Agency
Office of Current Intelligence

10 August 1961

Memorandum

SUBJECT: THE EAST GERMAN REFUGEES

Composition of Refugee Flow

1. West Germany has registered more than 2,600,000 refugees from East Germany since 1949 (and a total, including expellees, of more than 3,500,000 since the end of World War II.) The flow has included persons of all ages and classes, but since September, 1949, when West Germany first began compiling detailed statistics, almost 50 percent have been less than 25 years old, and another 25 percent in the 25-45 age bracket.

2. From 1956 through 1959, the refugee flow declined as a result of improved economic conditions in East Germany and a sense of political stabilization. The flow to the West, moreover, was counteracted by a growing West-to-East migration of returnees and West Germans, estimated to have reached its peak at about 62,000 in 1959. [redacted] statistics compiled by the East German regime for the period 1951-59 reportedly show a total West-to-East migration of 520,423 but admit an East-to-West flow of 2,286,417. In 1960, increased international tensions and, the East German collectivization drive stimulated an increased flow of refugees and sharply curtailed the number of returnees. Published East German statistics acknowledge a steady slow decline of the total population from 19,066,000 in 1948 to approximately 17,200,000 at the end of last year.

3. So far this year the volume of refugees is the highest since 1953. The high proportion of professionals, engineers, and intellectuals has been of particular concern to the regime. From 1954 through 1960, the refugees included 4,334 doctors and dentists, 15,536 engineers and technicians, 738 professors, 15,885 other teachers, and more than 11,700 other college graduates. In addition, industrial managers have been leaving East Germany in significant numbers, many of them Socialist Unity Party (SED) members of long standing. The proportion of young people aged 21-25 has risen from about 13 percent throughout 1960 to 15.6 percent in May, 1961, the last month for which this breakdown is presently available The percentage of males of military age appears unusually high. Except for this shift in age groups, the composition of the refugee flow has remained basically the same from year to year. Economic status, family status, and religion of the refugees show roughly the same proportions as the total East German population.

4. Some individuals have managed to accumulate savings in West Berlin with a view to eventual flight. Others depend on reaching relatives or friends in *West* Germany. The abundance of job opportunities in West Germany has generally permitted all to earn a livelihood.

Motivation of Refugees

5. In general, the refugee leaves the Soviet Zone because he has grievances against the Communist system. In the past, this usually meant feelings of oppression and frustration over political and economic conditions. For example, the children of professional men have been denied equal access to higher education and subjected to other discriminations because of their "bourgeois" origin. In recent weeks, however, an additional element seems to have been the developing crisis over West Berlin, which has led to widespread fear not only of war but also that chances for escape might soon disappear. With the start of school vacations on 8 July the refugee flow showed a marked increase. At the same time popular resentment was building up against unsatisfactory living conditions in East Germany—sporadic food shortages and undesirable housing—and the regime's failure to live up to its promises to improve these conditions. Prospects of better conditions in West Germany were attractive. American officials in Berlin have noted that even among East German party and Government circles a feeling exists that the economic reorganization announced in July offers little prospect of solving the large and basic economic problems.

Effect on East Germany

6. The steady drain of technical and managerial skills and of manpower, added to the regime's overall economic difficulties stemming from shortages of capital and raw materials, have forced curtailment of the annual plan twice in the past six months and seriously reduced the possibility that the East German economy will attain the goals of the Seven Year Plan ending in 1965. The present level of escapes, if continued, would mean a loss of about 1,400,000 workers out of a labor force of approximately 8,400,000, between 1958 and 1965. This would require further cuts in production goals, although not necessarily in per capita productivity or consumption.

7. The flight of medical men has obstructed the government program of free medical care for all its citizens. It has also hampered the training of new East German doctors. Such devices as importing Bulgarian doctors to fill the places of East German escapees have proved unsatisfactory both because of their lower level of medical skill and because of language difficulties. The escape of professors and teachers has lowered educational standards.

8. In political terms, the picture is embarrassing for the regime. The loss of population points up the regime's unpopularity, its inability to control its own people, and mocks the declared East German goal of overtaking the West German standard of living. To attempt, as Ulbricht is doing, to blame the flow on West German and Allied "recruiting" and "head hunting" has generally invited ridicule among the East German populace.

East German Countermeasures

9. To date, the East German regime has relied upon scare propaganda—including show trials—and an intensification of normal police controls in its effort to reduce the refugee flow. Even these intensified controls have been applied only sporadically and mainly between East Germany and West Berlin. On the East-West Berlin sector border, police measures have been minimal. However, the regime has instituted new measures in an attempt to force the 54,000 "border crossers"—East Germans and East Berliners who work in West Berlin—to take jobs in the East. This has only increased the proportion of border crossers among the refugees. Apart from severe economic sanctions, police action has been directed mainly against those 13,500 border crossers who live in areas of the East Zone adjacent to West Berlin.

10. There is some evidence that the regime is considering harsher measures to reduce the flow. [redacted] East German propaganda on 10 August suggested that a decree promulgating new and more vigorous control measures would be forthcoming from the meeting of the East German Peoples Chamber on 11 August.

Effect on Ulbricht and Khrushchev

11. East German leader Ulbricht is faced with the dilemma that the actions necessary to halt the refugee flow would in all likelihood cause a sharp and dangerous rise in public discontent. The East German population is already openly critical of the bloc's policies on West Berlin and internal conditions in East Germany, However, it remains unlikely that the population would presently rise up against the Communists unless even more repressive political, economic and security policies are instituted and the escape route through West Berlin closed. Ulbricht, who has successfully weathered Soviet criticism of past failures in East German policies, probably had to account at the 3-5 August Warsaw Pact meeting for the present situation and may have received instructions as yet to be implemented.

12. Ambassador Thompson in Moscow considers that the refugee flow is a source of embarrassment to Khrushchev. Apart from possible adverse consequences on the bloc's economy, Khrushchev doubtless is concerned at the great publicity that the subject has received in the Western press and feels that his bargaining position is thereby weakened. While such considerations might lead him to endorse more repressive East German measures to reduce the flow, they may also increase his desire for an early agreement to resume negotiations on a Berlin settlement.

Document 4

CONGRESSIONAL RECORD — SENATE
August 1, 1961

I have read the transcript of the "Issues and Answers" program of Sunday. In it, Senator Fulbright outlines some suggestions as to how this country might take the diplomatic offensive on the Berlin issue. ... Mr. President, in order that the record made by the distinguished Senator from Arkansas [Mr. Fulbright] may be clarified completely, I ask unanimous consent to have the text of the *Issues and Answers* program of July 30 printed In the body of the Record at this point.

There being no objection, the text was ordered to be printed in the Record. As follows:

Issues and Answers (Sunday. July 30. 1961)
Guest: Senator James W. Fulbright. Democrat, of Arkansas, chairman of the Senate Committee on Foreign Relations.

Panel: Peter Clapper, ABC Capitol Hill correspondent, and John Scali, ABC diplomatic correspondent.

Mr. Scali: In any negotiations over Berlin, Senator, would you be willing to accept any concessions on the part of the West which closed West Berlin as an escape hatch for refugees in any way?

Senator Fulbright: Well, I think that that might certainly be a negotiable point. The truth of the matter is I think the Russians have the power to close it in any case. I mean we are not giving up very much because I believe next week if they chose to close their borders, they could, without violating any treaty right I know of. We have no right to insist that they be allowed to come out. As I said I don't understand why the East Germans don't close the border because I think they have a right to close it. So why is this a great concession? You don't have that right now.

Congressional Record — Senate, August 1, 1961, pp. 14222-14224.

Document 5

Department of State Airgram

Aug 3, 1961

FROM: BONN

TO: SECSTATE WASHINGTON

Rarely has a statement by a prominent American official aroused as much consternation, chagrin and anger as Senator Fulbright's recent television interview. He is quoted as favoring disengagement in Central Europe, ban on nuclear-capable weapons for Bundeswehr, free-city status for Berlin and large peace conferences. Although all of these proposals are anathema to West German officials and political leaders, their greatest wrath was direct against the Senator's alleged proposal to make concessions to Communist Bloc whereby stream of refugees from Soviet Zone would be stopped. Senator Fulbright is quoted as saying, in this connection, "I believe one would not give up very much because they (the Russians) in my opinion could close the borders whenever they wished without violating a contractual right. We do not have the right to demand from them that they permit refugees to come over." Subsequent editions of various papers did carry a denial by Senator and member of his staff that he had recommended closing door to refugees. They also reported unnamed source in State Department as stating that Fulbright was a member of Congress and that his suggestions, consequently, imposed no obligation on Executive.

Government circles in Bonn were quoted as terming Fulbright's alleged proposal on refugees as "morally and politically, completely unrealistic." A relatively junior Foreign Ministry official said privately that he and his colleagues thought that Fulbright's remarks constituted greatest mistake yet made by Western leader apropos of Berlin situation. Mayor Willy Brandt of Berlin is quoted as saying that he could not believe that Fulbright had really made such a statement regarding refugees. He went on to reject, however, any thought that refugees provided a useful concession, and he said freedom of travel between divisions of German had to be maintained. Federal Minister for All-German Affairs Lemmer said flatly that Fulbright's suggestions were "unacceptable." FDP leader Erich Mende also rejected Senator's reputed proposal. Influential but non-governmental reaction was illustrated by the phone call of leading West German publisher, Axel Springer to Embassy Press Attaché, in which Springer asked for text of remarks and expressed his dismay and indignation.

More ominous conclusion was drawn by editorial writer in *Süddeutsche Zeitung* who implied strongly that Fulbright's ideas would have considerable impact on American government because of Senator's influence, and that his concepts were realities as Germans might discover after German elections were over.

While Embassy has not as yet received the text of Senator's remarks, and they may prove more innocuous than reported by German press, it seems clear that suspicion and uneasiness regarding U.S. position on Berlin will persist for some little time in German governmental and political circles.

LIMITED OFFICIAL USE

Document 6

THE WHITE HOUSE
WASHINGTON
July 31, 1961

Minutes of Meeting of Inter-Departmental Steering Group on Berlin, July 26, 1961, 5:15 p.m.

Present: The President. the Secretary of State, Mr. Dean Acheson, Mr. Kohler, Mr. Nitze. Under Secretary Fowler, Mr. Hillenbrandt, Mr. Owen, Mr. Bundy

The President opened the meeting by asking about progress 'on our negotiating position. The Secretary responded saying that timing was a major problem. Should we propose a meeting before the 22nd Congress? The Germans might not approve, and he thought the topic should be one for discussion in the Paris working sessions.

The Secretary asked if Mr. Acheson had supplemental comments. Mr. Acheson said the problem was tough. He would advise against calling a peace conference, since that would bring many too many countries into the act. He also believed that it would be wrong at this stage to go to the United Nations.

Mr. Acheson believed that the outlines of any proposal would amount to a dressed-up form of the *status quo*, that such a dressed-up *status quo* might eventually include a four-nation agreement that they are not going to fight over Berlin, perhaps endorsed by NATO and by the members of the Warsaw Pact. (This endorsement would give a certain indirect role to the DDR.) At a later stage in the negotiations, Mr. Acheson said later, we might go a little further — (1) there could be a discouragement of movements of population as distinct from acts of genuine political refuge; (2) there might be new trade arrangements; (3) we might give assurances on the Oder-Neisse boundary. Mr. Acheson advised against using this last counter unless it buys agreement, because in the view of the Germans It is a substantial issue. The Secretary of State argued that we might accept something like Solution C, in which each side might maintain its own theory with respect to an agreed factual situation.

Document 7

~~SECRET~~

Table of Contents

Berlin: A Political Program

Preface

Phase I: Until the German Elections

Phase II: Period Between German Elections and a Peace Treaty

Phase III: After a Treaty

Tab A: Proposed Revision of Western Peace Plan

Tab B: Proposed Revision of Solution "C"

July 31, 1961

PHASE II. PERIOD BETWEEN GERMAN ELECTIONS AND A PEACE TREATY

4. Next Steps: When we had strung out this negotiation for all it was worth, we would have to decide whether the Soviet attitude had been sufficiently affected by our political and military posture to make genuine negotiation feasible. If so, we should move toward our real negotiating positions, which would involve the following amplification on each of the three above changes in the Western Peace Plan:

(a) Berlin. The Berlin proposal in the Western Peace Plan should be expanded to provide for declarations that activities which threaten peace or the interests of other parties would — consistent with fundamental human rights and freedoms — be avoided in Berlin, plus perhaps a general undertaking to discourage excessive movements of population, so long as a reasonable freedom of movement is permitted within the city, including freedom to live in one part and work in another without economic or other penalty. We should try to bargain for some form of international control over the access routes in return for these and the further concessions indicated below.

~~SECRET~~

Document 8

Translation of the text that was expunged from the 1981 edition of Jürgen Petschull, *Die Mauer: August 1961 — 12 Tage zwischen Krieg und Frieden* (page 205) when it was republished in 1990 as *Die Mauer: August 1961 — November 1989 vom Anfang und vom Ende eines Deutschen Bauwerks.* (page 259)

STERN: There was some domestic and international political blowback about this letter. Adenauer complained that the Governing Mayor had, so to speak, bypassed official channels by writing directly to the US President. Kennedy must have also been a bit surprised, and even annoyed.

BAHR: I can imagine that an American President seldom gets written to by the mayor of a foreign city who demands that he finally do something.

STERN: But then Berlin is not a city like any other.

BAHR: That is probably true. But Brandt was not a mayor like any other. What was hard was to make Bonn and the other Western capitals realize what had really happened in Berlin, and that it was very important.

STERN: Wasn't the trust of the Berliners in the Allied guarantees of safety eroded before the Wall was built?

BAHR: No, but if you are referring to the communiqué from the NATO Ministerial Meeting in Oslo in April 1961: I took the communiqué to the Governing Mayor, put it on his desk, and said: "This is unsettling — this formulation is almost an invitation to the Soviet Union to do what it wants with its sector." Because the previous guarantees that had been given for Berlin were reduced to access, presence, and the viability of the three Western sectors of the city.

STERN: That was a message that was well understood in Moscow. Just like the TV interview that the influential Senator Fulbright gave in July 1961, in which he said that he would understand if Ulbricht closed the borders to stop the refugee exodus.

BAHR: That's why some of us called him "Fulbricht."

*****

On the one hand, the redaction spares Bahr the embarrassment of his mistake in identifying the source of the shift in American policy on Berlin to **presence**, **viability**, and **access**; but on the other hand, it denies the reader the insight of Bahr's perceptive analysis of this shift, and of his evaluation of Fulbright's television interview.

Bahr's attribution of this policy shift to "the communiqué from the NATO Ministerial Meeting in Oslo in April 1961" is incorrect. The NATO Ministerial Meeting in Oslo took place from 8 to 10 May, and paragraph 6— the one on Germany and Berlin—says that NATO is determined "to maintain the freedom of West Berlin and its people."[17]

These essential US interests in Berlin were only first articulated in an outline of the US position prepared by the State Department for the critical National Security Council meeting on 19 July, the day after the US response to the Soviet *aide memoire*. It listed them as:

1. Presence and security of Western forces in Berlin
2. The security and viability of West Berlin
3. Physical access to West Berlin[18]

The day after the Security Council meeting, Kennedy sent a message to Adenauer, de Gaulle and Macmillan, in which he laid out his decision on Berlin. In this message, Kennedy said:

Our mutual interests require the continued presence of Western forces in Berlin. These interests also require that we maintain the security and viability of West Berlin and physical access thereto.[19]

While the policy of presence, viability, and access is widely attributed to Kennedy's television speech of 25 July (in *Background Berlin*, page 170 of this volume), Kennedy does not use the word *viability* in that speech. The message to Adenauer is most likely the source of Bahr's information.

These key policy elements are also found in the ~~TOP SECRET~~ "United States Outline Plan for Berlin" revised 3 August 1961 that says:

2. Mission: The United States and her Allies will employ political, economical, psychological, and military means to:
a. Assure the continued presence of Western forces in Berlin.
b. Maintain the security and viability of West Berlin and physical access thereto.[20]

The same three goals of access, presence and viability are repeated in the *Berlin Handbook* (page 64 of this volume) in the entry for the NATO Council Meeting of November 1961.

---

[17] www.nato.int/docu/comm/49-95/c610508a.htm lvo 7 March 2014.
[18] Fabian Rueger, *Kennedy, Adenauer and the Making of the Berlin Wall, 1958-1961*, Stanford University, 2011, p. 192.
[19] Rueger, p. 195.
[20] www.foia.via.gov document 1961-08-03b.pdf lvo 7 March 2014.

Index

Y

Z

US Army Checkpoint Charlie

The corner of Friedrichstraße with Zimmerstraße
Across Zimmerstraße, to the left of the sign that says:
"You are leaving the American Sector,"
is a small sign that says:
"*Der Sozialismus siegt.*" (Socialism will be victorious)

About the Author

T.H.E. Hill served with the U.S. Army Security Agency at Field Station Berlin in the mid-1970s, after a tour at Herzo Base in the late 1960s. He is a three-time graduate of the Defense Language Institute (DLIWC) in Monterey, California, the alumni of which are called "Monterey Marys". The Army taught him to speak Russian, Polish, and Czech; three tours in Germany taught him to speak German, and his wife taught him to speak Dutch. He has been a writer his entire adult life, but now retired from Federal Service, he writes what he wants, instead of the things that others tasked him to write while he was still working.

Some of the awards for his novels include:

The 9539th T.C.U. does to the secret Cold War what the 4077th M.A.S.H. did to the Korean War.

Voices Under Berlin: The Tale of a Monterey Mary is the tale of one of the early skirmishes of the Secret Cold War told with a pace and a black humor reminiscent of that used by Joseph Heller (*Catch-22*) and Richard Hooker (*M*A*S*H**). It is set against the backdrop of the CIA cross-sector tunnel operation to tap three Russian telecommunications cables in Berlin in the mid-1950s.

It is the story of the American soldiers who worked the tunnel, and how they fought for a sense of purpose against boredom and the enemy both within and without. One of them is the target of a Russian "honey-trap," but which one? Kevin, the Russian transcriber, Blackie, the blackmarketeer, or Lt. Sheerluck, the martinet?

The other end of the tunnel is the story of the Russians whose telephone calls the Americans are intercepting. Their end of the tale is told in the unnarrated transcripts of their calls. They are the voices under Berlin.

• Dr. Wesley Britton, author of *Spy Television, Beyond Bond: Spies in Fiction and Film,* and *Onscreen and Undercover: The Ultimate Book of Movie Espionage,* calls *Voices Under Berlin* "a spy novel that breaks all the molds."

• Po Wong writing at *bookideas.com* says "Kevin is a hero in the mold of McMurphy, the rebellious asylum inmate who is the protagonist in Ken Kesey's *One Flew over the Cuckoo's Nest.* Kevin manages to do his job despite the blind obedience to stringent regulations that frequently overrides common sense and intelligence in large military operations, and despite the widespread ineptness around him. ... *Voices under Berlin* is a coherent, funny, and often sardonic look at real espionage work. The detail is so realistic that you may find yourself wondering, as I did, whether this is a novel or the memoirs of an actual intelligence agent. Of course, if you're looking for James Bond, you won't find him here. What you will find is a fascinating account of what it must have been like to be toiling away at an important but often dreary job underneath the streets of Berlin during the Cold War years.

• *Midwest Book Review* says one of the things that sets this novel apart is "the author's combining a genuine gift for humor with a deft literary astuteness in telling a story that fully engages the reader quite literally from first page to last."

For more information about this novel, please visit:

www.VoicesUnderBerlin.com

Want to learn more about Berlin in the early 1950s?

Then read *Berlin in Early Cold War Army Booklets.*

This is a reprint of a series of six army booklets on Berlin, covering the period from 1946 to 1958, two years after the Russians shut down the CIA cross-sector tunnel that served as the background for the novel *Voices Under Berlin.*

When read in parallel, the booklets create a sense of living history, because, while they cover the same topics of interest about Berlin, their coverage of these topics changes as time goes by. The value added to the booklets by reprinting them in a single volume is that the single-volume reprint makes it possible to compare the texts and see the changes.

As the series progresses, the role of Hitler and the Nazis moves further and further into the background, as does the amount of war damage noted. At the same time, the relationship between the USSR and the USA can be seen to rearrange itself. The reprint is indexed and the changes in the text from one edition to the next of the individual booklets are highlighted for ease of comparison. To help better define the historical context of the booklets, the reprint is provided with a Berlin Chronology.

The decision to reproduce these booklets was based on a number of considerations, number one of which was preservation. A number of the copies in the author's collection are distressed, and this project will put a stop to their deterioration. In addition, not a single one of these booklets is to be found in a search of WorldCat, the on-line catalogue of a consortium of libraries, headed by the Library of Congress. Reprinting will make them available for research libraries to add to their collections.

To learn more about *Berlin in Early Cold War Army Booklets,* we invite you to visit:

www.voicesunderberlin.com/1950.htm.

Also by this author:

Reunification: A Monterey Mary Returns to Berlin

Mike Troyan got to know the divided city of Berlin as a Monterey Mary at the Army Security Agency Field Station there. His peaceful retirement from the CIA is derailed when he returns to post-Wall, reunified Berlin to write a book about the Stasi, and one of the ghosts of his Berlin past sends him to the ER to be stitched together on the evening of his first day back. This does not bode well for his project, because this ghost is Ilse, the mother of the Director of the Stasi Archive where Mike will be working. She used to be Mike's long-haired dictionary. She is clearly not happy to see him.

The plot thickens when Mike reads his own Stasi file, and discovers that someone was reporting on him to the Stasi while he was at the Field Station. Standard counter-intelligence logic suggests that the Stasi source was Ilse, but Mike does not want that to be the case, because it would mean that he was wrong, and Security was right. He scours the darkened recesses of his memory in search of other suspects for the title of MUSIK, the covername for the Stasi asset reporting on him. Wearing his case-officer hat, Mike imagines how easy it would have been for him to recruit each of the rogues' gallery of characters he served with in ASA at Field Station Berlin.

Mike's search for MUSIK is complicated by the fact that the MUSIK files were shredded when the Berlin Wall fell. Shredding, however, was only secure before today's computers, so Mike and the reader have to be patient while the computer pieces together the MUSIK files from the piles of shredded Stasi documents so that Mike can identify the penetration at Field Station Berlin.

Then add an IRA informant in witness protection who thinks that Mike is a hit man sent to settle an old score. Serve stirred, not shaken in the form of a classic espionage whodunit, garnished with a dash of moral ambiguity provided by the people that Mike meets in his travels around Berlin who force him to compare the Old Berlin to the New, and the CIA to the Stasi.

Who was MUSIK?

That would be telling, and that's Mike's rice bowl. He's the narrator. You'll have to hear it from him.

The illustrations, except as noted, are from documents in the public domain. The quality of the reproductions of the illustrations is a function of the quality of the originals, some of which were showing their age. Walter Ulbricht - Bundesarchiv Bild 183-76791-0001 by Horst Sturm via *Wikimedia Commons*; U.S. Senator J. William Fulbright (D-AR) — the National Archives; Kennedy and Khrushchev — Department of State photo via *Wikimedia Commons*; Khrushchev and Ulbricht — Bundesarchiv Bild 183-B0115-0010-082 by Helmunt Schaar via *Wikimedia Commons*; Checkpoint Charlie — Bundesarchiv Bild via *Wikimedia Commons*; Warning Sign - original work by the author with logo elements from *Wikimedia Commons*; scale from *Wikimedia Commons*; Berlin Wall I from *Die Flucht aus der Sowjetzone und die Sperrmassnahmen des kommunistischen Regimes vom 13. August 1961 in Berlin*, published by Bundesministerium für Gesamtdeutsche Fragen, p. 157; Six Book Awards Logo - original work by the author, and Army of Occupation Medal, original work by the author.

Berlin Wall I (1961) at the corner of Lindenstraße and Zimmerstraße

Generations of the Wall

Each succeeding generation made it harder to cross.

I - 1961-1962: concrete block and barbed wire.
II - 1962–1965: concrete panels replace concrete blocks.
III - 1965–1975: concrete slabs held in place by H-shaped steel supports,
    capped by a round concrete pipe to make it harder to climb over the top.
IV - 1975–1989: pre-cast L-shaped concrete segments with a rounded top.